REDEEMING THE TIME
ESSAYS FOR THE CHURCH IN AN AGE OF CONFESSION

Redeeming the Time
Essays for the Church in an Age of Confession

James D. Heiser

Repristination Press
Malone, Texas

2014

Dedication:

To my brother, **Phillip**, with affection, and with thanksgiving for
our kinship both in blood and in the waters of Holy Baptism,
and,

to Jakob and Gunilla Fjellander,

with whom I had the privilege of beholding the literary treasures
of Lutheran Orthodoxy in Sweden—including original copies of
the *Decretum Upsalensis* (1593)

REPRISTINATION PRESS
716 HCR 3424 E
MALONE, TEXAS 76660

www.repristinationpress.com

ISBN-13: 978-1891469428
ISBN-10: 1-891469-42-8

Table of Contents

Foreword:
Apology in an Age of Confession

A few years before his death in 1894, the Rev. James MacGregor,
D.D. wrote what was arguably his most significant work, *The
Apology of the Christian Religion*. In this book, MacGregor began with
a striking contrast between the brutality of Mohammedanism and
the apologetic character of the Christian verity:

> When the taciturn Caliph Omar was entering Jerusalem
> now taken, he was pertinaciously assailed by an aged Chris-
> tian priest with refutation of Mohammedanism and proof
> of Christianity. "Cut me off," said the Saracen commander,
> "that old man's head, unless he be silent." That old man,
> with no shield but faith, no sword but the word, setting
> himself alone to stem the then raging lava torrent of fanati-
> cism, with its brutish alternative of the Koran or death, is
> typical of the fact, that Christianity is an *apologetic* religion.

In point of fact, MacGregor further declared that "Christianity is
the apologetic religion. No other religion has ever seriously set itself
to the endeavour to subdue a hostile world by apology (from *logos*,
'reason,' or 'reason,' *ratio* vel *oratio*, 1 Pet. iii. 15), to *reason* the sinful
world out of worldliness into godliness."

If one labors with the purported apologetic goal "to reason
the sinful world out of worldliness into godliness," then MacGregor
(a divine of the Presbyterian Church of Otago and Southland) did
not need to travel to the land of the Saracen to encounter occasions
for such apologetics, for the apologetic task is often undertaken
within the confines of visible Christendom. Thus, for example, our
forefathers confessed the faith in the Augsburg Confession and its
Apology, and in the other documents of which the Book of Concord (1580) consists.

In point of fact, only the Holy Spirit, working through the Word of God and the Holy Sacraments, can work such a conversion in the hearts of men.

In Colossians 4:5, St. Paul admonished the Church: "Walk in wisdom toward those who are outside, redeeming the time." And St. Peter wrote in his first Epistle, "But sanctify the Lord God in your hearts, and always be ready to give a defense to everyone who asks you a reason for the hope that is in you, with meekness and fear; having a good conscience, that when they defame you as evildoers, those who revile your good conduct in Christ may be ashamed." (3:15) Redeeming the time, we often are called upon to confess the Catholic verity against those who would deny it or even oppose it.

The title chosen for this volume, *Redeeming the Time*, is, in part, an expression of the hope that these essays have offered such a confession toward "those who are outside" as well as comfort and instruction to the faithful. The title was also chosen to pay homage to a worthy volume of essays by the late Dr. Russell Kirk which was published in 1996—two years after his death. My appreciation for the scholarly endeavors of this great teacher of modern American Conservatism has only grown with the passage of years—not least because, though he beheld the darkness of the present age, he did not despair because he took to heart the words of T. S. Eliot:

> If we take the widest and wisest view of a Cause, there is no such thing as a Lost Cause because there is no such thing as a Gained Cause. We fight for lost causes because we know that our defeat and dismay may be the preface to our successors' victory, though that victory itself will be temporary; we fight rather to keep something alive than in the expectation that anything will triumph.

Thus we are ever striving to redeem the time.

The essays of which this little volume consists were originally presented in a variety of circumstances over the years. Several ("The Use of Irenaeus' *Adversus Haereses* in Martin Chemnitz' *Loci*

9

Theologici" and "The Limits of Liturgical Innovation in light of Martin Luther's *Exhortation to the Christians in Livonia Concerning Public Worship and Unity [1525]*") began as seminary papers written in the early to mid-1990s, and were later published (one in a journal and the other as a tract). Another ("The Art of Rhetoric and the Art of Hymnody") was written while undertaking my S.T.M. studies, and later became a conference paper presented to the ELDoNA. Yet another ("The Church-State Relationship and Augustana XVI in the Writings of C. F. W. Walther and S. S. Schmucker") was published, and then received special commendation in 1997 from the Concordia Historical Institute.

Several other papers (including "The Role of Philosophy in the Theology of Philipp Melanchthon: Is There a Need for Reappraisal?," [1997] "The Balance of Word and Sacrament in the Divine Service," [2000] "An Overview of the Distinction of Grades of Sin in the Book of Concord and the Early Lutheran Fathers," [2001] "Confessionalism and Pluralism in our Post-Modern World," [2003] and "The *Decree of Uppsala* (1593) and the Confessional Lutheran Church in Sweden" [2007]) began as papers prepared for various conferences. One paper ("Capital Punishment: A Scriptural Perspective" [2008]) was written for a secular audience.

If the reader seeks a thread which binds together the essays of this little volume, it is this: that being ready to give a defense of our hope will bring one into various contentions for the truth. In some circumstances, the contentions are particularly heated; on other occasions, the errors which are confronted may be dealt with more gently. But in all circumstances, contending for the truth is at the heart of redeeming the time.

+*James D. Heiser, M.Div., S.T.M.*
Bishop, the ELDoNA
Pastor, Salem Lutheran Church

Festival of St. Andrew, A.D. 2014

"An Overview of the Distinction of Grades of Sin in the Book of Concord and the Early Lutheran Fathers"[*]

Introduction.

The situation has deteriorated to the point that some might even question what we are doing here tonight—why have a conference on *sin*? Shouldn't the Church go about proclaiming the Gospel? We read in the Apology of the Augsburg Confession:

> The world is full of blasphemies against God, and of wicked opinions; and the devil keeps entangled in these bands those who are wise and righteous in the sight of the world. In other persons, grosser vices manifest themselves. But since Christ was given to us to remove both these sins and these punishments, and to destroy the kingdom of the devil, sin and death; it will not be possible to recognize the benefits of Christ unless we understand our evils. (II:49–50)

And Martin Chemnitz declared in his *Loci Theologici*: "...the benefits of Christ cannot be understood if we do not know what sin is."[†] If we are to believe the Gospel, we must have knowledge of the Law, and by the Law comes the knowledge of sin. As St. Paul wrote to the Romans: "What shall we say then? Is the law sin? Certainly not! On the contrary, I would not have known sin except through the law." (Rom. 7:7) Pastoral necessity compels a knowledge and exposition of the Scriptural teaching concerning sin. Much more needs

---

[*] This essay was originally presented at the "Sin Conference," hosted by the Lutheran Student Center of the University of Texas-Arlington in November 2001.

[†] Chemnitz, Martin, *Loci Theologici*, (St. Louis: Concordia Publishing House, 1989), vol. 1, 2 vols., p. 265.

to be said than can be set forth by the speakers presenting at this conference, but it is our hope that we will at least make a beginning.

Our approach this evening will be to look at several issues. We will begin by asking the most central question, "What is Sin?"—that is, how do we define the term "sin"? In addition, on the basis of Holy Scripture, the Church has wisely made distinctions between different grades of sin. As Leonard Hutter, one of our sixteenth century fathers, once wrote: "There are various distinctions made between sins. The principal divisions are into 1, original and actual; 2, into mortal and venial."* Because knowledge of these grades is helpful for the Christian, we will proceed from a definition of sin to examine the primary categories of sin: the distinction between original sin and actual sin. Next, we will look at the fundamental distinction of categories of actual sin: the distinction between venial sin and mortal sin. Lastly, we will touch briefly on the topic of the sin against the Holy Ghost.

Our concern is, of course, to present the biblical teaching. The labors of the Church to make a faithful confession of the teachings of Holy Scripture, as well as the Lutheran pastor's ordination oath to conform all of his teaching to the faithful exposition of Holy Scripture contained in the Book of Concord, lead the presenter to center his treatment of the topic in various articles of the Lutheran Confessions. Because of their faithfulness to Scripture and the Confessions, he will also utilize three writings from the sixteenth century Lutheran fathers: the 1543 *Loci Communes* of Philip Melanchthon, the *Loci Theologici* of Martin Chemnitz, and the *Compend of Lutheran Theology* of Leonard Hutter.[†]

1. What is Sin?

If we are going to speak about sin, it behooves us to ask, "What is sin, anyway?" How should we define it? Holy Scripture

---

* *Compend of Lutheran Theology*, trans. by H.E. Jacobs, (Philidelphia: Lutheran Book Store, 1868) p. 61.

[†] Melanchthon and Chemnitz were, of course, authors of substantial portions of the Lutheran Confessions. Leonard Hutter was a professor at the University of Wittenberg in the period following the completion of the Book of Concord.

teaches us, "Whoever commits sin also commits lawlessness, and sin is lawlessness." (1 John 3:4) Again, St. John wrote in his first Epistle: "All unrighteousness is sin..." (4:17). We read in Romans 14: "...for whatever is not from faith is sin." (v. 23) St. James declared, "Therefore, to him who knows to do good and does not do it, to him it is sin." (4:17) Therefore we see that sin is everything which is not the fruit of faith, for as Hebrews 11:6 teaches us, "without faith it is impossible to please Him," that is, God; without faith, every thought, word, and deed is motivated by something other than fear, love, and trust in God above all things. Sin is the violation of the Law of God; it is unrighteousness and the failure to do good.

Larson's *Concordance to the Book of Concord* lists 694 occurrences of the word "sin," and 752 occurrences of the word "sins" in the Tappert translation of the Book of Concord.* Many of these references occur in the context of differentiating original sin from actual sin (a distinction we will get to shortly), but one rarely encounters any dogmatic definition of sin, *per se*. In Article IV of the Apology of the Augsburg Confession, Melanchthon cited Romans 14:23: "Whatsoever is not from faith is sin." In this context, Melanchthon made the point that *every* thought, word or deed of an unbeliever is sinful because, "If the carnal mind is enmity against God, the flesh sins, even when we do external civil works. If it cannot be subject to the Law of God, it certainly sins even when, according to human judgment, it possesses deeds that are excellent and worthy of praise." (AP IV.33) In the Formula of Concord, in its treatment of the third use of the Law, we read: "But sin is everything that is contrary to God's Law." (FC SD VI.13)

In his *Loci*, Melanchthon defined sin as follows: "Sin is a defect or an inclination or an action in conflict with the law of God, offending God, condemned by God, and making us worthy of eternal wrath and eternal punishments, unless there be forgiveness."† Melanchthon explained that by including "defect or inclination" in this definition, original sin is included, and that by speaking of "ac-

---

* Please note that all quotations are taken from the H. E. Jacobs edition of the Book of Concord.

† trans. by J.A.O. Preus, (St. Louis: Concordia Publishing House, 1992) p. 48.

tion" all actual sins are also incorporated in this definition. Chemnitz incorporates Melanchthon's entire locus on sin within his own *Loci*, and Hutter approved of Melanchthon's definition.[*] Indeed, one is hard pressed to imagine a better definition than that which Melanchthon offers, and so we will let it stand as our own for this paper: *Sin is a defect or an inclination or an action in conflict with the law of God, offending God, condemned by God, and making us worthy of eternal wrath and eternal punishments, unless there be forgiveness.*

2. The Fundamental Distinction: Original Sin and Actual Sin.

In his *Loci*, Chemnitz observed that all men have some knowledge of sin, "For no race is so savage and barbaric that it does not have some understanding of vices or sins and speaks of them."[†] Indeed, Romans 2 says that the Gentiles "show the work of the law written in their hearts, their conscience also bearing witness, and between themselves their thoughts accusing or else excusing them" (v. 15).

Nevertheless, the world's understanding of sin and its corruption is woefully inadequate. As Melanchthon explained in his *Loci*,

> But the Church points out the wrath of God and teaches that sin is a far greater evil than human reason thinks. Nor does the Church reprove only external actions which are in conflict with the law of God or reason, as philosophy does; but it reproves the root and the fruit, the inner darkness of the mind, the doubts concerning the will of God, the turning away of the human will from God and the stubbornness of the heart against the law of God. It also reproves ignoring and despising the Son of God. These are grievous and atrocious evils, the enormity of which cannot be told.[‡]

In short, the Church teaches, based on Holy Scripture, that the outward actions (which even unbelieving men recognize as sinful)

---

[*] Hutter, p. 60.

[†] p. 265.

[‡] p. 47.

spring from an inner corruption—a "defect or inclination," as was said above in the definition of sin. As our Lord declares in Matthew 15, "But those things which proceed out of the mouth come from the heart, and they defile a man." (v. 18) This corruption of the heart is called original sin. Man's natural powers detect that certain actions of man are sinful; Holy Scripture reveals original sin to be the source of all actual sins. "This hereditary sin is so deep a corruption of nature, that no reason can understand it, but it must be learned and believed from the revelation of Scriptures, Ps. 51:5; Rom. 5:12sqq.; Ex. 33:3; Gen. 3:7sqq." (SA III.I.3)

Although one will not find the terms "original sin" and "actual sin" in Holy Scripture, a proper understanding of the distinction between original sin and actual sin is thoroughly biblical and vital to grasping the depth of man's corruption and his need for a Savior. As we teach in the Apology of the Augsburg Confession: "But the recognition of Original Sin is necessary. For the magnitude of the grace of Christ cannot be understood, unless our diseases be recognized. The entire righteousness of man is mere hypocrisy before God, unless we acknowledge that our heart is naturally destitute of love, fear and confidence in God." (AP II.33) The failure of the Roman Church to teach correctly concerning original sin is intrinsically connected to its failure to teach correctly concerning the grace of God; as we confess in the Apology of the Augsburg Confession: "it will not be possible to recognize the benefits of Christ, unless we understand our evils." (II.50)

Because of its centrality to the whole of Christian doctrine, the article on original sin is given prominent placement in the Augsburg Confession (Article II), the Apology (Article II), the Smalcald Articles (Section III, Article 1), and the Formula of Concord (Article I). In the Augsburg Confession, the article on original sin necessarily precedes the articles on the Son of God (Article III) and Justification (IV); the sending of the Son of God to atone for the sins of the world is God's gracious response to man's sin. In the Augsburg Confession, original sin is described as follows: "since the Fall of Adam, all men begotten according to nature, are born with sin, that is, [1] without the fear of God, [2] without trust in God, and [3] with concupiscence; and that this disease, or vice of origin, is truly sin, even now condemning and bringing eternal death upon those not born again through baptism and the Holy Ghost." (§1-2) Man is thus born without fear and trust in God—he is born in a state of violation of the first commandment, and he is born with concupiscence, which is the desire to sin. The Formula of Concord explains:

> Original Sin (in human nature) is not only such an entire absence of all good in spiritual, divine things, but that it is at the same time also, instead of the lost image of God in man, a deep, wicked, horrible, fathomless, inscrutable and unspeakable corruption of the entire nature and all its powers, especially of the highest, principal powers of the soul in understanding, heart, and will; that now, since the fall, man receives by inheritance *an inborn wicked disposition, an inward impurity of heart, wicked lusts and propensities;* that we all have by nature inherited from Adam such a heart, feeling and thoughts, as according to their highest powers and the light of reason, are naturally inclined and disposed directly contrary to God and His chief commands, yea, they are at enmity with God, especially as to what concerns divine and spiritual things. (SD I.11–12)

Both the Confessions and the writings of the fathers point us to Romans 5:12 as a clear passage of Scripture teaching the doctrine of original sin: "Therefore, just as through one man sin entered the world, and death through sin, and thus death spread to all men, because all sinned—". Martin Luther wrote in the Smalcald Articles, "Here we must confess, as Paul says in Rom. 5:12, that sin originated from one man Adam, by whose disobedience all men were made sinners, and subject to death and the devil. This is called original or capital sin." (III.I.1) Or as Melanchthon wrote in his *Loci:* "If only actual transgressions are sins, then each would be guilty only of his own deed. Now since it clearly says that we are guilty because of the transgression of Adam, it testifies that there is some other sin in nature besides actual transgressions. And lest this sin be understood as only an imputation of guilt, the import of the words ought to be noted. 'All have sinned,' [Rom. 5:12ff.] that is, the evil which is sin is passed on to all.'" Thus the sin of Adam spreads to all of fallen mankind, and it is, in and of itself, enough to bring the sinner into condemnation. Hutter wrote regarding original sin: "Original sin is a natural, contagious disease and imperfection, with which all men are born, not only causing us to be destitute of the fear of God, and of confidence in Him, and likewise through wicked desires to be entirely depraved, but also making us subjects of eternal condemnation, unless we are born again."† The Formula of Concord condemns Matthias Flaccius' teaching that man's substance or essence is sin; however, it does teach that original sin is "so deep a corruption of human nature, that nothing healthy or uncorrupt in man's body or soul, in inner or outward powers, remains, but, as the Church sings, 'Through Adam's fall is all corrupt, nature and essence human.'" (FC Ep. I:8)

While original sin pertains to the corruption of the sinner, the term "actual sin" refers to the sinful thoughts, words, and deeds through which original sin is expressed in the life of a sinner. Chemnitz and Hutter approved of Melanchthon's definition of actual sin: "Actual sin is every action, whether internal or external, which conflicts with the law of God; as *in the mind*, doubts concerning God; *in the will* and heart, the flames of wicked desires; *and in the members*, all motions and actions contrary to the Divine Law."‡

Writing in the Smalcald Articles, Luther identified such actual sin as the 'fruit' of original sin (analogous, if you will, to the way in which good works are the fruit of faith):

> The fruits of this sin [original sin] are afterwards the evil deeds which are forbidden in the Ten Commandments, such as unbelief, false faith, idolatry, to be without fear of God, arrogance, blindness, and, to speak briefly, not to know or regard God;

---

* p. 49.
† p. 61.
‡ Chemnitz 312–313; Hutter 69.

secondly, to lie, to swear by [to abuse] God's name, not to pray,
not to call upon God, not to regard God's Word, to be dis-
obedient to parents, to murder, to be unchaste, to steal, to
deceive, etc. (III.I.2)

This understanding of actual sin as the fruit of original sin is consistent
with the biblical witness. As St. James observed: "when desire has con-
ceived, it gives birth to sin; and sin, when it is full-grown, brings forth
death." (1:15) Our Lord declared in Matthew 15: "For out of the heart
proceed evil thoughts, murders, adulteries, fornications, thefts, false
witness, blasphemies." (v. 19)

There is a very close relationship between the corruption
caused by original sin and the fruit of that corruption which is man-
ifested in actual sin. Chemnitz observed that "in adults original and
actual sin are so closely connected that it is not easy for a person to
show the precise or mathematical point of comparison (so to speak)
at which the two should be distinguished."* Toward clarifying the
respective roles of original sin and actual sin, Chemnitz set forth the
flow from original sin into actual sin in five steps.

And the difference can be even more clearly understood
from the distinction between the degrees of sin which we
have received from antiquity: (1) an inherent tinder, the inclination or depravity which includes our lack of righteousness; (2) suggestions or urgings on the part of our thoughts
and emotions, that is, when our original corruption gets
into motion under the impulse of some urging; (3) pleasure; (4) consent; (5) the work itself.

Of these degrees or steps, the first two apply to
original sin and the other three to actual. †

It is important that Christians are correctly instructed concerning
the relationship between the sin which is in them from Adam and
the sins which they commit on a daily basis. Again, it is as we teach

---

* p. 314.
† ibid.

in the Apology of the Augsburg Confession: "it will not be possible to recognize the benefits of Christ, unless we understand our evils." (II.50) If Christians view their own sinfulness only in terms of discreet, individual acts—rather than understanding themselves to be thoroughly corrupted by sin—there is a danger they will minimize sin to the point of considering it to be merely individual acts to be avoided. Where there is a biblical understanding of original sin, the Christian begins to understand the utter hopelessness of the sinner's plight, apart from Jesus Christ. Confessing himself to be *by nature* sinful and unclean *and* to have sinned against God by thought, word, and deed opens the eyes of faith to the poignancy of St. Paul's words, "O wretched man that I am! Who will deliver me from this body of death?" (Romans 7:24)

The great strength of the traditional general confession is that it reflects a biblical understanding of the nature of the relationship between original and actual sin. Some pastors have sought to make confession more "relevant" by replacing the general confession with a list of specific sins which varies from week to week. There is certainly a place for a person to confess his individual, actual sins—privately, to his pastor—and such private confession has a proper role to play in the Church. It is for this reason that Augsburg Confession Article XI says that, "Private Absolution ought to be retained in the churches," and the Apology of the Augsburg Confession says, "it would be wicked to remove private absolution from the Church." (XII:100) But when the general confession is replaced by a list of specific sins, we risk depriving God's people of something which they need: first, to confess that their sinfulness exceeds their ability to enumerate; and, second, to specifically confess actual sins which particularly trouble them. The fifth chief part of the Small Catechism takes for granted that private confession and absolution will be occurring in the Church, and that is the place for specificity: the Christian confesses the sin which troubles him, and the pastor absolves him, assuring him that the Lord has forgiven *that* sin, too. It is as Luther teaches in the Small Catechism, "In the presence of God we should acknowledge ourselves guilty of all manner of sins, even of those which we do not ourselves perceive; as we do in the Lord's Prayer. But in the presence of the pastor we should confess those sins alone of which we have knowledge and which we feel in our hearts." A biblical understanding of original and actual sin leads us both to confess ourselves to be thoroughly sinful, and also to have sinned through specific thoughts, words, and deeds.

3. The Distinction between Venial Sin and Mortal Sin.

Modern Lutherans are not as familiar as their forefathers were with the distinction between venial and mortal sins. In fact, the distinction is never mentioned in the 1991 edition of *Luther's Small Catechism with Explanation* published by Concordia Publishing House. The failure to teach this vital distinction would have greatly disappointed the Lutheran fathers, who strongly emphasized it over against the "once-saved, always saved" theology proclaimed by some of the false teachers of their age.* Chemnitz observed in his *Loci*: "For example, in the teaching of the Anabaptists there are some who clamor that this distinction between mortal and venial sin is a device of the scholastics. But Scripture does have certain very clear illustrations of this distinction, so that it cannot be denied."†

The point at issue in the distinction between venial and mortal sins is that there are some sins which are so grievous that they can cause a person to lose his salvation. Melanchthon observed that among the unbelievers, *all* sins are mortal: "It is not necessary for the unregenerate to inquire into the distinction between mortal and venial sins, because 'Whatsoever is not of faith is sin,' Rom. 14:23. ... But for the regenerate it is necessary to ask the question who has venial sins and

---

* The fathers of the Lutheran Church-Missouri Synod also emphasized this important distinction. C. F. W. Walther's famous lectures on *The Proper Distinction Between Law and Gospel* emphasize this distinction. As Walther observed in the thirty-first lecture: "We have already seen that a distinction must be made between mortal and venial sins. A person failing to make this distinction does not rightly divide Law and Gospel." (325)

† p. 671.

why the fall from these are called mortal sins."* In other words, for the unbelieving, there is no forgiveness of sins, and so all sins lead to damnation. But for the believers, it is necessary to know what sins will cause a Christian to fall from grace.

We read in Ezekiel 18: "But when a righteous man turns away from his righteousness and commits iniquity, and does according to all the abominations that the wicked man does, shall he live? All the righteousness which he has done shall not be remembered; because of the unfaithfulness of which he is guilty and the sin which he has committed, because of them he shall die." (v. 24) Thus, the Lutheran Confessions teach, based on Holy Scripture, that the distinction between venial and mortal sins is found in the cooperation of the will in the commission of the sin. As Luther observed in the Smalcald Articles:

> ...it is necessary to know and teach that if saints who still have and feel original sin, and also daily repent, and strive with it, fall in some way into manifest sins, as David into adultery, murder and blasphemy, faith and the Holy Ghost are then absent from them. For the Holy Ghost does not permit sin to have dominion, to gain the upper hand so as to be completed, but represses and restrains it so that it must not do as it wishes. But if it do what it wishes, the Holy Ghost and faith are not there present. (III.III.43-44)

This teaching is also emphasized in the article in the Formula of Concord concerning the righteousness of faith: "We believe, teach and confess that although the contrition that precedes and the good works that follow, do not belong to the article of justification before God, yet such a faith should not be imagined as can coexist with a wicked intention to sin and to act against conscience." (SD EP III.11)

The Church chastised the Romanist teachers for claiming that faith and willful sin could coexist: "The adversaries feign, that faith is only a knowledge of history, and, therefore teach that it can coexist with mortal sin." (AP IV.48) In other words, the Roman-

---

* p. 126.

ists reduced faith to simply assenting to the factual validity of Holy Scripture, rather than understanding that the faith which saves is a trust which takes hold of the promises of God. The Church responds to the Romanists: "But since we speak of such faith as is not idle thought, but of that which liberates from death and produces a new life in hearts, and is the work of the Holy Ghost; this does not coexist with mortal sin, but, as long as it is present, produces good fruits..." (AP IV.64) Again, "Nor indeed is this faith an idle knowledge, neither can it coexist with mortal sin, but it is a work of the Holy Ghost, whereby we are freed from death, and terrified minds are encouraged and quickened." (AP IV.115)

In light of the above, Hutter's definition of mortal sin (again, borrowed from Philip Melanchthon) seems quite adequate: "In those who have not been born again, every sin is mortal, whether it be original or actual, internal or external. But in those who have been born again, a mortal sin is either a fundamental error, or an internal action, contrary to the law of God, committed against conscience, and depriving its subject of the grace of God, faith and the Holy Ghost."*

In the case of venial sin, one is dealing with actual sins where the sinner is not deliberately acting against conscience; "At this point if you fight against sin so that you do not give way against your conscience, you shall retain grace and the Holy Spirit."† In this context, Melanchthon directs his readers to St. Paul's words in Romans 7: "But I see another law in my members, warring against the law of my mind and bringing me into captivity to the law of sin which is in my members." In such a person, sin is not being willfully tolerated; rather, its unwelcome presence torments the Christian. As Chemnitz explained, "Therefore there is sin dwelling in us which tries to keep us in captivity, and those who hold hands with it and are overcome by it are led to damnation. But if they fight against it and are in Christ Jesus, even though sin is still in their members, yet for them there is no condemnation."‡

---

* Hutter, p. 69.

† Melanchthon, 127.

‡ Chemnitz, 672.

In contrast to mortal sin, Hutter defined venial sin as follows: "A venial sin, therefore, is a fall or action of the regenerate, which conflicts with the law of God, but does not cause the loss of grace, the Holy Ghost, and faith; for those who have been born again, in their spirit strive that they may not be led astray contrary to conscience, and they grieve over their corruption, and believe that for the sake of their Mediator, God regards them with favor, and gratuitously forgives them all their sins, through and on account of Christ."* Such is the nature of venial sin, that Luther observed we "should acknowledge ourselves guilty of all manner of sins, even of those we do not ourselves perceive; as we do in the Lord's Prayer."

The distinction between venial sins (which we often commit without even being aware of it) and mortal sins (which are sins against conscience) is well summarized by David in the nineteenth Psalm: "Who can understand his errors? Cleanse me from secret faults. Keep back Your servant also from presumptuous sins; let them not have dominion over me. Then I shall be blameless, and I shall be innocent of great transgression." (v. 12-13) We pray that God would cleanse us from the secret faults which we may not even understand (venial sin), but we also pray to be kept from presumptuous (mortal) sins.

Comparing different portions of St. John's first Epistle, Chemnitz draws a useful example of the distinction between mortal and venial sins:

> 1 John 1:8, "If we say that we have no sin, we deceive ourselves and the truth is not in us"; and yet he says in 3:6, "Whoever sins has not known God." These statements seem to contradict each other, but they are easily reconciled. In ch. 1 he is speaking of those who have been washed in the blood of Christ, but still have sin in them. But in ch. 3 he is speaking of premeditated sins which thus are a different kind of sin. Again the same John says in the same epistle, 3:8, "He who commits sin is of the devil," and in v. 9, "Whoever is born of God does not sin." Thus John is dem-

---

* Hutter, 70.

onstrating that there is a difference between having sin and committing sin. The latter is more serious than the former, although sometimes they are treated as one. For sin still clings in all of us, and no one can say that he is absolutely pure of all sin. Yet the godly through the grace of the Spirit resist sin. But he who carries out his calling and brings evil lusts into his work, in a sense is training himself in the art of sinning.[*]

The most important thing for us to remember as Christians is that the door of repentance remains open for all who repent and believe in Jesus Christ as their Savior. David's adultery and murder offer a striking example of mortal sin, but his restoration demonstrates for us that even those who fall away in mortal sin can be restored. As we are promised in 1 John 1, "If we confess our sins, He is faithful and just to forgive us our sins and to cleanse us from all unrighteousness." (v. 9) The teaching of the distinction between mortal and venial sins is fundamentally necessary for pastoral care: first, so that Christians may understand the nature of sin, and the danger which it poses to their faith, that they would turn to the means of grace for strengthening against temptation; second, so that pastors may properly rebuke hardened sinners (who believe they are 'good Christians' despite their willful sin) and comfort repentant sinners, assuring them of God's grace. As Chemnitz observed:

> It is beneficial that we always have before us this warning, for unless we support the Spirit in His struggle against the flesh, it will be easy for us to fall and lose our salvation. But by this admonition or the bridles of the Holy Spirit we can be kept under control so that we are not drawn into mortal sin. ... But if a man is 'overtaken in some fault,' Gal. 6:1, through the wickedness of Satan and the weakness of his own flesh, he must seek the remedy in this doctrine and rise again through repentance."[†]

---

[*] Chemnitz, 672.
[†] Chemnitz, 681.

4. The Sin against the Holy Ghost.

Our examination of the fundamental distinction of grades of sin would not be complete without a few words regarding the sin against the Holy Ghost. Concerning this sin, our Lord says in Matthew 12: "Therefore I say to you, every sin and blasphemy will be forgiven men, but the blasphemy against the Spirit will not be forgiven men. Anyone who speaks a word against the Son of Man, it will be forgiven him; but whoever speaks against the Holy Spirit, it will not be forgiven him, either in this age or in the age to come." (v. 31-32) Many pious souls have been concerned regarding the nature of the unforgivable sin. However, there is not an extensive examination of this in the Lutheran Confessions.

In their private writings, however, there is much agreement among the Lutheran fathers concerning this sin. Hutter defines it as "a voluntary apostasy or denial of either a portion or the whole of Gospel truth, made by one who has acknowledged his faith in it, and who, with deliberate purpose, contrary to the testimony of his own heart and conscience, hostilely attacks and despises the ministry of the Holy Ghost, or the means of grace." *Chemnitz agreed, writing in his *Enchiridion*:

> For those who, after they once have been enlightened and made partakers of the Holy Spirit, knowingly and in obstinate wickedness again deny the acknowledged truth and completely fall away from Christ, and so persevere therein that, as it were, they crucify Christ anew, regard [Him] as a joke, and tread [Him] underfoot, and insult the Spirit of grace—for those, I say, there remain no remission of sins, but the prospect of the judgment of God and of eternal fire. For they do not return to repentance, and without Christ there remains no offering for sins.†

---

* Hutter, 70-71.
† *Ministry, Word and Sacraments—An Enchiridion*, trans. by Luther Poellot, 1981 (St. Louis: Concordia Publishing House,) 108.

Johann Gerhard (1582-1637) is also worth citing with regard to this sin:

> The Sin against the Holy Ghost, therefore, is an intentional denial of evangelical truth, which has been acknowledged and approved by conscience, connected with a bold attack upon it, and voluntary blasphemy of it. For we must observe that this kind of sin was proved against the Pharisees by Christ; for, although they were constrained by the force of the truth uttered by Him, and were convicted in their consciences by its illumination, yet they raged against Him by their wicked impiety, to such a degree that they blushed not to ascribe His doctrines and miracles to Satan.*

Hutter made the point that this sin is unforgivable "not, indeed, because the impossibility of its forgiveness as such, that the greatness of its guilt exceeds and surpasses the mercy of God and merit of Christ."† The reason the sin is unforgivable, Hutter explained, is because:

> 1. He voluntarily forsakes Christ, without whom there is no sacrifice for sin; 2. He persistently neglects, despises, and, as it were, treads under his feet, the instruments or means of grace, without which no one can obtain forgiveness of sins; 3. and lastly. This sin is connected with final hardening of the heart, so that with confirmed purpose, the sinner at length knowingly, willingly and recklessly proceeds to attack and blaspheme that truth which he had at one time acknowledged.

Conclusion.

We have seen that *Sin is a defect or an inclination or an action in conflict with the law of God, offending God, condemned by God, and making us worthy of eternal wrath and eternal punishments, unless there be forgive-*

---

* quoted in Heinrich Schmid, *The Doctrinal Theology of the Evangelical Lutheran Church* (Philadelphia: United Lutheran Publication House, 1961) p. 256.
† Hutter, 71.

ness. For us to correctly understand the depth of our wickedness, it is necessary that we recognize that original sin is the 'font' from which actual sins 'bubble up' in us; our wickedness is far greater than the sum total of our actual sins; the heart of man is desperately wicked on account of Adam's fall. A correct understanding of original sin reveals to us the scope of the miracle which God accomplishes in us in holy Baptism, forgiving our sin, and granting us grace to begin turning away from actual sin. The influence of concupiscence will be with us throughout this life, however, so that we will continue to be afflicted by venial sin. The Christian can, however, by the grace of God avoid mortal sin. All sin needs to be repented of, and there is a particularly pressing need in the case of a lapse into mortal sin that we repent and believe again the promises of the Gospel.

My little children, these things I write to you, so that you may not sin.
And if anyone sins, we have an Advocate with the Father, Jesus Christ the
righteous.
And He Himself is the propitiation for our sins,
and not for ours only but also for the whole world. (1 John 2:1–2)

The Use of Irenaeus' *Adversus Haereses* in Martin Chemnitz' *Loci Theologici**

Introduction.

If one were to ask the average American Lutheran layman how his faith had been influenced by a second century bishop and a sixteenth century theologian, one might well imagine a reaction of utter incredulity—the entire question would be so far removed from his frame of reference that it would be essentially meaningless. In a society steeped in materialism, individualism, and a universalistic view of religion, an interest in such figures seems like an impractical, quaint antiquarianism. In an age obsessed with finding one's "own path to God" (or gods, or goddess, or Gaia, etc.), certainly the early church seems like a dead end.

Likewise, Martin Chemnitz, if his name is recognized at all, belongs to a dimly-remembered "Reformation Day" sermon—an item for the theological equivalent of "German/October Fest." And yet: *Si Martinus non fuisset, Martinus vix stetisset.* If this is true, and the second Martin is now unknown, can the first be far behind?

Chemnitz and the theologians of the Age of Lutheran Orthodoxy (1580-1713) possessed a vision of the Church which has been essentially lost today: "Consequently, you are no longer foreigners and aliens, but fellow citizens with God's people and members of God's household, built on the foundation of the apostles and prophets, with Christ Jesus Himself as the chief cornerstone. In Him the whole building is joined together and rises to become a holy temple in the Lord." (Eph. 2:20-21 NIV) To believe in the holy catholic and apostolic Church professes unity with the whole Church throughout the ages. Although the voices of some of the faithful may not resonate as clearly in our age, they still speak to

* This essay was first published in Epiphany 1998 (VII:1) issue of *Logia.*

us today, rebuking at one time, encouraging at another. Lutherans such as Martin Chemnitz saw the great riches to be uncovered in the fathers:

> ...I decided that the safest way to educate and remedy my own simplicity would be to consult the fathers of the Church who, in the times of pristine purity and learning directly after the apostles, were active in expounding this subject publicly and with characteristic diligence, and to hear them as they conferred among themselves and shared their well-considered and pious opinions on the basis of God's Word. For in this way, like Gregory's pygmies sitting on the shoulders of giants, we can more easily and correctly form a judgement on the basis of God's Word concerning this difficult question, we can acquiesce with more conviction to sound and simple teaching, and we can more safely escape the danger of falling. [*]

The following pages will offer some brief thoughts concerning the place of the fathers within Lutheran theology, followed by an examination of the place St. Irenaeus occupied in the theology of Martin Chemnitz' *Loci Theologici*.

I. The Place of the Church Fathers within Lutheran Theology—The Harmony between the *Sola Scriptura* principle and the use of the Fathers.

There is a mentality at work within modern American Lutheranism which automatically turns a wary eye toward anyone who would study the Church Fathers. The image of Luther's confrontation with the emperor at the Diet of Worms and the *sola Scriptura* principle are wedded together into a mentality which, in turn, merges quite easily with modern secular notions which turn the individual conscience into the final judge on all moral questions.

[*] Chemnitz, Martin, *The Two Natures in Christ*, trans. by J.A.O. Preus (St. Louis: Concordia Publishing House, 1971), p. 19.

Luther becomes a role model not on the positive basis of his fidelity to the Scriptures, but only negatively, in his rejection of "authority." The result is a theological shell game in which either the iconoclastic Carlstadt or the fanatic Münzer is swapped for the Reformer.

Such a modern reinterpretation does not yield a historical picture of Luther and the Reformation, nor does it do justice to the 1,500 years of catholic teaching which the Reformers fought to uphold. True, there was an effort to correct an excessive emphasis on 'tradition,' which had taken away from the teaching authority of the Scriptures, but the Reformation self-consciously chose to emphasize its adherence to the teachings of the fathers. Although the quantity of patristic citations in the Confessions is not numerically large (14 in the *Augustana*, 29 in the Apology, for example),[*] one should not be misled into believing this implies a lack of interest. As J.A.O. Preus observed:

> The comparatively small number of actual quotations or references to the fathers in the Confessions does not indicate a lack of interest in, or respect for, the fathers on the part of the Lutheran theologians, but rather reflects the intended purpose of the Confessions. Confessions are the symbols or rallying points for the whole church: for the laity, for parish pastors, and for officials; they are not intended only for theologians.[†]

Instead of emphasizing a particular quantity of citations, the overall orientation of the Confessions bespeaks the catholicity of the Lutheran teaching—"This is about the Sum of our Doctrine, in which, as can be seen, there is nothing that varies from the Scriptures, or from the Church Catholic, or from the Church of Rome as known from its writers. This being the case, they judge harshly who insist that our teachers be regarded as heretics."[‡] Again, one

---

[*] Preus, J.A.O., "The Use of the Church Fathers in the Formula of Concord," *Concordia Theological Quarterly*, April-July 1984 (48:2-3), p. 98.

[†] ibid.

[‡] *The Book of Concord; or, the Symbolical Books of the Evangelical Lutheran Church*, ed. by Henry Eyster Jacobs, (Philadelphia: General Council Publication Board, 1911), p. 46.

finds at the *Augustana*'s conclusion: "Only those things have been recounted, whereof we thought that it was necessary to speak, so that it might be understood that, in doctrine and ceremonies, nothing has been received on our part, against Scripture or the Church Catholic, since it is manifest that we have taken most diligent care that no new and ungodly doctrine should creep into our churches."* The fathers and the early councils are repeatedly appealed to in the *Augustana* and the Apology as witnesses against innovations in the Roman Church, an appeal which only increased as the Reformation progressed, as can be seen in Martin Chemnitz' and Jakob Andreae's *Catalog of Testimonies* appended to the Book of Concord.† The use of the fathers was even more extensive in the private writings of the Lutheran dogmaticians.

The question remains, however, why did *sola Scriptura* Lutherans "bother" to refer to the fathers? J.A.O. Preus' identifies eight reasons:

> 1. ... There is a strong desire to remain within the tradition of the ancient pure church not only in teaching, but even in terminology.
> 2. There was a desire to show the unbroken tradition of teaching. ...
> 3. There was the desire to identify with the ancient purer church and its interpretation of Scripture. *The point is often made that the closer one can get to the time of the apostles, the closer one gets to the correct teaching.*
> 4. The Lutheran theologians of the Reformation and confessional period wanted to establish authority for their own teaching. ...
> 5. The fathers were used by Lutherans to refute errors, both in the Roman camp, as Chemnitz does so brilliantly in his *Examen*, and also in the Reformed camp, as both the Formula and the writings of the Lutherans of the confessional period demonstrate.

---

* ibid., p. 67.

† Preus, "The Use of the Church Fathers in the Formula of Concord," p. 102.

6. The Lutheran confessors used the fathers to distinguish between the Scriptures and the writings of men, even the highly honored fathers themselves. ...

7. The fathers were cited to help in establishing a normative interpretation for certain key doctrines and passages. ...

8. Finally, it does not seem beyond the realm of possibility that the Lutherans were a little impressed with their own learning and wanted to display it to the supercilious and sophisticated Romanists, as well as to the ignorant and uneducated fanatics.[*]

In the *Catalog of Testimonies*, Chemnitz and Andreae explain their use of the fathers as follows:

Christian reader, these testimonies of the ancient teachers of the Church have been here set forth, not with this meaning that our Christian faith is founded upon the authority of men. For the true saving faith is to be founded upon no church-teachers, old or new, but only and alone upon God's Word... But because fanatical spirits, by the special and uncanny craft of Satan, wish to lead men from the Holy Scriptures—which, thank God! even a common layman can now profitably read—to the writings of the fathers and the ancient church-teachers as into a broad sea, so that he who has not read them cannot therefore precisely know whether they and their writings are as these new teachers quote their words, and thus is left in grievous doubt,—we have been compelled by means of this Catalogue to declare, and to exhibit to the view of all, that this new false doctrine has as little foundation in the ancient pure church-teachers as in the Holy Scriptures, but that it is diametrically opposed to it.[†]

The fathers provided the Lutherans with terminology, helped frame their exegesis, and helped both to formulate and to

---

[*] ibid., p. 106-108. Italics added.

[†] *The Book of Concord*, (St. Louis: Concordia Publishing House, 1922), p. 307.

support Lutheran doctrine. This did not mitigate against *sola Scriptura*, since the Lutherans often disagreed with the fathers when they felt so obligated by God's Word. But the early Lutherans did not view themselves in isolation from the preceding history of the Church. They were at ease citing the fathers in agreement or disagreement because they saw themselves within the continuity of catholic thought.

2. The Place of Irenaeus in the Theology of Lutheran Orthodoxy.

2.1 Irenaeus and the Lutheran Confessions.

Irenaeus of Lyons was born in Asia Minor, quite possibly in Smyrna, sometime between 140 and 160 A.D. Having heard Polycarp, the Bishop of Smyrna and former student of St. John, as a boy, "Irenaeus was in touch with the Apostolic age."[*] Irenaeus became presbyter of the Church of Lugdunum and was sent to Rome in 177, returning the next year to find that Bp. Photinus had been martyred during his absence. Having succeeded Photinus, Irenaeus made his lasting mark upon the Church primarily through his writing *Adversus Haereses*, a work of five books, directed primarily against Gnosticism, and *The Demonstration of the Apostolic Teaching*, another apologetic work.[†]

At first glance, Irenaeus of Lyons might not seem particularly influential in Lutheran thought. A survey of the Confessions reveals only five references to Irenaeus, two of which occur in parallel sections of the German and Latin versions of the *Augustana*. No reference is made to Irenaeus in the *Catalog of Testimonies*. In fact, Irenaeus is only directly quoted in Augustana XXVI—"Disagreement in fasting does not destroy unity of faith"—the other three references only allude to Irenaeus' writings. Irenaeus' view on the "image of God" is declared in Apology II (Original Sin).19 to be in keeping with the understanding expressed by the Lutherans: "What

---

[*] Quasten, Johannes, *Patrology*, vol. 1 (Westminster, Maryland: The Newman Press, 1950), 4 vols., p. 287.

[†] ibid., p. 288-289, 292.

else is this than that a wisdom and righteousness was implanted in man that would grasp God and reflect him, that is, that man received gifts like the knowledge of God, fear of God, and trust in God? So Irenaeus interprets the likeness of God." In Formula of Concord VII (Lord's Supper).14 the reference is contained in a quote from Luther,* with Irenaeus cited in defense of the Lutheran teaching that "there are two things in this sacrament, one heavenly and one earthly." Finally, Irenaeus, together with Hilary, Athanasius, Basil and Gregory of Nyssa, Theodoret and John of Damascus, is cited in FC VIII (Person of Christ) as using the terms "communion" and "union" to describe the relationship of Christ's two natures. Altogether, while Irenaeus had a place in official Lutheran teaching, it is possible to imagine the Confessions holding together quite nicely without making any of these references.

2.2 Luther's and Melanchthon's use of Irenaeus in their Private Writings.

However, Irenaeus is seen in a different light when the *private* writings of the Lutherans are examined. Although the index of the American Edition of Luther's works contains few references to Irenaeus, Luther cited him in defense of his teaching on the Lord's Supper (e.g. LW 37:115-120), and also against Erasmus concerning original sin and the righteousness of the Law. As Luther wrote to George Spalatin in October, 1516:

> ... Moreover [Erasmus] does not clearly state that in Romans, chapter 5, the Apostle is speaking of original sin, although he admits that there is such a thing. Had Erasmus studied the books Augustine wrote against the Pelagians (especially the treatises *On the Letter and the Spirit, On Merits and Forgiveness of Sinners, Against the Two Letters of the Pelagians,* and *Against Julian,* almost all of which can be found in the eighth volume of his works), and had he recognized that nothing in Augustine is of his own wisdom *but is rather that of the most outstanding Fathers,* such as Cyprian [Greg-

---

* Thus a second hand allusion to *Adversus Haereses,* IV, 18, 5!

ory of] Nazianzus, Rheticus, Irenaeus, Hilary, Olympius, Innocent, and Ambrose, then perhaps he would not only correctly understand the Apostle, but he would also hold Augustine in higher esteem than he has so far done. (LW 48:24. Italics added.)

Melanchthon also thought highly of Irenaeus, referring to him as "in his time the only theologian in the Western Church who was still filled with the Apostolic spirit."* Melanchthon was particularly drawn to Irenaeus' doctrine of the person of Christ. "Repeatedly [Melanchthon] declares that he wants to be in line with Irenaeus" because of his scriptural presentation of the doctrine of the Trinity.† A good example of Melanchthon's enthusiastic use of Irenaeus can be found in Locus II, "The Person of the Son of God" of his *Loci Communes*:

> And if someone objects that the divine nature does not suffer or die, but Christ died, the answer is well-known, true, and necessary. Since there are two natures in Christ, the things which are proper to one nature do not hinder the presence of the other nature. Further, these are properties of the human nature, that its members become mutilated, suffer, and die. Therefore Peter clearly said, "Christ suffered in the flesh," 1 Peter 4:1. And Irenaeus with learning and piety says, "Christ was crucified and buried with the Word in quiescence, so that He could be crucified and die" [Bk. 3.19; MPG 7.941], that is, the divine nature indeed was not mutilated or dead but was obedient to the Father, remained quiet, yielded to the wrath of the eternal Father against the sin of the human race, did not use its power or exercise its strength. If you carefully consider this statement of Irenaeus, you will understand that the differences between the

---

* "Irenaeus, qui vir unus illis temporibus mihi reliquus fuisse videtur in occidentis Ecclesia, qui vere Apostolico spiritu fuerit." P. Fraenkel, *Testimonia Patrum*, p. 84, as cited in E.P. Meijering, *Melanchthon and Patristic Thought*, (Leiden: E.J. Brill, 1983), p. 67.

† Meijering, *Melanchthon and Patristic Thought*, p. 70.

natures are reverently described, and that at the same time
light is shed both on the greatness of God's anger against
sin poured out against Christ and on the humility of the
Son who remained quiet and obedient to the Father and
did not exercise His power.[*]

2.3 Chemnitz' Estimation of Irenaeus of Lyons.

It has been observed that for Martin Chemnitz (1522-
1586), "dogmatics is the combination of two specific disciplines: history (church history and the history of dogma) and Biblical study
(exegesis)."[†] This approach can be seen in his *Loci Theologici*. Structured as a commentary on Melanchthon's *Loci Communes*, Chemnitz'
Loci was never finished, but instead was published posthumously by
Polycarp Leyser in 1591.[‡]

Chemnitz' *Loci* contains a special essay entitled "Treatise on
the Reading of the Fathers or Doctors of the Church."[§] Largely built
around summaries of the teachings of various fathers, Chemnitz pointed out the virtues and shortcomings of these fathers to demonstrate
how best to learn from them without falling into the same doctrinal
errors which occasionally snared them. Although later Lutherans
continued emphasizing the study of the fathers, Robert Preus determined that "never again in a dogmatics was there a special section
like this one on the importance of reading the church fathers. This
innovation of Chemnitz' is not insignificant: Chemnitz is the first
to bring the systematic study of church history and the history of
doctrine into a book dealing specifically with Christian doctrine."[C]

Chemnitz' reason for writing such a treatise is quite practical, even pastoral, coming in response to the request of friends:

* Chemnitz, Martin, *Loci Theologici*, (St. Louis: Concordia Publishing House,
1989), vol. 1, 2 vols., p. 88. [Citation from Melanchthon's text.]
† Preus, Robert, *The Theology of Post-Reformation Lutheranism*, vol 1. (St. Louis:
Concordia Publishing House, 1970), p. 98.
‡ ibid., p. 48.
§ *Loci Theologici*, vol. 1, pp. 27-33. The treatise will be referred to as TRFDC in
this paper for the sake of brevity.
C ibid., p. 93.

For although one could with great usefulness speak at length on the way to read the fathers safely, and could demonstrate the fruitfulness of such study in addition to the study of the sacred canonical Scriptures, yet in this present instance it is necessary to speak only briefly concerning the writings of certain individual fathers. For it is useful, even necessary, that one who is about to read them has in advance a method worked out in his mind and knows what is especially important in the individual fathers and what stands out, where dangers need to be avoided, and in which areas they speak correctly and usefully.*

In essence, Chemnitz cautions his reader to know the context of the work in question. With an understanding of the general "thrust" of the particular father, as well as both his strengths and weaknesses, the reader is better prepared to use such research beneficially. Fortunately, Irenaeus is one of the fathers Chemnitz examines in this treatise, and he does so as follows:

Irenaeus [*Adversus Haereses*, MPG 7(1-2)] is by far the oldest among those whose writings are extant and of whom there is nothing doubtful. He sat at the feet of Polycarp, the disciple of John. Moreover, he wrote many things which were preserved by Jerome. But in our day only five books remain, and these indeed are rather badly translated, since Irenaeus in his own language speaks with great elegance. Epiphanius cites several portions from his Greek original. There is the rumor that somewhere a Greek copy is in existence, and it would be a worthy effort to try to bring it to light. For many things which are inadequately translated could then be understood more exactly. However, these books are most worthy of our reading because they deal with the main points of the Christian faith in a most fundamental way. For in those days heretics were rejecting the Scripture and obtruding onto the churches their own ab-

---

* *Loci Theologici*, p. 27.

surd ravings under the name of apostolic tradition. Therefore Irenaeus sets forth the true tradition which had been
commended to the church by the apostles, namely, that the
summary of the faith is comprehended in the creed (for he
often cites the creed in almost the precise words), and he
says that the tradition in all the apostolic churches is the
same. To this he adds the text of Scripture and in many
ways demonstrates which of the writings of the apostles
are canonical. He summarizes the matter in two points,
tradition or the creed, and the text of Scripture; and what
does not agree with these, he rejects as heretical. We must
carefully observe this in opposition to our adversaries who
are trying to get the church to accept notable errors and
manifest abuses on the grounds that the only traditions are
the things which they say. In the second place, the pious
mind will be greatly comforted when it sees that in the description of the heretics of that time the face of the papacy
is already becoming evident with all its errors and abuses,
such as anointing, extreme unction, and many other matters. Furthermore, a great many fine doctrinal points are
contained in the writings of Irenaeus concerning nearly
every article of faith, such as the two natures in Christ,
the Eucharist, which is not a sacrifice as our adversaries
imagine, and that the fathers in the Old Testament were
saved by the same faith as the saints of the New Testament.
Again, however, because even at that time he was disputing against the same notion which the Manichaeans later
embraced, he speaks harshly and unfortunately concerning
the free will. Again, because he was opposed by those who
dreamed that there is one God who is the righteous God of
the Law and another God who is the merciful God of the
New Testament, he sometimes speaks carelessly regarding
the distinction of Law and Gospel. But in other places he
makes a proper and careful statement concerning faith in
Christ and justification. He does not set forth a sufficiently

accurate definition of original sin because he is speaking in opposition to those who attributed the cause of sin to God. We can read these points in many places in Irenaeus and, when we see clearly both the cause and the occasion of what he says and why he speaks the way he does, then his words can be read without offense and with real profit. There are some rather superficial statements, as in his explanation of Elohim, Adonai, Sabaoth, which are lacking in grammatical foundation. And when he says that Christ was almost 50 years old, he has no historical basis. The ancient church noted in him one basic error, namely, his holding to chiliasm, and there are in Bk. 5 a few seeds of this error in his handling of certain chapters of the Apocalypse.*

In summary, Chemnitz highlights four central points on which to praise Irenaeus and five to criticize. On the positive side, Irenaeus' *Adversus Haereses*: (1) "deal with the main points of Christian faith in a most fundamental way," (2) "In the second place, the pious mind will be greatly comforted when it sees that in the description of the heretics of that time the face of the papacy is already becoming evident with all its errors and abuses," (3) "a great many fine doctrinal points are contained in the writings of Irenaeus concerning nearly every article of faith," and particularly, (4) "he makes a proper and careful statement concerning faith in Christ and justification." Chemnitz identifies Irenaeus' short-comings as: (1) speaking "harshly and unfortunately concerning the free will," (2) speaking "carelessly regarding the distinction of Law and Gospel," (3) "He does not set forth a sufficiently accurate definition of original sin," (4) "there are some superficial statements" and, finally, (5) chiliasm.

The question remains whether Chemnitz actually followed these guidelines in practice. It has been estimated that Irenaeus is the father cited sixth most often in Chemnitz' writings.† How did

* ibid., pp. 28-29.

† Kelly, Robert A., "Tradition and Innovation: The Use of Theodoret's *Eranistes* in Martin Chemnitz' *De Duabus Naturis in Christo*," in *Perspectives on Christology: Essays in Honor of Paul K. Jewett*, ed. Marguerite Shuster and Richard Muller

Irenaeus benefit Chemnitz' work? The following section seeks to offer a preliminary answer to this question by examining the *Loci Theologici* of Martin Chemnitz. The chief aim will be seeing whether Chemnitz' evaluation of Irenaeus' teaching in *Loci Theologici* matches that given in the treatise.

3. Chemnitz' Use of Irenaeus in *Loci Theologici*.

3.1 General Observations.

However, before turning to the precise content, certain general observations seem warranted concerning Chemnitz' use of Irenaeus. First of all, virtually all attributed references to Irenaeus' writings come from his *Adversus Haereses*. Obviously Chemnitz could not have utilized *The Demonstration of the Apostolic Teaching*, since its text was not re-discovered until 1904.* No other surviving fragment of Irenaeus' work is quoted, but Chemnitz does make reference to works no longer extant, such as *De monarchia*.†

All five books of *Adversus Haereses* are utilized. Book 2, however, is only cited in the sections carried over from Melanchthon's *Loci Communes*. Book 4 is the book used most extensively by Chemnitz. Irenaeus citations occur in the following loci: I (God), II (The Person of the Son of God), IV (Creation), V (The Cause of Sin and Concerning Contingency), VI (Human Powers or Free Choice), VII (Sin), XIII (Justification), XIV (Good Works), and XVII (The Church).‡

(Grand Rapids: Zondervan Publishing House, 1991), p. 107. Kelly estimates that those fathers cited more often than Irenaeus are: John of Damascus, Cyril, Athanasius, Augustine and Theodoret.

* "For a long time not more than the title of this work (Euseb. *Hist. eccl.* 5,26) was known. In 1904 the entire text was discovered in an Armenian version by Ter-Mekerttschian who edited it for the first time in 1907." Quasten, p. 292.

† *Loci Theologici*, vol. 1, p. 189.

‡ It should be remembered that since loci IX, X, XI, XII, XX and XXI were not included in the CPH translation, they were not included in this study. This means that only loci III, VIII, XV, XVI, XVIII and XIX are believed not to contain any reference to Irenaeus' writings.

3.2 Irenaeus' explanation of the "the main points of the Christian faith."

[T]hese books are most worthy of our reading because they deal with the main points of the Christian faith in a most fundamental way. For in those days heretics were rejecting the Scripture and obtruding onto the churches their own absurd ravings under the name of apostolic tradition. Therefore Irenaeus sets forth the true tradition which had been commended to the church by the apostles, namely, that the summary of the faith is comprehended in the creed ... To this he adds the text of Scripture and in many ways demonstrates which of the writings of the apostles are canonical. He summarizes the matter in two points, tradition or the creed, and the text of Scripture; and what does not agree with these, he rejects as heretical. We must carefully observe this in opposition to our adversaries who are trying to get the church to accept notable errors and manifest abuses on the grounds that the only traditions are the things which they say.[*]

Irenaeus provided Chemnitz with a vital window into the dogmatic history of the early church, highlighting the course of early creedal development and profiling the struggle against the early heresies. Chemnitz considers the Apostles' Creed to be the "most important" of the early summaries of Christian doctrine, "For it is extant under the traditional name of the Apostles' Creed in almost the same words in Irenaeus and Tertullian, the oldest writers of the church. It is given the honorable name, 'the canon and rule of faith.'"[†] In fact, Chemnitz ends Locus I, chapter III, "The Definition [of God]" with Irenaeus' rendering of the creed:

> The church has been planted throughout the world and to the uttermost ends of the earth by the apostles and their disciples and has received from them this faith which believes in the one God the Father, the Almighty who made the heaven and the earth, the sea, and all that is in them. And in the one Jesus Christ, the Son of God who became incarnate for our salvation. And in the Holy Spirit, who

---

[*] *Loci Theologici*, pp. 28-29.
[†] ibid., p. 38.

through the prophets predicted the mysteries and coming of this dispensation, and His birth of the Virgin, His suffering and resurrection from the dead, and the bodily ascension into heaven of our Lord Jesus Christ, our God and Savior and King, according to the pleasure of the invisible Father, every knee shall bow of things in heaven and things on earth and things under the earth, and every tongue confess Him, and He will bring a righteous judgment to all [*Adv. Haer.* 1.10, MPG 7(1).550].*

The parallel between this passage and elements of the creed as it is known today is striking, and the beauty of the formulation clearly had an impact on Chemnitz, since he made it his "last word" on the definition.

Chemnitz also praises Irenaeus for his role in determining the parameters of the biblical canon because he is well aware of the numerous pseudopigrapha circulated by heretics in the early church as they sought to legitimize their teachings. The canonical books had been challenged because:

Against these canonical writings the fanatics wrote opposition documents, which went under the titles of traditions, and they brought in many other and different teachings in which they alleged the apostles had taught in public meetings and private discussions with their followers whom they claimed as living witnesses. But Irenaeus and Tertullian prove from the form of the churches founded by the apostles that the true traditions or teachings of the apostles were not different but were absolutely the same as those signed by them and included in the apostolic writings. Therefore the form of the traditions in the apostolic churches in every way agrees with the apostolic writings. In this way the reliable canon of the New Testament Scriptures was established. But very quickly spurious writings began to be spread. However, those who were true disciples of the

* ibid., p. 62.

apostles exercised their judgment and rejected these adulterated writings.*

Chemnitz often returns to the wealth of knowledge in *Adversus Haereses* concerning the early heresies. This interest is not an idle curiosity, but is based on the conviction that yesterday's heresies will be back tomorrow. Chemnitz observes, for example, a common Christological error in Valentius, Marcion and the Anabaptists of the so-called "Kingdom of Münster":

> First Valentius, Marcion, and very many others contended that Christ did not assume a true human nature or flesh consubstantial with Mary and with us but brought with Him from heaven a sidereal, heavenly, and elemental body.
>
> And to prove their opinion they misinterpret the following passages: 1 Cor. 15:47; John 6:62; 3:13.
>
> But at this point we are not contending merely against condemned ghosts of heretics, but the devil in our own time, under new colors, is recalling to light from hell heresies which long ago had been totally stamped out. For that horrible monster of most repulsive views in Münster had in its first line of battle an article which would destroy the true human nature in Christ. Therefore we must cling to the sure testimonies which confirm this part of the rule as a basic statement, that the Son of God assumed a human nature consubstantial with Mary and with us.†

Chemnitz also notes early heretical notions concerning the necessity of good works. In Locus XIV, Chemnitz again draws a

---

* *Loci Theologici*, vol. 2, p. 468.

† *Loci Theologici*, vol. 1, p. 106. Lewis Spitz observes: "The wildest adventure of the militant Anabaptists was the proclamation of the Kingdom of Münster. ... Münster was declared the New Jerusalem which would be spared when all the rest of the world was destroyed, before Easter of that year. ... In August 1534, after beating off an attack of the bishop's mercenary army, John [of Leiden] had himself proclaimed king of the New Jerusalem and the Messiah or anointed one of the last days foretold by the prophets of the Old Testament." *The Renaissance and Reformation Movements* (St. Louis: Concordia Publishing House, 1987), vol. 2, 2 vols., p. 401-403.

parallel between the early heretics and 16th century Anabaptists:

It would be difficult to believe that such abominable filth could be brought into the church and mixed with its doctrine at the very beginning of the Gospel, if we in our own age had not experienced almost the same things in the case of the Anabaptists. Lest anyone think that we are doing them an injustice, we shall quote the words of the fathers with which they described the aberrations of their own era. Irenaeus [*Adversus Haereses*, 1.23 (new 24), MPL 7.678], discusses the statements of Basilides and his shameless life, and among other things he says that Basilides was indifferent to the practice of lust. Irenaeus, in discussing the heresy of the Carpocratians, says [ibid., 1.24 (new 25), MPL 7.682], "They are so uncontrolled in their raving that they say they can do whatever irreligious and ungodly things they want to do. They say that good and evil are only matters of human opinion, since by nature nothing is evil." In 1.32 (new 29) [MPL 7.691], he describes the wild lusts of Basilides and Carpocrates thus: "Some people take the occasion from their association with Basilides and Carpocrates to practice promiscuous sexual relations, enter into multiple marriages and the neglect of their own families, and they say that such things as eating meat sacrificed to idols is a matter of indifference to God."*

Thus we see that Chemnitz makes use of Irenaeus just as he had outlined: Irenaeus is cited for his concise statement of the faith, his efforts in establishing the scope of the biblical canon, and his refutation of the heretics addresses the faith "in a most fundamental way" which still speaks against modern heresies.

3.3 Irenaeus' Foreshadowing of "the face of the Papacy."

In the second place, the pious mind will be greatly comforted when it sees that in the description of the heretics of that time the face of the papacy is already

* *Loci Theologici*, vol. 2, p. 577.

46

*becoming evident with all its errors and abuses, such as anointing, extreme unction, and many other matters.**

A survey of *Loci Theologici* and the *Examen* found no citations of Irenaeus in reference to anointing and extreme unction, and none of the Irenaean quotes collected from the *Loci* yielded any such links between early heresies and the sixteenth century papacy. Rather, what was found was a large number of links between the ancient heresies and the Anabaptists, as was shown above in 3.2.

3.4 "A great many fine doctrinal points are contained in the writings of Irenaeus..."

Furthermore, a great many fine doctrinal points are contained in the writings of Irenaeus concerning nearly every article of faith, such as the two natures in Christ, the Eucharist, which is not a sacrifice as our adversaries imagine, and that the fathers in the Old Testament were saved by the same faith as the saints of the New Testament.†

As noted above (section 2.2) Melanchthon was particularly drawn to Irenaeus' Christology. This affection carries over into Chemnitz' theology, with the result that both the *Loci Communes* and *Loci Theologici* drew upon Irenaeus in the formulation of this locus. Melanchthon (whose *Loci Communes* Chemnitz incorporated into *Loci Theologici*) praised Irenaeus' understanding of the two natures:

> And if someone objects that the divine nature does not suffer or die, but Christ died, the answer is well-known, true, and necessary. Since there are two natures in Christ, the things which are proper to one nature do not hinder the presence of the other nature. Further, these are properties of the human nature, that its members become mutilated, suffer, and die. Therefore Peter clearly said, "Christ suffered in the flesh," 1 Peter 4:1. And Irenaeus with learning and piety says, "Christ was crucified and buried with the Word in quiescence, so that He could be crucified and die" [Bk. 3.19; MPG 7.941], that is, the

* *Loci Theologici*, vol. 1, p. 29.
† ibid.

divine nature indeed was not mutilated or dead but was obedient to the Father, remained quiet, yielded to the wrath of the eternal Father against the sin of the human race, did not use its power or exercise its strength. If you carefully consider this statement of Irenaeus, you will understand that the differences between the natures are reverently described, and that at the same time light is shed both on the greatness of God's anger against sin poured out against Christ and on the humility of the Son who remained quiet and obedient to the Father and did not exercise His power.*

As if this were not a strong enough endorsement of Irenaeus' formulation, Melanchthon adds that "Care behooves the pious, for the sake of harmony, to speak in line with the church. And it was not without good reasons that the ancient church approved some ways of speaking and rejected others."† Irenaeus' formulation is the *Church's* formulation; his words are 'pious' and 'reverent.'

Since Locus XX (The Lord's Supper) was not included in the English translation of *Loci Theologici*, we have not examined Chemnitz' use of Irenaeus within that context. However, Irenaeus was used extensively in Chemnitz' *De coena Domini*. In chapter 10, "Arguments from the Testimonies of the Ancient Church," Irenaeus is a key church father quoted in support of the Lutheran position over against those of Rome and Geneva. For example,

But there is no need for conjecture or books of divination, for Irenaeus himself clearly and specifically calls the bread also the body of Christ, the cup also the blood of Christ. ... Nor are the words "body and blood" ambiguous. For Irenaeus in *Adversus haereses*, Bk. 5, ch. 2, adds a completely clear explanation. He says that the blood is nothing less than what flows from the veins, the flesh, and the rest of human substance, which was truly made the Word of God who redeemed us by His blood.‡

* ibid., p. 88.
† ibid.
‡ Chemnitz, Martin, *The Lord's Supper*, trans. J.A.O. Preus (St. Louis: Con-

And later Chemnitz notes:

> ...Further, the reader should note that Irenaeus does not base his argument, as the adversaries do, on our bodies receiving only the external symbols of the body of Christ and that from the soul a power afterwards redounds to our body. But Irenaeus argues in this way: "Just as that which is bread from the earth, when it receives the call of God is no longer common bread but the Eucharist, consisting of two parts, the earthly and the heavenly, so also our bodies when they share in the Eucharist which consists of these two things are no longer subject to corruption but possess the hope of the resurrection."[*]

As can be seen even from this small sample, Chemnitz utilizes Irenaeus' writings to support Lutheran teaching concerning the "real presence."[†] At the same time, the second citation, by referring to the Eucharist "consisting of two parts, the earthly and the heavenly" also wreaks havoc on the Roman doctrine of transubstantiation.

---

cordia Publishing House, 1979), p. 152. Chemnitz' 'paraphrase' of Irenaeus is almost a verbatim quote, for the passage in book 5, chapter 2 reads as follows: "For blood can only come from veins and flesh, and whatsoever else makes up the substance of man, such as the Word of God was actually made. By his own blood he redeemed us, as also His apostle declares, 'In whom we have redemption through His blood, even the remission of sins.' ... He has acknowledged the cup (which is part of the creation) as His own blood, from which He bedews our blood; and the bread (also a part of the creation) He has established as His own body, from which He gives increase to our bodies." *The Ante-Nicene Fathers of the Church*, ed. Alexander Roberts and James Donaldson (Grand Rapids: Wm. B. Eerdmanns Publishing Company, 1989) vol. 1, 10 vols., p. 528.

[*] ibid., p. 169.

[†] Chemnitz also quotes Irenaeus in this context in the *Examen*: "Irenaeus says 'When to the cup with its mixture and the bread which has been broken the Word of God is added, it becomes the Eucharist of the body and blood of the Lord.' And that he understands this of the word of institution he explains when he says that the earthly bread receives the call of God, namely, when Christ declares concerning the bread, 'This is My body.'" *Examination of the Council of Trent*, vol. 1, p. 227.

Finally, Chemnitz asserts that Irenaeus teaches that "the fathers in the Old Testament were saved by the same faith as the saints of the New Testament..." Certainly this is an accurate estimation of Irenaeus' teaching, since one finds in 4.21:

> 1. But that our faith was also prefigured in Abraham, and that he was the patriarch of our faith, and, as it were, the prophet of it, the apostle has very fully taught [Gal. 3:5-9 are cited] ... For which [reason the apostle] declared that this man was not only the prophet of faith, but also the father of those who from among the Gentiles believe in Jesus Christ, because his faith and ours are one and the same: for he believed in things future, as if they were already accomplished, because of the promise of God; and in like manner do we also, because of the promise of God, behold through faith that inheritance [laid up for us] in the [future] kingdom.*

However, Chemnitz does not hold up this teaching in *Loci Theologici*, but instead writes in Locus XIII (Justification):

> An excessive amount of admiration for outward discipline and for natural human powers in the unregenerate brought great darkness over this article. Thus Irenaeus 4.30 [new 4.16, MPG 7(1).107], says, "The fathers before the promulgation of the Law were righteous by the natural law. ... In short, Pelagianism was built out of many unfortunate statements of this kind."†

3.5 Irenaeus' "careful statement concerning faith in Christ and justification."

But in other places he makes a proper and careful statement concerning faith in Christ and justification.‡

A significant proportion of Chemnitz' Locus XIII (Justification) is devoted to defending the Lutheran use of the terms

---

* *The Ante-Nicene Fathers*, vol. 1, p. 492.

† *Loci Theologici*, vol. 2, p. 471.

‡ *Loci Theologici*, vol. 1, p. 29.

'faith' and 'grace.' It is precisely in defense of the expression "by faith alone" that Chemnitz praises Irenaeus. Chemnitz declares that "The expression 'by faith alone' in the article of justification was not dreamed up as something new and for the first time by our theologians, but it was always used in the complete consensus of all antiquity in connection with this article, as examples from the writings of the fathers testify." Chemnitz cites Ambrose, Basil, Hilary, Chrysostom and several other ancient writers before observing, "Therefore we can correctly say with Erasmus: 'This word *sola*, which has been attacked with so much noise in the era of Luther, was reverently heard and read among the fathers.'"[†] It is after this point that Chemnitz cites Irenaeus: "Note the clear use of the exclusive concept in Irenaeus [*Adv. Haer.*], 4:37-38 [MPG 7(1).1031-46], 'Men are saved from the ancient serpent in no other way than that they believe in Him.'"[‡] This citation is not given the prominence of many of the other patristic citations, being tacked on after his citation from Erasmus, and one almost wonders if Chemnitz hesitated to use it. It is certainly one of the shortest references to the fathers in this section. Nevertheless, while one would not wish to defend the entire Lutheran appeal to the fathers on this one quote, the overall argument is quite impressive, allowing Chemnitz justification for claiming patristic support for the phrase "by faith alone."

3.6 Irenaeus spoke "harshly and unfortunately concerning the free will."

Again, however, because even at that time he was disputing against the same notion which the Manichaeans later embraced, he speaks harshly and unfortunately concerning the free will.[§]

As would be expected, Chemnitz' citations from Irenaeus on the "free will" are found in Loci V (The Cause of Sin and Concerning Contingency) and VI (Human Powers or Free Choice).

* *Loci Theologici*, vol. 2, p. 541-542.
† ibid., p. 542.
‡ ibid.
§ *Loci Theologici*, p. 29.

Chemnitz notes at the outset of Locus V, chapter II, "The Chief Controversies...Regarding the Cause of Sin," that "First we must explain the controversies which in and outside of the church have corrupted and perverted the true meaning of this locus as given to us in the Word of God."* Irenaeus is praised in this context for writing his *De monarchia* or *That God is Not the Author of Sin* against the Marcionite heresy, which "attributed the cause of sin to a god who ... compelled men against their will to commit crimes..."†

Irenaeus is again cited in chapter IV ("Explanation of Certain Scripture Passages Which Can Be Raised in Objection") as Chemnitz argues against a Calvinistic double predestination. Chemnitz notes that certain Scripture passages were misused "even in antiquity... in opposition to the true teaching concerning this question, as we read in Irenaeus, Bk. 4."‡ The first passage Chemnitz treats—"I will harden the heart of Pharaoh" (Ex. 4:21)—was also used by the Marcionites in defense of their teaching. Here the statements of Irenaeus needed to be "glossed" in later generations. As Chemnitz observes:

> The ancients with earnest and feasible interpretations tried to soften statements such as that of Irenaeus, where he says regarding the hardening of Pharaoh's heart: "Therefore God has given them up unto their unbelief and turned His face away from people of this kind, leaving them in the darkness which they have chosen for themselves" [*Adv. Haer.* 4.29, MPG 7.1064] ... Thus these expressions really refer to permission. But this permission is not to be understood in the sense that... God wills, approves, or aids crimes, or that God does not really care when men commit crimes such as the permission of tryants [sic], but God is not the efficacious cause, aiding, moving, or forcing our wills to sin.§

---

* ibid., p. 186.

† ibid., p. 189. Chemnitz cited Eusebius' *Hist. eccl.* as his source of information concerning this non-extant work.

‡ ibid., p. 192.

§ ibid., p. 194-195. Irenaeus continues in 4.29: "If, therefore, in the present time also,

In chapter VIII, "The Modes of Speaking," Chemnitz notes that "We ought to be careful in our ways of speaking on all subjects, but especially when we are speaking about God. ... Therefore we shall first review at this point some of the formulas for speaking used by those who have upset the teaching of this locus."* Because of their historical setting, Justin Martyr and Irenaeus were most susceptible to poor terminology on this point:

> Before the time of the Manichaeans those who corrupted this locus used this method of speaking, as Justin describes: "All things which happen happen out of the necessity of fate. The wicked have been made such by fate." [MPG 6.392]

> Irenaeus gives us this formula: "When man sins, the power comes from God."†

Irenaeus' statements strike the modern reader (and obviously the sixteenth century reader, as well!) as inconsistent, rejecting Marcionite claims which "attributed the cause of sin to a god" and yet proclaiming, "When man sins, the power comes from God." Such statements need careful interpretation for the danger of false doctrine to be avoided. Thus the explanation of "permission." Chemnitz' thrust here is as stated in TRFDC: "Again, however, because even at that time he was disputing against the same notion which the Manichaeans later embraced, he speaks harshly and unfortunately concerning the free will."‡

Chemnitz addresses Irenaeus' "carelessness" again in Locus VI

God, knowing the number of those who will not believe, since He foreknows all things, has given them over to unbelief, and turned away His face from men of this stamp, leaving them in the darkness which they have themselves chosen for themselves, what is there wonderful if He did also at that time give over to their unbelief, Pharaoh, who never would have believed, along with those who were with him?" *The Ante-Nicene Fathers*, vol. 1, p. 502.

* ibid., p. 215.

† ibid.

‡ ibid., p. 29.

(Human Powers or Free Choice). Chemnitz acknowledges that "This locus is very complicated and includes many questions which need verification,"* and he begins by determining the *status controversiae*:

> What kind of power does man possess after the Fall to render obedience to the Law, since our mind is darkened and our will turned away from God, and in our own hearts there is a stubborn resistance to the law of God? And since the law of God demands not only external, civil obedience but also the continuous and perfect obedience of our entire human nature, the question is what and how much the human will can do. And thus the title "Human Powers" is preferable to "Free Choice" or "Free Will."†

Chemnitz next determines to "say something about the term 'free choice,' for many perplexing matters are related to this expression."‡ Chemnitz explains that:

> Justin uses three words: 1. *autexousion* (possessing a free will); 2. *eleuthera proairesis* (free will); 3. *to eph' hemin* (that which is in us). The same words were used by Irenaeus, as we can gather from the Latin translation. For he says that man is of a free opinion and that he has the power of choosing, and that that power is in us. ...
>
> The translation of Irenaeus uses the terms "free choice" and "the power of free choice." Hence among the Latin writers the term "free choice" always continues in use.
>
> ...
>
> Irenaeus, 4.37 [MPG 7.1099], puts it this way, "God has put into men the power of choice (*proairesis*), which He also has given to the angels."§

---

* ibid., p. 226-227.
† ibid., p. 227-228.
‡ ibid., p. 228.
§ ibid. The emphasis in Irenaeus is against notions of the "compulsion of God": "For there is no coercion with God, but a good will [toward us] is present with Him continually. And therefore does He give good counsel to all. And in man, as well as in angels, He has placed the power of choice (for angels are rational

Chemnitz chooses not to argue directly against these fathers at this point, but instead notes the modifications in terminology which occurred during the confrontation with the Pelagians. When one is speaking of the state of the sinner before God, Chemnitz urges that "the words which Augustine correctly used in opposition to the Pelagian praise of freedom, such as: the enslaved will, the captive will, the destroyed, the loose will, the damnable handmaiden, stubbornness, and nonfreedom."* The term "free choice" should be limited to civil righteousness.

Chemnitz raises the matter of contradictory patristic citations in the final section of the locus, "Refutation of Arguments." Again, Chemnitz' concern is with the Pelagians:

> We must say something about the testimonies of the ancients by which Pelagius tried to prove that he had the agreement of the church of all antiquity. A consideration of this point has many uses. For there is no more illustrative example as to how imprecisely the fathers, outside of the controversies, spoke than on this locus. Likewise, it shows how the imprecise statements of the ancients have to be interpreted according to the analogy of faith. For when we read the arguments of Justin, Irenaeus, and Tertullian regarding free choice—which they used in opposition to the Marcionites and others like them—if the titles of the works did not tell us by which authors the books had been written, we would think that we were hearing the very words of Pelagius.
>
> Justin, *Apologia* [2.6, MPG 6.455], "Good works would not be praised, nor evil ones condemned, if man does not have an equal power to turn himself from one direction to the other." Pelagius spoke almost exactly the same words. Irenaeus, 4.71 [MPG 7.1099], "The power is not from God, but a good intention is always in man. And because of this condition

beings), so that those who had yielded obedience might justly possess what is good, given indeed by God, but preserved by themselves." *The Ante-Nicene Fathers*, vol. 1, p. 518.

* ibid., p. 229.

He gives some good quality to all. Further, He has given to man the power of choosing, just as to the angels." Ch. 72 [MPG 7.1100], "All men are of the same nature, capable of keeping and doing the good, and able to lose and not do the good." Many more statements of this kind can be found.*

The intent here is certainly not to accuse Irenaeus of being Pelagian, since Chemnitz states the historical reasons why such "free choice" terminology was selected. Rather, Chemnitz' focus is on the need for precision in one's theological terminology, which is precisely the criticism raised in the TRFDC. Such imprecise terminology must be explained according to the analogy of faith. Irenaeus' incautious use of "free choice" allowed the Pelagians to distort his teaching into a weapon against the orthodox faith. Indeed, the Pelagian controversy eliminated the freedom to use this term in the way Irenaeus did. While it was possible for Irenaeus to give such terminology an orthodox meaning before the Pelagian controversy, such freedom does not exist now.

If a person does not recognize that these statements are improper, he is a manifest Pelagian. Nor was Pelagius merely a stammering child. For he could not only list testimonies from the ancients, but he could pile them up and amplify them. All those whose writings are extant, from the time of the apostles, he cited as sharing his views and speaking the same way. And for Augustine it was much easier to refute Pelagius and to establish the true doctrine from Scripture than to refute him from the fathers. Likewise, it proved to be of more importance to Pelagius to pile up citations from the ancient writers than passages of Holy Scripture. For this reason I have often marveled, since the writings of the ancients were held in such honor at that time, that Augustine could defend his own teachings which he drew from Scripture, while Pelagius had for himself such a long series of fathers who asserted the dogma of Pelagius in almost the

* ibid., p. 259.

same words. There is no doubt that Augustine had been divinely endowed with so great authority that his teaching was upheld and preserved against these corruptions.

But we should observe by what line of reasoning Augustine dealt with this matter so as to ward off attacks. (1) From the clear testimonies of Scripture he established the true doctrine and refuted Pelagius. (2) He retracted many of his own statements which he had injudiciously made and quietly noted statements among the writings of others which were not quite correctly set forth. Finally, he freely approached the statements of the fathers which Pelagius used, and with a certain degree of helpful interpretation, which was often rather painstakingly discovered, he softened certain of these citations. And what he could not soften or where a better interpretation could not be made, he clearly rejected it.[*]

Augustine serves to make precisely the point raised by Chemnitz and Luther (e.g. *The Bondage of the Will*) over against the "semi-Pelagian" Romanists: do not attempt to refute the Lutheran teaching on this doctrine by appealing to the fathers' use of inappropriate terminology, since these usages predate the controversies establishing the correct manner of speaking of the human will. Doctrine should be established on the basis of Scripture, not the incautious overstatements of fathers who were confronting a different heresy within a specific historical context.

3.7 Irenaeus' carelessness "regarding the distinction of Law and Gospel".

Again, because he was opposed by those who dreamed that there is one God who is the righteous God of the Law and another God who is the merciful God of the New Testament, he sometimes speaks carelessly regarding the distinction of Law and Gospel.[†]

---

[*] ibid., p. 259-260.
[†] ibid., p. 29.

As in previous sections ("Free Will," for example), Chemnitz attributes Irenaeus' confusing terminology to his struggle against the Marcionites. Chemnitz' tone is almost apologetic during his discussion of "unfortunate statements of the fathers" in Locus XIII (Justification):

> We have made the point regarding the reading of the history of the church so that we might consider how the ancient writers, when they were involved in controversies on the articles of faith, failed to deal with the doctrine of justification carefully and circumspectly. For often, when they were occupied with something else, they made many unfortunate statements that later on gave occasion for a gradual and serious departure from the purity of this article. ...
>
> But it is not our purpose to be like Ham, who uncovered his father's shame. Thus we shall not deal with the lapses of those by whose labors we have been aided and whose gray hairs we ought to honor, but we will refer to them only as warnings so that we may be cautioned by their examples to be more careful and diligent in preserving the purity of this doctrine, so that we never give occasion to anyone to follow in these footsteps. ...*

This having been said, however, Chemnitz notes that such confusion was "widespread" and "the statements are very unfortunate" at best:

> 3. The confusion of Law and Gospel was widespread in the church, and even if we speak charitably, the statements are very unfortunate. They did not distinguish accurately enough as to what kind of righteousness the Law was describing, nor the purpose of the Law, nor did they define what the doctrine of the Gospel is, properly speaking, or what the righteousness of faith before God is, and why we must have another kind of righteousness than that of the Law.

---

* *Loci Theologici*, vol. 2, p. 469-470.

... So as not to prolong the list, even Irenaeus, Tertullian, Origen, and Eusebius, when they tried to distinguish the righteousness of the Law and the Gospel, only refer to the doctrine of works and only distinguish according to what is greater and what is less. As Clement says in his *Stromata*, 6.18 [MPG 9.398], the righteousness of the Pharisees was rejected because they only refrained from evils. And in Book 7 he says, "The Law prohibits only evil actions, but the Gospel also prohibits evil thoughts." We can read similar ideas in Irenaeus [*Adversus Haereses*, 4.42], Tertullian, *Adversus Marcionem* [4.9], Eusebius, *Demonstratio Evangelica*, 4.2, and Chrysostom, *Homilia 16 in Matt.*.*

Irenaeus' alleged confusion rests on an incomplete understanding of Matthew 5:20: "For I tell you that unless your righteousness surpasses that of the Pharisees and the teachers of the law, you will certainly not enter the kingdom of heaven." (NIV) In 4.13, Irenaeus explains the passage as follows:

In the first place, [we must] believe not only in the Father, but also in His Son now revealed; for He it is who leads man into fellowship and unity with God. In the next place, [we must] not only say, but we must do; for they said, but did not. And [we must] not only abstain from evil deeds, but even from the desires after them. Now He did not teach us these things as being opposed to the law, but as fulfilling the law, and implanting in us the varied righteousness of the law.†

On this occasion, however, it is difficult to judge Irenaeus too harshly, particularly if one sees this statement not as three tasks to be completed for salvation, but in terms of Justification and Sanctification. The passage stresses faith in the Son of God for salvation "who leads man into fellowship and unity with God," and only then are "good works." In addition, the stress throughout this chapter is on works performed in the freedom of the Gospel:

---

* ibid., p. 470.
† *Ante-Nicene Fathers*, vol. 1, p. 477.

For the law, since it was laid down for those in bondage, used to instruct the soul by means of those corporeal objects which were of an external nature, drawing it, as by a bond, to obey its commandments, that man might learn to serve God. But the Word set free the soul, and taught that through it the body should be willingly purified. ... the working of the liberty is greater and more glorious than that obedience which is rendered in slavery.*

Chemnitz was also clearly alarmed by the severity of the practice of church discipline in the early church, no doubt in part because he saw in those practices the groundwork for what would become the Roman system of satisfactions, but also because he feared it inculcated the view that penitence and faith were not enough, thus depriving the penitent of hope:

The older writers judged that with severity of discipline in receiving the lapsed, people could be held to the work of pious devotion and be deterred from security and levity which lead to sin. ... Irenaeus 4.45 [4.27, MPG 7(2).1036ff.], cites the statement of a certain elder who had heard the apostles preach: "To those of former times the death of the Lord was the cure and remission of their sins, but in the case of those who sin now, Christ does not die for them any longer, but the Son will come as a judge. Therefore we ought to fear lest after knowing Christ we do something which is not pleasing to God, for we do not have the remission of sins again, but shall be excluded from His kingdom." These statements of this elder are sufficiently hard and unyielding.

... And they tormented the souls of the penitent over a period of several years with their teachings regarding satisfactions before they were received back into the church. Hence the true doctrine of repentance, grace, faith, and the free remission of sins was greatly obscured, something the

---

* ibid.

fathers failed to notice because of their over concern with discipline.*

Once again, when errorists (the Montanists and the Novatians this time) arose and "destroyed hope and brought shame upon Christ," the fathers found it necessary to study Scripture and "study the unfortunate statements they and others had made which supplied the seeds for Novatianism. They retracted these statements and corrected them according to the norm of the Word of God."† Again, Chemnitz' clear criticism is the danger posed by inadequate doctrinal formulations.

3.8 An Inadequate Definition of Original Sin.

He does not set forth a sufficiently accurate definition of original sin because he is speaking in opposition to those who attributed the cause of sin to God.‡

Chemnitz appears to have virtually ignored Irenaeus during his defense of Lutheran teaching concerning original sin. In fact, there is only one citation from Irenaeus in the relevant sections of *Loci Theologici* and the *Examen* combined! In his chapter on the "Definition of Original Sin," Chemnitz remarks that, "Irenaeus says that it is a trap of the old serpent from which human beings are saved through Christ. Again, 'Bound by the chains of Adam, we were dead.'"§ Obviously the quote is used in supporting of Lutheran teaching, thus avoiding a negative use of Irenaeus, as was the case in other articles.

3.9 Irenaeus' "Superficial Statements."

There are some rather superficial statements, as in his explanation of Elohim, Adonai, Sabaoth, which are lacking in grammatical foundation. And when he says that Christ was almost 50 years old, he has no historical basis.₵

* ibid., p. 472.
† ibid.
‡ *Loci Theologici*, vol. 1, p. 29.
§ ibid., p. 280.
₵ *Loci Theologici*, vol. 1, p. 29.

It should be seen as a mark of Chemnitz' respect for the fathers than he excludes references to such "superficial statements" from *Loci Theologici* (TRFDC excluded, of course). As Chemnitz remarked in his discussion of the fathers' views on Justification:

> But it is not our purpose to be like Ham, who uncovered his father's shame. Thus we shall not deal with the lapses of those by whose labors we have been aided and whose gray hairs we ought to honor, but we will refer to them only as warnings so that we may be cautioned by their examples to be more careful and diligent in preserving the purity of this doctrine, so that we never give occasion to anyone to follow in these footsteps. ...[*]

Perhaps because no one would likely fall into the errors cited by Chemnitz in TRFDC, he excluded further reference to them from *Loci Theologici*.

3.10 Irenaeus' Chiliasm.

The ancient church noted in him one basic error, namely, his holding to chiliasm, and there are in Bk. 5 a few seeds of this error in his handling of certain chapters of the Apocalypse.[†]

Since Chemnitz does not examine this error within the English translation of *Loci Theologici*, Irenaeus' chiliasm is not brought up in this context. When one consults the *Examen*, however, one finds Chemnitz' assessment of Irenaeus on this point. In his discussion of the sixth kind of tradition ("the catholic concensus of the fathers"), Chemnitz cites Irenaeus' Chiliasm as a teaching rejected by the Church: "Lastly, when these mitigations or suitable interpretations of those things which had not been stated aptly or could not find a place, then the fathers expressly disapproved and condemned those things which did not agree with the rule of

---

[*] *Loci Theologici*, vol. 2, p. 469-470.
[†] *Loci Theologici*, vol. 1, p. 29.

Scripture. ... Thus the opinion of the Chiliasts is freely condemned in Irenaeus."* And only a few pages later, in the discussion of the eighth kind of tradition ("traditions which pertain both to faith and morals and which cannot be proved with any testimony of Scripture"†), Chemnitz mentions Papias, who caused "very many men after him in the church to fall into the chiliastic error. ... For the chiliastic opinion was embraced as being apostolic tradition by Irenaeus, Apollinarius, Tertullian, Victorinus, and Lactantius, as Jerome recorded."‡ Chemnitz clearly identified the closing chapters of book 5 of *Adversus Haereses* with charges of "chiliastic error." Indeed, Irenaeus cites Papias in 5.33.4 quite favorably concerning the end times, since "these things are borne witness to in writing by Papias, the hearer of John, and a companion of Polycarp, in his fourth book..."

Conclusion.

It has been demonstrated that in most cases Chemnitz' use of Irenaeus' writings in *Loci Theologici* was consistent with his analysis of the Irenaeus' strengths and weaknesses in the "Treatise on the Reading of the Fathers or Doctors of the Church." On occasions when other works such as *Examen* or *De coena Domini* were consulted, Chemnitz' use of Irenaeus was generally in keeping with the TRFDC profile. Chemnitz' work shows a remarkable consistency in this respect.

Of even greater interest to this writer, however, is Chemnitz' attitude toward the church fathers. A deep respect is communicated in the way in which Chemnitz treats passages which he finds less than satisfactory. Careful attention is paid to the way in which the historical setting may have led to a less than desirable formulation. Chemnitz allows the fathers to speak for themselves as far as possible, which lends toward a feeling that the fathers are not being manipulated to prove a point.

---

* Chemnitz, Martin, *Examination of the Council of Trent*, trans. by Fred Kramer, vol 1 (St. Louis: Concordia Publishing House, 1971), 4 vols., p. 265.

† ibid., p. 272.

‡ ibid., p. 279.

All this having been said, however, Chemnitz clearly points out the dangers found in certain formulations, often appealing to Scripture or a later church father to provide a better manner of speaking. As one writer has noted, "As there are rules for reading Scripture, there are also rules for reading the fathers *cum iudicio*. For example when writers in the tradition speak carelessly and incautiously before a doctrine has come into controversy, their word cannot be pressed to defend matters which are not in agreement with Scripture."* A love for the ancient fathers is not allowed to impinge upon the clear meaning of Scripture, but Chemnitz' adherence to the *sola Scriptura* principle was not, as one writer has claimed is sometimes the case today, "to ward off any appreciation of Christendom's great dogmatic tradition..."† Instead, for Chemnitz, to be faithful to *sola Scriptura* means that one should not neglect all the study, meditation and struggle which has ensued over the ages precisely over the question of what Scripture says.

Finally, it has been observed that "We are approaching a time that has many more similarities with the time before Constantine the Great than it does with the time of the Reformation."‡ In fact, this writer continues, "What is needed now is *a renaissance of Irenaeus*."§ If this is the case, then we must begin to learn from that which has been handed down from the saints of that age, while remaining faithful to Scripture and the Lutheran Confessions. These are not mutually exclusive aims, but will instead deepen our faith and our knowledge of the Church catholic. Chemnitz provides a superb teacher in this task because this is the same task in which he, and the other Lutheran fathers who followed him, engaged. As Robert Preus observed:

---

* Olsen, Arthur, "The Hermeneutical Vision of Martin Chemnitz: The Role of Scripture and Tradition in the Teaching Church," in *Augustine, the Harvest, and Theology (1300-1650)*, ed. by Kenneth Hagen (Leiden: E.J. Brill, 1990), p. 325.
† Johnson, John F., "Authority and Tradition: A Lutheran Perspective," *Concordia Journal*, September 1982, p. 185.
‡ Wingren, Gustaf, "The Doctrine of Creation: Not an Appendix but the First Article," *Word & World*, Fall 1984 (4:4), p. 370.
§ ibid., p. 361.

It would be a grave mistake for any serious theologian to consign the theology of Lutheran orthodoxy to the limbo of irrelevant and outdated matters that concern only the antiquarian. For orthodoxy not only works under the Scriptures as the only source of theology, but it also is eminently catholic and confessional in its approach to theology.

... They did not... whimsically jump on theological bandwagons, overwork precarious theological or philosophical motifs, or impose alien philosophical schemata on theology...they were eminently catholic in all their work. A tremendous amount of labor was plied by the orthodox Lutherans in presenting the contributions of the church fathers on every point of theology. For they claimed the church fathers as their own.[*]

---

[*] Preus, *The Theology of Post-Reformation Lutheranism*, p. 35.

Confessionalism and Pluralism in our Post-Modern World[*]

I have no greater joy than to hear that my children walk in truth.
(3 John 4)

I. Introduction: A Church and Culture in Crisis.

Christianity and Western civilization have undeniably reached a moment of profound crisis. To call our situation a "crisis" is by no means a new development, of course; theologians, philosophers and poets have sounded the warning for generations. But our culture and the Church have now reached the point where one can no longer ignore this crisis; to refuse to address it is to concede to the death of the West and the reduction of confessional Christendom[†] to a vanishing remnant. In the December, 2002 issue of *Concord*, an unofficial publication distributed within the Lutheran Church—Missouri Synod, it was astutely observed:

> The controversies we face in Synod today are symptomatic of a deeper war between two principles, the confessional principle versus the pluralistic principle. The confessional principle seeks unity through agreement in doctrine and practice. The pluralistic principle seeks unity through agreement to disagree. ... The confessional principle itself is under severe attack in our church as it is in the world. Confessionalism and pluralism are incompatible principles. They cannot coexist in the church.[‡]

---

[*] This paper was originally presented at a Free Conference at Faith Lutheran Church in Plano, Texas in January 2003.

[†] By "Confessional Christendom" we refer to all those Christians adhering to a creedal expression of the faith and who uphold the conviction that the truth proclaimed in God's Word is immutable.

[‡] "We Believe, Teach, And Confess," Concord (XVI:3) December 2002, page 3.

The crisis is fundamentally different from any of those which have confronted the Church in over 1,500 years. The Church has often addressed competing truth claims—conflicting confessions—throughout her history. In such controversies, the issue was, in essence, "Which side is proclaiming the truth?" Our modern (or, more accurately, "Post-modern") crisis strikes at a much deeper level: "Is there truth at all?" The answer to this question is the fundamental division between Confessionalism and Pluralism. Confessionalism believes that there is truth and that truth can be known (even through different confessions may vary widely concerning what they believe the truth to be). Pluralism (as well as Unionism and Syncretism, its theological offspring) teaches that either there is no single truth, or that, ultimately, truth is unknowable.

II. The "Loss of Moral Meaning" and the Triumph of "Tolerance."

The loss of belief in the existence of truth is the most profound shift in the modern mind. Even in the debate between Christianity and Rationalism, both parties believed in the existence of truth—and denied that their opponent possessed the truth (or at least, the whole truth). Now, however, the debate is over the existence of truth itself. In the prevailing mindset of our culture, a good citizen (or churchman) is to be 'sensitive' or 'tolerant' of the beliefs of others. The only sinful view in such a worldview is to be 'intolerant'— intolerance will not be tolerated! The general moral ambivalence of Pluralism, Paul Griffiths observes in a recent article, is the heart of the drive for "tolerance." Tolerance (Pluralism) is placed in opposition to proselytism (Confessionalism). Proselytism (whether for a Lutheran, Roman Catholic, Marxist or Buddhist worldview) acts on the premise that the respective worldview is true, and that proselytes will be better off for coming to faith in their confession. Tolerance/Pluralism does not allow judgments to be made between worldviews; one may not conclude that another person is lacking because they do not share your faith. Griffiths observes:

* "Proselytizing for Tolerance," *First Things* (November 2002) p. 30-34.

Tolerance is like proselytism in being a concept of the moral order. Both imply the same judgment about the alien: that the alien's beliefs are false, and/or that the alien's practices are improper. But where the proselytizer wants to transform the alien into kin by making a proselyte of him, the practitioner of tolerance wants to let him alone in his error, to permit him to continue to do or think what he does or thinks.*

But for toleration to endure, it must ultimately come to the position where it no longer believes that the alien is in error (unless, of course, his error is intolerance!). Psychologically and spiritually, the burden of tolerance—believing another person is wrong, even in danger of eternal condemnation, but refusing to offend them through proselytism—is a burden which cannot be endured indefinitely. One must either become a Confessionalist, or surrender to a Pluralism which maintains, in essence, "You've got your truth, and I've got mine." In the estimation of Griffiths, "The grammar and syntax of toleration propose as destination a place that cannot be arrived at, that no-place from which all particular religious proselytisms can be tolerated (endured, put up with, let be)."†

The implications of Pluralism for daily life are quite profound. A culture which is pluralistic and tolerant must still be governed by laws, but the basis of the laws is perceived to no longer be transcendent, but arbitrary. A pluralistic, tolerant culture no longer consciously bases its law upon a perceived higher Law; a Church which is pluralistic and tolerant turns away from reliance on Scripture and Confessions to bylaws and procedures. In losing a sense of divine Law, man's law is made absolute, but arbitrary. The natural end of such arbitrary legalism is a political and spiritual totalitarianism which dehumanizes citizens and Christians. As C.S. Lewis observes in *The Abolition of Man*, when men reject natural law, it

> is not one among a series of possible systems of value. It is
> the sole source of all value judgements. If it is rejected, all

---

* ibid. p. 32.
† ibid.

value is rejected. If any value is retained, it is retained. ... If my duty to my parents is a superstition, then so is my duty to posterity. If justice is a superstition, then so is my duty to my country or my race. ... The rebellion of new ideologies against the Tao [the natural law] is a rebellion of the branches against the tree: if the rebels could succeed they would find that they have destroyed themselves.[*]

Thus it is as Francis Schaeffer observed in 1969:"Today we are left not only with a religion and a church without meaning, but we are left with a culture without meaning. Man himself is dead."[†]

As a culture succumbs to pluralism and toleration, it finds itself increasingly unable to comprehend Confessionalism. Thus, cultural elites uncomprehendingly label Southern Baptists and Islamic militants with the same term:"Fundamentalists." Those who are so identified are the only members of Church or State who are truly alien and frighteningly incomprehensible. The loss of a common faith in a divine origin of law and all other order is literally dissolving the bonds which hold together both the Church and the culture. As Turner observed in *Without God, Without Creed—The Origins of Unbelief in America:*

> The option of godlessness has dis-integrated our common intellectual life, both in formal disciplines like philosophy, science, literature and in those informal habits of mind by which we, as a culture, experience and order our world. God used to function as a central explanatory concept. As cause and purpose, the idea of God shaped and unified natural science, morality, social theories, psychology, and political thought into one vaguely coherent (though very loosely assembled) approach to understanding humankind and the cosmos. ... But at the most fundamental level, God provided the frame of an agreed-upon universe in which to argue. Our web of shared assumptions has not unrav-

---

* (New York: Macmillan, 1947), p. 56.
† Schaeffer, *Death in the City*, p. 18.

eled altogether—without some unity, a culture collapses. But the traditional linchpin is missing; our culture, in this sense, now lacks a center.[*]

A culture which has become godless is a culture which, ultimately, must abandon all sense of transcendent meaning or truth. Our culture lacks such a center, and is threatened with dissolution by the release of centrifugal forces centered in the self-interests of self-indulgent individuals and groups.

One result of this disintegration of society is the rise of moral indifference. In his 2001 book, *Landscapes of the Soul, The Loss of Moral Meaning in American Life*, sociologist Douglas Popora observes that the triumph of post-modernism is fundamentally tied to the moral indifference of our age. Porpora declares, "Strangely, many of my students seemed morally indifferent to the plight of others, morally unmoved even when we ourselves were collectively contributing to that plight."[†] Even for many of those who still claimed a religious affiliation, the ability of the worldview to shape their moral conviction was gone: "If I had sought to connect with the values contained in my students' own religious traditions, I soon learned that my students—whatever their religion—were somehow disconnected from those values and traditions themselves."[‡] As a result of this disconnection from faith, "Most Americans continue to believe in God. Many just do not find God someone to whom they are particularly attached. ... What has withered is not principally belief in cosmic meaning but concern with cosmic meaning."[§] This moral disconnection is witnessed in countless number of parishes throughout the West. It burdens faithful Christians who weep to see the baptized who are ambivalent to either moral living or orthodox teaching. Many, if not most, of those within the visible Church simply no longer feel themselves absolutely bound to fidelity to

---

* (Baltimore: The John Hopkins University Press, 1985) p. 263-4.
† (Oxford: Oxford University Press, 2001), p. 3.
‡ ibid.
§ ibid. p. 4.

God's revelation of Law and Gospel. The loss of confessional fidelity has led to self-indulgence:

> As the more Christian-dominated consensus weakened, the majority of people adopted two impoverished values: personal peace and affluence.
>
> Personal peace means just to be let alone, not to be troubled by the troubles of other people, whether across the world or across the city—to live one's life with minimal possibility of being personally disturbed. Personal peace means wanting to have my personal life pattern undisturbed in my lifetime, regardless of what the results will be in the lifetime of my children and grandchildren. Affluence means an overwhelming and ever-increasing prosperity—a life made up of things, and more things—a success judged by an ever-higher level of material abundance.*

Because of the rise of such idolatrous 'values', many have become as vacuous as one of Porpora's students, who declared: "I'm Catholic. So the meaning of life for me is just to enjoy ourselves."†

Such an empty worldview is refuted by Alexandr Solzhenistyn's famous words,

> If, as claimed by humanism, man were born only to be happy, he would not be born to die. Since his body is doomed to death, his task on earth evidently must be more spiritual: not a total engrossment in everyday life, not the search for the best ways to obtain material goods and then their carefree consumption. It has to be the fulfillment of a permanent, earnest duty so that one's life journey may become above all an experience of moral growth: to leave life a better human being than one started it.‡

For even a sociologist observes: "Morality is not only about what we

---

* Francis Schaeffer, *How Should We Then Live?* (Wheaton: Crossway Books, 1976) p. 205.

† Porpora. p. 3

‡ *A World Split Apart* (New York: Harper & Row, 1978), p. 57–59.

should do, however. It is also supposed to provide positive guidance as to what we should be doing. ... The fact is that moral purpose is less something we choose than something that chooses us. Before we ever choose to devote our lives to one or another moral purpose, that purpose must first move and inspire us."* Ultimately, one cannot speak more correctly than to use our Lord's words: "He who finds his life will lose it, and he who loses his life for My sake will find it." (Mat. 10:39) Again, "For whoever desires to save his life will lose it, but whoever loses his life for My sake will find it. For what profit is it to a man if he gains the whole world, and loses his own soul? Or what will a man give in exchange for his soul?" (Mat. 16:26-27) We are a culture which is losing its soul for the sake of material wealth and might. "There is only one perspective we can have of the post-Christian world of our generation: an understanding that our culture and our country is under the wrath of God. Our country is under the wrath of God! Northern European culture is under the wrath of God. It will not do to say how great we are. It will not do to cover up the difference between the consensus today and the consensus of a Christian world."†

III. The Triumph of Syncretism and Indifference in the Post-Modern Age.

As was observed at the beginning of this paper, the crisis in our culture and within Christ's Church is essentially unprecedented. The history of the Church's controversies has been one of competing truth claims (e.g., Pharisee vs. Christian, Arian vs. Catholic, Catholic vs. Orthodox, Lutheran vs. Romanist, etc.). The post-modern victories in the conflict between Confessionalism and Pluralism have led men to turn away from the very idea of immutable truth. Porpora notes:

How ironic that the second millennium closed with a post-modern loss of meaning. In the first century, by contrast, the common era began with a plenitude of meaning. Be-

---

* Porpora, p. 8–9.
† Schaeffer, *Death in the City*, p. 15–16.

sides the birth of Christianity and Rabbinic Judaism, there were also in Israel the independent movements of the Essenes and the Baptist. In the far east, Buddhism had just crossed over from India into China. And throughout the Roman Empire, there were mystery cults for the many and, for the intellectual few, the high philosophies of Stoicism, Cynicism and Epicureanism. All addressed the question, How am I to live? Then, perhaps, there were too many answers; today, there are too few. Today we have lost even the question.[*]

The centuries between Pentecost and Constantine's Edict of Toleration were an age in which toleration and Pluralism ruled the pagan world—and made it vulnerable to Confessional Christianity. In the words of Ramsay MacMullen: "From the throne—occupied every decade or so by the particular favorite of some different deity—down to the marketplace of some individual town in which might be seen both the thoroughly skeptical Celsus or Lucian and the thoroughly credulous customers of the latest wizard, the empire seemed positively to invite a sharply focused and intransigent creed—if only to round out an embrace that was so infinitely tolerant."[†] The Church, although almost certainly small, poor, and weak in terms of worldly power, was utterly uncompromising in its Confessionalism.

By contrast, Christianity presented ideas that demanded a choice, not tolerance; and while some lay easily within the bounds of the acceptable, others were a lot harder to swallow. ...

... [T]he one point of difference that seems most salient was the antagonism inherent in it [Christianity]—antagonism of God toward all other supernatural powers, of God toward every man or woman who refused allegiance, and (we shall see) of those who granted their al-

---

[*] Porpora, p. 23.

[†] *Christianizing the Roman Empire, A.D. 100-400*, (New Haven: Yale University Press, 1984) p. 16.

legiance toward all the remaining stubborn unbelievers. It was not the church's liturgy, nor morals, nor monotheism, nor internal organization (when these things were correctly understood) that seemed to non-Christians much different from other people's or at all blameworthy. ...

... Christianity did present a kind of polarization to its audience at various points in what may be called pagan theology—a polarization that pricked or alarmed the observer.[*]

Today, much of the visible Church has discarded the 'intolerance' (Confessionalism) which was so important to her existence in the early days of the Church. In the words of Francis Schaeffer:

> But if we are looking across the history of the world to see those times when men knew the truth and turned away, let us say emphatically that there is no exhibition of this anywhere in history so clearly in such a short expanse of years as in our own generation. ... Men of our time knew the truth and yet turned away not only from the biblical truth, the religious truth of the Reformation, but turned away from the total culture built upon that truth, including the balance of freedom and form which the Reformation brought forth in northern Europe in the state and in society, a balance which has never been known anywhere in the world before.[†]

The collapse is certainly as profound as Schaeffer saw in 1969. Although the triumph of the pluralistic apostasy has seemed sudden, its roots are buried deep in the soil of Western civilization. The crisis of our age is by no means sudden in its onset. Again, Schaeffer declares:

> What caused such a breakdown in our culture? The two world wars? Don't believe it. If the house had been strong,

---

* ibid., p. 17, 19.
† Schaeffer, *Death in the City*, p. 14

it would not have come down with the earthquake. If the heart had not been eaten out of the culture, the world wars would not have broken it. 'Don't worry,' some say, 'It's only a technological problem, and technology will be a solution.' But that is not true. Man would not be in the position he is simply because of technological problems if he had had a really Christian base. A population explosion? Of course it is serious, but it is not the heart of the problem. The fact that the United States is now urban rather than agrarian? Is this the final problem? No. To solve only the urban problem is to heal 'slightly.' You can hear it over and over again—all kinds of secondary solutions to secondary problems. Of course these are problems, but they are not the central problem. And men who use theological language to fasten our eyes upon them as the central problem stand under the judgment of God, because they have forgotten that the real reason we are in such a mess is that we have turned away from the God who is there and the truth which He has revealed. The problem is that the house is so rotten that even small earthquakes shake it to the core.

Schaeffer's observations have profound implications for the Church today: we must not confuse secondary problems for the primary problem. Lives and fortunes can be expended on secondary causes; if the primary cause is left unaddressed, the war would still be lost, while God's people are left exhausted and embittered. If we are to meaningfully address the primary cause of our troubles, we must not imagine that our crisis is a "fluke" or the result of one (or several) men "somehow" getting elected.

What is being lost is a reliance on the Word of God. What is vanishing is belief in the necessity of faith in Christ alone. Within much of the Church, subtle philosophical asterisks are being placed at the end of confessional-sounding statements, with the result being confessions which are essentially, 'Jesus is the only way of sal-

* Schaeffer, *Death in the City*, p. 58.

vation... unless there's another way God hasn't revealed yet.' The Church must confess Christ: "Therefore whoever confesses Me before men, him I will also confess before My Father who is in heaven. But whoever denies Me before men, him I will also deny before My Father who is in heaven. Do not think that I came to bring peace on earth. I did not come to bring peace but a sword." (Mat. 10:32–34) Where the heart of the faith has been lost,

> As men have turned away from God, who alone gives a basis for absolutes in truth, men have become untruthful, and hypocritical with each other. ... Ours is a plastic culture, and often ours is a plastic church. Men are simply carrying on by memory. They are living only by habit, not because they have a firm, rational, Christian base for their actions, and it is indeed ugly.*

Where, by words or deeds, the Church does not confess with St. Peter, "Nor is there salvation in any other, for there is no other name under heaven given among men by which we must be saved," (Acts 4:12) men do indeed "simply carry on by memory."

Increasingly, rite is reduced to a secular husk; the holy days of the Church are made to serve idolatrous ends. As Porpora observes,

> Some commentators have argued that as we have become disconnected from what is more ultimate, the tendency today is to make the family itself an object of worship. Indeed, survey data reveal that for many today, holidays such as Christmas and Passover are less celebrations of religious meaning than of family togetherness. If so, then it is not the decline of family values that is the problem today but rather their apotheosis.†

Anyone who does not believe this trend exists is welcome to attend the divine service on the Feast of the Holy Nativity. Where

---

* Schaeffer, *Death in the City*, p. 41.
† Porpora, p. 65.

will you find most Christians: standing in front of Christ's altar, receiving Him in Word and Sacrament, or gathered around plastic Christmas trees in their living rooms? Christ's Word remains true: "He who loves father or mother more than Me is not worthy of Me. And he who loves son or daughter more than Me is not worthy of Me. And he who does not take his cross and follow after Me is not worthy of Me." (Mat. 10:37-38)

The rises of Pluralism and Syncretism are intertwined. Unionism and Syncretism are marks demonstrating that a Church no longer believes it has the truth. It is no accident that the triumph of historical critical interpretation of the Sacred Scriptures has occurred in most of the visible Church at the same time that the unionistic agenda of the ecumenical movement has come to dominate.

Elsewhere, the presenter has reviewed the terrifying 'fruit' which are the harvest of Syncretism in the Third World.[*] The horrible perverting of Christian theology—ranging from the most extreme examples of 'prosperity theology' and Pentecostalism, to crass Syncretism which mixes animal sacrifice and ancestor worship—are readily observable, even dominant, in many of the new Third World (or "Southern") churches. Rather than seeking to correct such false teaching, some Western observers praise such abominations, and commend them to the spiritually weakened Western church: "In the present day, it may be that it is only in the new churches that the Bible can be read with any authenticity and immediacy, and the Old Christendom must give priority to Southern voices."[†] Such an empty assertion demonstrates how far the West has fallen. That such a flawed analysis is promoted by the president of the Lutheran Church—Missouri Synod as "powerfully packed with prophetic prognostication"[‡] reveals the degree to which the syncretistic sickness has spread in our own circles.

---

[*] see the book review of *The Next Christendom, The Coming of Global Christianity* in *Concord*, December 2002, (XVI:3), p. 5–7.

[†] Jenkins, *The Next Christendom*, p. 217.

[‡] August 2002 "Pastoral Letter" as quoted in review in Concord, p. 5.

IV. Traveling the Road which Returns to Faithfulness.

As bleak as our review of the current state of the Church might seem, far more might be said which is just as bad or worse. What is certain is that the state of denial must come to an end among Confessional Christians. As dire as the situation truly is, the battle is not yet lost. "The LORD is my light and my salvation; whom shall I fear? The LORD is the strength of my life; of whom shall I be afraid? When the wicked came against me to eat up my flesh, my enemies and foes, they stumbled and fell. Though an army may encamp against me, my heart shall not fear; though war may rise against me, in this I will be confident." (Psa. 27:1-3)

In the 1940s, English author Dorothy Sayers declared to her countrymen:

> The thing I am here to say to you is this: that it is worse than useless for Christians to talk about the importance of Christian morality, unless they are prepared to take their stand upon the fundamentals of Christian theology. It is a lie to say that dogma does not matter; it matters enormously. ... It is hopeless to offer Christianity as a vaguely idealistic aspiration of a simple and consoling kind; it is, on the contrary, a hard, tough, exacting, and complex doctrine, steeping in a drastic and uncompromising realism. And it is fatal to imagine that everybody knows quite well what Christianity is and needs only a little encouragement to practice it. The brutal fact is that in this Christian country not one person in a hundred has the faintest notion what the Church teaches about God or man or society or the person of Jesus Christ.*

The importance of dogma—of Christian doctrine—is unchanged. Holy Scripture is filled with exhortations such as that which is found in Titus 2: "But as for you, speak the things which are proper

* Dorothy L. Sayers, *Creed or Chaos? Why Christians Must Choose Either Dogma or Disaster*, (Manchester: Sophia, 1999) p. 44.

for sound doctrine" (v. 1). In a world of change and death, the immutable, eternal Word of God is our strength and consolation; "The grass withers, the flower fades, but the word of our God stands forever." (Isa. 40:8) The Christian need not worry whether he is winsome enough, whether his Church has enough money and worldly power to 'effectively' go about proclaiming the Word of God—the efficacy is in the Word itself. "All Scripture is given by inspiration of God, and is profitable for doctrine, for reproof, for correction, for instruction in righteousness, that the man of God may be complete, thoroughly equipped for every good work." (2 Tim. 4:16–17) Armed with that unchanging Word, the faithful Christian may go forth with boldness, trusting that Word to accomplish that which the Lord intends.

But to be a confessional Lutheran is not to give a nod to the Lutheran Confessions, and then rely on the means of man and party politics to 'get the job done.' When "confessional Lutherans" rely on the same means and methodologies as the Pluralists; when the appeal is to "our" party versus "their" party; and when both parties appeal to ignoring doctrinal differences to create the broadest possible power base, the 'best' outcome one can hope for is a truly Phyrric victory. Such a victory means despair, when the faithful discover (again) the differences between parties is one of degree, not kind.

It has been observed: "In an age of relativity the practice of truth when it is costly is the only way to cause the world to take seriously our protestations concerning truth."* In both the culture and in the Church, too often the easy road, not the faithful road, has been the road most often traveled. When one speaks of Western society or of Western Christendom, the false solution which has been pursued over and over again is that which posit that if we "elect the right man" everything will change. Such a solution ignores the fact that the corruption has come through the apostasy of individuals; the road back to faith must be taken one soul at a time. As Turner describes the rise of atheism in the West: "It was not the inexorable

---

* Schaeffer, *Death in the City*, p. 73.

juggernaut of history that crushed belief. It was, rather, the specific responses to modernity chosen by thousands of specific believers which made belief vulnerable."[*]

At present, we are living in the suburbs of Laodicea. To the Church at Laodicea, the Lord declared:

> I know your works, that you are neither cold nor hot. I could wish you were cold or hot. So then, because you are lukewarm, and neither cold nor hot, I will vomit you out of My mouth. Because you say, 'I am rich, have become wealthy, and have need of nothing'—and do not know that you are wretched, miserable, poor, blind, and naked—I counsel you to buy from Me gold refined in the fire, that you may be rich; and white garments, that you may be clothed, that the shame of your nakedness may not be revealed; and anoint your eyes with eye salve, that you may see. As many as I love, I rebuke and chasten. Therefore be zealous and repent. (Rev. 3:15-19)

Our affluence has blinded Christians to their doctrinal impoverishment. We have become so smug and comfortable in our padded pews and middle class comforts that we are prepared to turn a 'blind eye' to a lot of false teaching and wicked practice in the Church before we'll let our slumber be disturbed.

There must be repentance in our individual lives, and in our congregations and pulpits. The road back from Pluralism to Confessionalism is not traveled by simply making out a check, supporting an organization, or writing letters, and then trusting that someone else is going to set things right. The practice of truth is often costly. Again, in the words of Dorothy Sayers:

> Seeing that Christ went about the world giving the most violent offense to all kinds of people, it would seem absurd to expect that the doctrine of His Person can be so presented as to offend nobody. We cannot blink at the fact that gentle Jesus meek and mild was so stiff in His opinions and

---

* Turner, p. 268.

so inflammatory in His language that He was thrown out of church, stoned, hunted from place to place, and finally gibbeted as a firebrand and a public danger. ... That being so, nobody need be too much surprised or disconcerted at finding that a determined preaching of Christian dogma may sometimes result in a few angry letters of protest or a difference of opinion on the parish council.[*]

In anticipation of the obvious caution, clearly this does not mean one is supposed to be offensive as an end in itself; rather, the Christian knows that the Gospel of Jesus Christ will offend the world. "If the world hates you, you know that it hated Me before it hated you. If you were of the world, the world would love its own. Yet because you are not of the world, but I chose you out of the world, therefore the world hates you." (John 15:18–19) As confessional Lutherans, we need to return to God's Word and the Lutheran Confessions. Pastors must teach the faith both in season and out of season—that is, whether the flock wants to hear the truth or not. Faithful laity will welcome catechesis, and proclaim the Word within their own godly vocations.

We have a blessed opportunity before us in this pluralistic culture. Our situation is like that which Sayers describes in 1940s England:

Theologically, this country is at present in a state of utter chaos, established in the name of religious toleration, and rapidly degenerating into a flight from reason and the death of hope. We are not happy in this condition and there are signs of a very great eagerness, especially among the younger people, to find a creed to which they can give wholehearted adherence.

This is the Church's opportunity, if She chooses to take it. So far as the people's readiness to listen goes, She has not been in so strong a position for at least two centuries. The rival philosophies of humanism, enlightened self-interest, and mechanical progress have broken down badly;

* Sayer, p.56–7.

the antagonism of science has proved to be far more apparent than real, and the happy-go-lucky doctrine of laissez-faire is completely discredited.˙

We live in an age which pleads for faithful confession. We are living in a society which is dying to hear someone say, "There is still Truth!" Dying souls need that Truth which will set them free from bondage. A firm stand must be taken against the deadly Syncretism and Pluralism of our dark age so that men will behold the light of the holy Gospel and be drawn to Christ Jesus. There can indeed be no compromise between our Christian Confession and the emptiness of Pluralism and tolerance. "Let us hold fast the confession of our hope without wavering, for He who promised is faithful." (Heb. 10:23)

---

* Sayers, p. 45–46.

82

"The Balance of Word and Sacrament in the Divine Service."*

"Nothing can be spoken with such care that it can avoid detraction." (Apology VII & VIII:2)

Introduction

Addressing the assigned topic is by no means an easy task, for it lends itself toward either a one sentence response, or to several hundred pages. The balance of Word and Sacrament in the Divine Service rests at the very heart of the life of the Church. Therefore, this paper is written with the understanding that anything set forth herein examines but a small part of the entire matter and addresses only a few of the challenges which confront the Church in our age. It is the hope of the author that others will find this work at least a helpful step toward addressing this worthy topic, and will find motivation in it to further expand the examination. (It should be noted at the outset that this paper will not devote much time to specific details of the liturgy which reflect the balance between Word and Sacrament.)

In this study, we will begin by examining what is meant by the expression "balance of Word and Sacrament." We will then look at several ways in which our present practice may be remedied toward restoring a proper balance of Word and Sacrament in the Divine Service. Our primary resource in this task will be the Lutheran Confessions.

---

* This paper was originally presented to the Free Conference of the Texas Confessional Lutherans, August 4 and 5, 2000, at Grace Lutheran Church, Brenham, Texas.

1. What is meant by a "balance" of Word and Sacrament?

The word "balance" is one which can carry a variety of meanings, and so it is important that one understands the sense in which we are using the term. Often "balance" is used to discuss two or more ideas, persons, parties, and so on, which are opposed to one another; a balance must be struck, so that neither side overwhelms the other. Thus, for example, Americans appeal to the notion of "balance" in the media: the goal is that opposing views on an issue or political campaign would be given equal representation. Geopolitical theorists during the Cold War' often spoke of a "balance of power" between the United States, the Soviet Union and People's Republic of China; again, the idea of "balance" conveyed here was of parity between otherwise mutually exclusive options.

When we are speaking of Word and Sacrament, we are not talking about allowing equal time for things which are in opposition; the Church is not worried that the Word or the Sacrament will some how "gain the upper hand" over the other. Indeed, a church in which either Word or Sacrament appears to dominate the Divine Service to the exclusion of the other is almost certainly a church which rightly confesses and practices neither. In such a situation it is not that Denomination X does a good job of preaching the Gospel, but neglects the Sacraments, while Denomination Y "is right on the Sacraments," but fails to preach the Gospel. Gospel proclamation without the proclamation and faithful use of the Sacraments—Baptism, Absolution, and the Lord's Supper—is a proclamation which eliminates virtually every way in which God's grace comes to us. After the same fashion, a church which emphasizes the Sacraments while neglecting to proclaim the Gospel, almost certainly utterly misunderstands the Sacraments. Proclamation must not be separated from the Sacraments; rather, hearing the Word leads Christians to faithfully partake of the Sacraments. Addressing the question, "What benefits does Baptism give?," Luther joins Sacrament and Gospel proclamation as follows: "It [Baptism] works forgiveness of sins, rescues from death and the devil, and gives eternal salvation to all who believe this, as the words and promises of God declare."* The Sacrament conveys these great blessings to us, but we learn of the blessings through the proclamation of the "words and promises of God." Again, in answer to the question, "What is the benefit of this eating and drinking?," Luther responds, "These words, 'Given and shed for you for the forgiveness of sins,' show us that in the Sacrament, forgiveness of sins, life and salvation are given us through these words. For where there is forgiveness of sins, there is also life and salvation."† Again, Gospel proclamation— "Given and shed for you for the forgiveness of sins"—is inextricably joined together with the profitable use of the Sacrament. Gospel proclamation leads us to the Sacraments; the Sacraments are received to our benefit because of the Gospel which has been proclaimed to us.

In light of the above, it is easily understood why the Church is not aided when the imbalanced use of the Word and the Sacraments among the sectarian churches is spoken of in almost Hegelian terms. A dialectical structure is attempted when some speak of the Roman Church being a 'sacramental' church (the thesis), the Reformed sects being 'Word, not Sacrament' churches (the antithesis), while the Lutheran Church is the 'Word and Sacrament' church (the synthesis). The means of grace which the Holy Trinity established for our salvation are not opposing theses, principles, ideas or substances. Rather than treating Word and Sacrament as competitors, the Church rightly confesses: "For through the Word and Sacraments as through instruments, the Holy Ghost is given, who worketh faith where and when it pleaseth God in them that hear the Gospel, to wit, that God, not for our own merits, but for Christ's sake, justified those who believe that they are received into favor for Christ's sake." (AC V:2–3) Word and Sacrament are "opposed" in the same way that two hands of one body are opposed, and no one in their right mind is glad to be missing one or the other.

---

* *Luther's Small Catechism with Explanation*, (St. Louis: Concordia Publishing House, 1991) p. 22.
† ibid., p. 29.

The Lutheran emphasis on the balance of Word and Sacrament in the Divine Service is connected to our understanding of the nature of the Church. This Church is described in a profound manner in the Augsburg Confession: "Also they teach, that One holy Church is to continue forever. The Church is the congregation of saints, in which the Gospel is rightly taught and the Sacraments rightly administered." (AC VII:1) The Church, therefore, is found where the pure Word and Sacrament are found; where they are absent, we have no assurance of the presence of the Church because the means through which it is created and sustained are absent. As Luther wrote in the Smalcald Articles concerning the opponents of the Gospel: "We do not acknowledge them as the Church, and they are not; we also will not listen to those things which, under the name of Church, they either enjoin or forbid. For, thank God, today a child seven years old knows what the Church is, viz. saints, believers and lambs who hear the voice of their Shepherd." (Part III, Art. XII:1–2) Again, Luther identifies the location of the Church by the proclamation of the Gospel of Jesus Christ; but those who preach another Gospel: "We do not acknowledge them as the Church, and they are not;...". This might seem to us a harsh blow, but remember St. Paul's epistle to the Galatians: "but there are some who trouble you and want to pervert the gospel of Christ. But even if we, or an angel from heaven, preach any other gospel to you than what we have preached to you, let him be accursed. As we have said before, so now I say again, if anyone preaches any other gospel to you than what you have received, let him be accursed." (Gal. 1:7–9) The faithful Christian remembers the words of Augustana V: "That we may obtain this faith, the Office of Teaching the Gospel and administering the Sacraments was instituted. For through the Word and Sacraments as through instruments, the Holy Ghost is given, who worketh faith where and when it pleaseth God in them that hear the Gospel..." (§1-2) Or as we read in Article IX of the Apology: "Neither indeed does it [the promise of salvation] pertain to those who are outside of Christ's Church, where there is neither Word nor Sacraments, because the kingdom of Christ exists only with the

Word and Sacraments." (§52) Faith is only created in us through the Word and Sacraments, and these means of grace are found in the Church, given and distributed by Christ through the office of the holy ministry.

Word and Sacrament are both the means which the Holy Ghost uses to create and sustain faith, and they are the identifying marks of the Church. As Melanchthon declares in the Apology of the Augsburg Confession: "But the Church is not only the fellowship of outward objects and rites, as other governments, but it is in principle a fellowship of faith and the Holy Ghost in hearts; which fellowship nevertheless has outward marks so that it can be recognized, viz. the pure doctrine of the Gospel and the administration of the sacraments in accordance with the Gospel of Christ." (VII & VIII:5) Thus we see that the Church is a visible fellowship, whose location may be determined by the outward marks of pure doctrine and rightly administered Sacraments. By examining a church's public teaching (both according to its written confession, and the doctrine actually proclaimed in its pulpits) and its sacramental practice, a Christian can determine whether that church is orthodox or heterodox.

Thus, one begins to see the origin and purpose of the balance of Word and Sacrament in the Divine Service. Both will be found in the true Church because they are the means through which the Holy Ghost creates faith; if the means are absent, faith will also be missing. In addition, however, we see that it is precisely in the balance of the pure Gospel and rightly administered Sacraments that we have criteria for evaluating whether a church is part of the Church catholic (AP VII & VIII:10). If a balance of Word and Sacrament is not found—if either appears to be absent, distorted or (worse) perverted—there is an indication that such a church is drifting into heterodoxy, or may even be apostate, depending on the deviation from God's gift of Word and Sacrament. The Church should remember Luther's words of warning: "Therefore in regard to this we ought and must constantly maintain that God does not wish to deal with us otherwise than through the spoken Word and the Sacraments, and that whatever without the Word and Sacraments is extolled as spirit is the devil himself." (SA Part III, Art. X:10)

2. The Necessity of Sacramental Preaching.

At the time of the Reformation, our fathers in the faith could rightly declare:

> The people are accustomed to partake of the Sacrament together, if any be fit for it, and this also increases the reverence and devotion of public worship. For none are admitted except they be proved. The people are also advised concerning the dignity and use of the Sacrament, how great consolation it brings anxious consciences, that they may learn to believe God, and to expect and ask of Him all that is good. This worship pleases God; such use of the Sacrament nourishes true devotion toward God. It does not, therefore, appear that the Mass is more devoutly celebrated among our adversaries, than among us. (AC XXIV:5–9)

It was a matter of great joy that the Lutheran theologians knew the people of the Evangelical Church were thoroughly instructed concerning the "dignity and use of the Sacrament," concerning the "great consolation it brings anxious consciences"—truly, those people who so know the blessings of the Sacrament partake of it with great reverence and devotion. Instruction in the Sacrament (and all the articles of the faith) was a matter of great importance, "for none are admitted except they be proved." This instruction is done primarily through the preaching of the Word; thus, the preaching should regularly be concerned with the benefits and right use of the Sacraments.

"What does this mean?" It means that the pastor proclaims the blessings which we receive through Word and Sacrament as often as he proclaims the Gospel. Pastors should not laud "salvation by grace through faith" without preaching about the role and importance of Baptism, Absolution and the Lord's Supper; otherwise, there is a definite risk that hearers will believe they may possess faith without the means which create it. In short, what is needed is Sacramental Preaching.

Luther observes that preaching before the Reformation was marked by a similar failure:

> For I well remember the time—and it may even now be daily seen—when there were adults and even aged persons so uncultivated as to know nothing of these things, and who, nevertheless, went to Baptism and the Lord's Supper, and used everything belonging to Christians, notwithstanding the fact that those who come to the Lord's Supper ought to know more and have a fuller understanding of all Christian doctrine than children and new scholars. (Large Catechism, Short Preface, §5)

After setting forth the chief parts of Christian doctrine, Luther warned his hearers to make sure catechumens were required to memorize the chief parts, "For you must not depend upon that which the young people may learn and retain from the sermon alone." (Large Catechism, Short Preface, §24) Today, the problem is reversed: pastors rely on catechetical instruction regarding the Sacraments to substitute for regular preaching concerning the Sacraments. Preaching about the Sacrament of the Altar on Maundy Thursday and Baptism on Epiphany,* and Absolution on Quasimodogeniti is not enough, for it fosters an idea in the hearers that Baptism, Absolution and the Lord's Supper are occasional 'add-ons' to the Word. The preaching which is needed is of the sort found in the fifth part of the Large Catechism: preaching where the goal is filling the heart with a holy desire for the blessed Sacrament. As we confess in the Apology of the Augsburg Confession: "But with respect to the time, certainly the most of our churches use the sacraments, absolution and the Lord's Supper frequently in a year. And those who teach of the worth and fruits of the sacraments, speak in

---

* How many Lutherans remember that Epiphany is, along with a celebration of other "manifestations," a day for remembering Christ's Baptism?

such a manner as to invite the people to use the sacraments frequently." (XI:60) Such an invitation comes in Sacramental Preaching.

How should the preacher approach the task of Sacramental Preaching? Although time does not allow for an extensive examination of this question, several points can be offered. First, just as a pastor approaches the propers for a particular Sunday looking for the distinctive way in which the Gospel is set forth therein, he should also look at them for points which offer opportunity to remind and instruct his hearers concerning the means of grace. Second, as every sermon must be centered in the proclamation of Jesus' death and resurrection for us, so every sermon should then proclaim how the benefits of Jesus' suffering and death for us come to us. The sermon should address how it is that Baptism "now saves us" (1 Pet. 3:21), and what a consolation it is that Jesus declared "He who hears you hears Me" (St. Luke 10:16), and that "as often as you eat this bread and drink this cup, you proclaim the Lord's death till He comes." (1 Cor. 11:26) Sacramental Preaching is a powerful remedy against the sectarians' treatment of the Incarnate Lord as if He were 'locked up' in heaven; our sin-sick, ravaged world needs to know the blessed Savior who promises, "and lo, I am with you always, even to the end of the age." (St. Matthew 28:20) What joy there is for us, knowing that our risen Redeemer is always with us! What comfort to know that He comes to us with His grace, through Water and the Word, and that it is Christ who baptizes us! What peace that "The words which absolution give are His who died that we might live; The minister whom Christ has sent is but His humble instrument." (*The Lutheran Hymnal*, Hymn #331, Stanza 5) And what love our God has for us, that He purchased the Church "with His own blood" (Acts 20:28)—Body and Blood which we now receive with the bread and wine in the Sacrament of the Altar.

3. Proper Preaching is Preaching the Propers.

A fitting subtitle for this section would be a line for a revised litany: "From the endless barrage of 'free-text' sermons to push the pastor's personal agenda, deliver us." In a generation when it seems as if every Recognized Service Organization in synod wants a special Sunday celebration of their work in the Church (complete with creative worship service and sermon or sermon outline), it is almost as if there is a war being waged against use of the historic propers. Indeed, one Church Growth/contemporary worship advocate declared, "Even the traditional Divine Service may have to see modification or even the burial of the Introit, Gradual, and Prefaces or seek more meaningful worship expressions to replace these liturgical formulations which are increasingly experienced as archaic."[*] And yet it is the propers (along with a wise choice of hymns to reflect the theme of the week) which are to be the elements of change from one Sunday to the next, while keeping each Sunday in a continuity of teaching. Far from "archaic" (for when can the exposition of Holy Scripture be seen as "archaic?"), the propers provide structure and balance to the preaching of the Church. The propers establish the theme for the Sunday, and thus should determine the sermon for the Sunday.

But before we go further: what do we mean by "propers"? These are the parts of the liturgy which change from Sunday to Sunday; specifically, the Introit, Collect, Old Testament, Epistle, Gradual, and Gospel. (The Sentences and Proper Prefaces will also change by season or festival, but not, generally, Sunday to Sunday.) Concerning the development of these propers, Luther Reed wrote:

> The liturgical propers are an essential and characteristic feature of all Western liturgies. These liturgies, unlike the so-called "worship programs" prepared for a single service, provide complete and varied material for all the services of the ecclesiastical year. There is a fixed, invariable framework which is repeated every service. Into this are fitted variable "propers" pertinent to the particular service or festival.
>
> These propers contribute more than variety, color and interest. Their content focuses attention upon the specific message each Sunday and determines the thought and

---

* Waldo Werning, *Making the Missouri Synod Functional Again*, (Fort Wayne: Biblical Renewal Publications, 1992) p. 299.

mood underlying the celebration of the festivals. Taken as a whole they present the entire body of the Church's teaching during the cycle of the year.*

The propers, then, are a great source of stability against pastoral whims and fundraising desires of special interests within synod or district. Even more importantly, however, the propers are intended to guarantee that all of the central articles of the faith are taught to the faithful. Year after year, the cycle of readings and prayers repeats, causing them to be ingrained in the hearts of the people. Each year provides the pastor and people with another opportunity to revisit each element of the cycle, hearing again the truth of our salvation and the heart of Christian doctrine.

The lectionary, especially the historic, one-year lectionary, aids in joining our worship in a continuity with the Church of all ages. The historic lectionary was not the creation of an individual, or even a committee, but was the product of generations of God's people gathering for Word and Sacrament; occasionally, changes are introduced, but much of the history of the lectionary is one of continuity.

Early Christian worship was very simple. Scripture readings from the Old Testament, the Epistles, and later the Gospels were at first all lectio continua, that is, continuous readings of entire Books. Weekly celebration of the Lord's Day and annual commemorations of Good Friday and Easter, and later on of other events in Christ's life and the life of the Church, led to the development of the Christian year. This has two great divisions—the Half Year of our Lord and the Half Year of the Church. Saints' days and other minor festivals are distributed throughout both divisions. This system of corporate worship was born not of scientific exactness but of spiritual experience. It developed against a background of historic depth and consciousness with annually repeated commemorations of

---

* Luther D. Reed, *The Lutheran Liturgy*, (Philadelphia: Muhlenberg Press, 1947) p. 427.

scriptural facts and persons. The Christian year and the Christian liturgy together constitute an effective and beautiful way of preserving and presenting the whole body of fundamental Christian truths in devotional form. Together they embrace the whole Gospel, "the things most surely believed among us," the way of salvation, the rule of life. This regular and universal review of Christian essentials is theologically adequate, devotionally inspiring, and pedagogically sound. It also protects ministers and people against the intrusion of social and secular themes and personal preferences or prejudices into the services of worship.[*]

Just as the Small Catechism does not become of less use even though we read it and study it again and again, year after year, so it is with the lectionary. The constant swirl of "special Sundays" should terrify us as much as would an annual version of the Catechism and its explanation printed in missal form. The yearly cycle of the lectionary—indeed of all the propers—serves a purpose connected to that of the Catechism: that the people may be taught. The heart of the faith, the history of our Lord's life, suffering, death and resurrection, His continued blessings to His Church, are all matters which deserve annual repetition. Thus, preaching from the propers is an aid in retaining the proclamation of the Word in our midst, for it keeps the pastor from constantly becoming caught up in "contemporary issues" or preaching whatever suits his fancy on a given Sunday. It is far too easy to only preach about the topics in which we have a particular interest. Diligently studying the interconnections between the propers for the Sunday, laboring to choose hymns which match the theme, and for the sermon to give an exposition of God's holy Word in keeping with that Sunday, proclaiming Christ Jesus and His atonement for our sins, and His grace toward us given through Word and Sacrament—this is properly preaching the propers.

---

[*] ibid., p. 427-428.

4. The Need to Restore the Lord's Supper to Every Divine Service.

The frequency of communion celebration can easily become an extremely emotional issue within a parish. Any pastor who attempts to move from monthly or biweekly celebrations of the Sacrament toward weekly communion quickly finds that he is opposed for a whole host of reasons. Nevertheless, at the time of the Reformation, it was part of our confession that the blessed Sacrament of the Altar was offered at least on Sundays and other festival days. As we read in the Augsburg Confession: "Now forasmuch as the Mass is such a giving of the Sacrament, we hold one communion every holy day, and also other days, when any desire the Sacrament it is given to such as ask for it." (AC XXIV:34) This pattern of practice is reiterated in the Apology: "In the beginning we must again make the preliminary statement that we do not abolish the Mass, but religiously maintain and defend it. For among us masses are performed every Lord's Day and on the other festivals, in which the sacrament is offered to those who wish to use it, after they have been examined and absolved. And the usual public ceremonies are observed, the series of lessons, of prayers, vestments and other like things." (AP XXIV:1) The Lutherans found themselves under attack from the Roman party because the former had abolished private masses and had, in the process, moved away from Roman practice of the daily celebration of the Sacrament. Interestingly, the Lutherans appealed to the Eastern churches for support: "The fact that we hold only Public or Common Mass is no offense against the Catholic Church. For in the Greek churches even today private masses are not held, but there is only a public mass, and that on the Lord's day and festivals." (AP XXIV:6)

Whereas once the Lutherans had to explain celebrating the Sacrament only on Sundays and festival days, now, it would seem, that Lutherans must defend themselves for returning to this confessional standard. The resistance to weekly communion is, I must confess, utterly inexplicable to me. Some 'concerns,' such as lengthening service time, seem, frankly, godless: If you are worried the service will run another 15 minutes longer, you may save a whole hour by staying home. The notion that somehow the Sacrament will become "less special" by offering Christ's Body and Blood weekly seems to utterly misunderstand the gift of the Sacrament; would a Christian refuse weekly general Absolution? Will hearing a sermon every Sunday make preaching "less special"?

The reformers argued that the Lutheran Church received the Sacrament more frequently in true faith than the opponents. As we read in Apology XXIV, "But if the use of the sacrament would be the daily sacrifice, nevertheless we would retain it rather than the adversaries; because with them priests hired for pay use the sacrament. With us the use is more frequent and more sacred. For the people use it, but after having first been instructed and examined." (§49)

It might be argued that where there is not regular (even weekly) communion, the Church is not fully living up to the balance of Word and Sacrament in the Divine Service. The Church knows there are two parts to the Divine Service, whether one wishes to call them the Mass of the Catechumens and Mass of the Faithful, or Office of the Word and Office of the Blessed Sacrament,* or Service of the Word and Service of Holy Communion, as they are called in Lutheran Worship. One portion without the other easily lends itself to upsetting the balance between Word and Sacrament; just as we would, presumably, consider a Divine Service which lacks a sermon to be utterly inadequate, the same should be the case for a Divine Service which lacks the Sacrament of the Altar. Wilhelm Löhe observed:

> The arrangement of the parts in the Order for the Chief Service on the Lord's day may be compared to a twin mountain, one of whose heights is a little lower than the other. The former of these heights, and the lower, is the Sermon; and the other, and the higher, is the Sacrament of the Altar, without the celebration of which no public worship is complete. In public worship the soul is engaged in an ascent, the goal of which is reached at the Table of the

---

* F. R. Webber, *Studies in the Liturgy*, (Erie: Ashby Printing Co, 1938) p. 97.

Lord, than which there is nothing higher—nothing diviner
on earth, only Heaven remains above. In the Holy Supper
the deepest longings of the soul are satisfied, as the humble
worshiper joyfully declares in the Nunc Dimittis.*

Fortunately, the restoration of weekly communion is one area in
which there is hope for significant improvement in the near term.
Although one should always be dubious of the significance of any
synodical or district resolution, it is worth noting that resolution
2-08A of the 1995 LC—MS convention provided a firm endorsement of returning to the historic Lutheran practice of weekly communion. The resolution reads:

WHEREAS, The opportunity to receive the Lord's Supper each Lord's Day was a reality cherished by Luther and
set forth clearly with high esteem by our Lutheran Confessions (Article XXIV of the Augsburg Confession and of
the Apology); and

WHEREAS, Our Synod's 1983 CTCR document on the
Lord's Supper (p.28) and our Synod's 1986 translation of
Luther's Catechism both remind us that the Scriptures
place the Lord's Supper at the center of worship (Acts 2:42;
20:7; 1 Cor. 11:20,33), and not as an appendage or an occasional extra; therefore be it

Resolved, That The Lutheran Church-Missouri Synod
in convention encourage its pastors and congregations to
study the scriptural, confessional, and historical witness to
every Sunday communion with a view to recovering the opportunity for receiving the Lord's Supper each Lord's Day.†

---

* *Liturgy for Christian Congregations of the Lutheran Faith*, ed. by J. Deinzer, trans. by
F.C. Longaker, (Malone: Repristination Press, 1993) p. XII.
† *Convention Proceedings 1995*, (St. Louis: Concordia Publishing House), cited by
David Schoessow, "Holy Communion: Should We Offer It More Frequently?,"
Concordia Journal July 1998 (24:3). We heartily recommend Schoessow's article
for a thorough examination of this important topic.

As the resolution noted, the new explanation of the Small Catechism teaches: "In the New Testament, the Sacrament was a regular and major feature of congregational worship, not an occasional extra (Acts 2:42; 20:7; 1 Cor. 11:20, 33). In Reformation times our churches celebrated the Sacrament 'every Sunday and on other festivals' (Apology XXIV 1)."* Thus, every pastor is given opportunity to catechize his confirmands regarding the weekly communion.

In all of this, it must be stressed that while the Sacrament should be offered weekly, no one should feel compelled to receive it weekly. Rather, one should listen to Luther's advice on this point, "It is to be feared that he who does not desire to receive the Lord's Supper at least three or four times during the year despises the Sacrament and is no Christian. So, too, he is no Christian who neither believes nor obeys the Gospel; for Christ did not say, 'Omit or despise this,' but, 'This do ye, as oft as ye drink it,' etc. He commands that this should be done, and by no means to be neglected or despised." (SC Preface, §22) The Lutheran pastor should have confidence that where there is faithful Sacramental Preaching and a weekly celebration of the Sacrament of the Altar, there Luther's observation will be found to be correct: "Let it simply be your aim to set forth distinctly the advantages and losses, the wants and the benefits, the dangers and the blessings, which are to be considered in connection with the Sacrament; the people will, doubtless, then seek it without urgent demands on your part." (SC Preface, §24)

5. Returning the Third Sacrament—Holy Absolution—to Parish Life.

Mention a "third Sacrament" and the reaction of most Missouri Synod Lutherans is somewhere between shock and anger. Even though our Confessions declare, "no prudent man will strive greatly concerning a number or term [of sacraments], if the objects still be retained which have God's command and promises," (AP XIII:17) many Lutherans have fallen into an absolutism placing the 'count' of Sacraments at two with a rigidity which is as dogmatic as

* *Luther's Small Catechism with Explanation*, p. 233.

the Roman enumeration of seven Sacraments. Although the 1991 explanation of the Small Catechism alleviated the situation somewhat with the "note" to question 237—"Sometimes Holy Absolution is counted as a third sacrament, even though it has no divinely instituted visible element (Large Catechism IV 74; Apology XIII 4)"*—the third Sacrament is the most woefully, inexcusably ignored means of grace in our synod today.

One definition of the term "Sacrament" which is common in our circles today is as follows: "A Sacrament is a sacred act: A. instituted by God, B. in which God Himself has joined His Word of promise to a visible element, C. and by which He offers, gives, and seals the forgiveness of sins earned by Christ."† However, it is wise to begin by noting that this definition cannot be found in Scripture. Instead, it is based, roughly, in the Large Catechism, where Luther wrote, "Hence also it derives its character as a sacrament, as St. Augustine also taught: 'Accedat verbum ad elementum et fit sacramentum.' That is, when the Word is joined to the element or natural substance it becomes a sacrament, that is, something holy and divine, and a holy and divine sign." (LC IV:18) We may just as appropriately use the equally Lutheran definition provided by the Apology of the Augsburg Confession: "If we call the sacraments, 'rites which have the command of God and to which the promise of grace has been added,' it is easy to decide what are properly sacraments." (AP XIII:3) The elegance of this definition of a Sacrament is easily seen from the words which follow:

> For rites instituted by men will not in this way be sacraments properly so called. For it does not belong to human authority to promise grace. Wherefore signs instituted without God's command, are not sure signs of grace, even though they perhaps instruct the rude, or admonish as to something. Therefore Baptism, the Lord's Supper and Absolution, which is the sacrament of repentance, are truly sacraments. For these rites have God's command and the

---

* *Luther's Small Catechism with Explanation,* p. 198.
† p. 197.

promise of grace, which is peculiar to the New Testament. For when we are baptized, when we eat the Lord's body, when we are absolved, they ought certainly to assure us that God truly forgives us for Christ's sake. (AP XIII:3–4)

The definition of a Sacrament which has become so common today leaves Absolution—which we confess has "God's command and the promise of grace"—in a 'limbo' between Word and Sacrament. The Apology's definition, placing Absolution firmly within the category of 'Sacrament' is more fitting, given the placement of Absolution between Baptism and the Lord's Supper in the Small Catechism.

There was a time when Lutherans could boldly confess:
It is well known that we had so elucidated and honored the benefit of absolution and the power of the keys, that many distressed consciences have derived consolation from our doctrine; since they have heard that is it is the command of God, nay rather the uttrance peculiar to the Gospel, that we should believe the absolution, and regard it certain that the remission of sins is freely granted us for Christ's sake; and that we should believe that, by this faith, we are truly reconciled to God. (Apology XI:59)

The Lutheran Church once knew private confession and absolution to be a great gift which the Triune God gave to the Church. Indeed, so great is the value of this Sacrament that the confessors declared: "For we also retain confession, especially on account of the absolution, which is the Word of God, that, by divine authority, the power of the keys proclaims concerning individuals. Wherefore it would be wicked to remove private absolution from the Church. Neither do they understand what the remission of sins or the power of the keys is, if they despise private absolution." (AP, Ch. VI, §2–3.) Instead of treating courageous pastors who work to restore private confession and absolution as if they were some sort of 'Romanizers' or 'odd-balls', the Church should ask itself why, by its own confession, it has now lapsed into wickedness by removing private absolution from the regular life of the Church. The words of the Apology still stand: if someone despises private absolution, then he does not know what the remission of sins or the power of the keys is.

In Article XI of the Augsburg Confession, we teach, "that Private Absolution ought to be retained in the churches, although in confession an enumeration of all sins is not necessary." (§1) As long as private Absolution is absent from the vast majority of the Churches of the Augsburg Confession, one may rightly ask whether the Augustana is our confession, for the teaching of Article XI is only so many pious words if the practice is not continued. Times for private Absolution should be posted as faithfully as the time for the Divine Service. Churches which do not yet regularly offer private Absolution should begin to catechize their members regarding the great blessings and comforts of this holy Sacrament, and pastors should be willing to sit alone in the sanctuary waiting for penitents to come. Most importantly, Absolution should be clearly presented to catechumens, and they should be encouraged to partake of this Sacrament throughout their confirmation years. If they are rightly taught, and Confession and Absolution are rightly implemented, you will have many of them coming to you for Absolution for years to come. They will, God-willing, devote far less energy to hiding the 'real' parishioner from their pastor, and you will find yourself truly ministering to their hurts and sins and no longer guessing (or at least not as often) about what is really troubling them.

6. Protecting Word and Sacrament by eliminating "Useless, Foolish Spectacles" (FC X).

Much time has been devoted in this paper to what should be added to the Divine Service to strengthen the balance of Word and Sacrament. This final portion of this paper is devoted to something which needs to be removed for the sake of the Gospel. In our time, the term 'adiaphora' is used to excuse the inclusion of elements of worship which have no place within the Divine Service of the Lutheran Church.

At the time of the Reformation, Lutherans were careful to keep innovation in the order of service at a minimum, retaining as much of the historic liturgical practice as possible. However, that which detracted from the Gospel—the Word and Sacraments—or perverted them, had no place in the Lutheran Mass. We declare in Article XV of the Augsburg Confession:

> Of Rites and Usages in the Church, they teach, that those ought to be observed which may be observed without sin, and which are profitable unto tranquillity and good order in the Church, as particular holydays, festivals, and the like.

> Nevertheless, concerning such things, let men be admonished that consciences are not to be burdened, as though such observance was necessary to salvation. They are admonished also that human traditions instituted to propitiate God, to merit grace and to make satisfaction for sins, are opposed to the Gospel and the doctrine of faith. (§1–3)

Thus the Lutherans retained the propers with only modest modifications and retained the historic Latin rite, only removing portions of the rite which upheld the notion of the sacrifice of the Mass and the invocation of the saints. Thus Lutherans who have attended a traditional Episcopalian or Roman worship service are often struck by the similarities between rites.

The Lutherans understood that the establishment of adiaphoristic rites rests with the authority of the office of the holy ministry. As we read in Augustana XXVIII:

> What, then, are we to think of the Sunday and like rites in the house of God? To this we answer, that it is lawful for bishops or pastors to make ordinances that things be done orderly in the Church, not that thereby we should merit grace or make satisfaction for sins, or that consciences be bound to judge them necessary services, and to think that it is a sin to break them without offense to others. ...

It is proper that the churches should keep such ordinances for the sake of charity and tranquillity, so far that one do not offend another, that all things be done in the churches in order, and without confusion; but so that consciences be not burdened to think that they be necessary to salvation, or to judge that they sin when they break them without offense to others; ...

Of this kind, is the observance of the Lord's Day, Easter, Pentecost, and like holy days and rites. (§53, 55–56, 57)

A similar line of thought is followed in §31 of Article X of the Solid Declaration of the Formula of Concord: "According to this doctrine the churches will not condemn one another because of dissimilarity of ceremonies when, in Christian liberty, one has less or more of them, provided they otherwise are in unity with one another in doctrine and all its articles, and also in the right use of the holy sacraments, according to the well-known saying: 'Disagreement in fasting does not destroy agreement in the faith.'"

Therefore, a great deal of responsibility and authority rests with bishops and pastors regarding the rite, since it is entrusted to their care, and there have been many in our age who have abused this authority to borrow heavily from the practices of other confessions. However, Article X of the Formula of Concord is of profound significance over against the intrusion of enthusiastic Protestant elements into the Divine Service. Because the primary focus of Article X is on the adaptation of alien rites in times of persecution, little attention is paid to the overall article. The specific historical setting of the article (compromises with the Roman Church under the Augsburg and Leipzig Interims) is perhaps thought to limit the applicability of the article to those times when the Church faces open persecution. In a case of persecution, it is true that adiaphora do not, of themselves, conflict with the Word and Sacrament, but,

every Christian, but especially the ministers of the Word, as the presidents of the congregation of God, are bound, according to God's Word, to confess the doctrine, and what belongs to the whole of religion, freely and openly, not only in words, but also in works and with deeds; and that then, in this case, even in such adiaphora, they must not yield to the adversaries, or permit these adiaphora to be forced upon them by their enemies, whether by violence or cunning, to the detriment of the true worship of God and the introduction and sanction of idolatry. (§9)

In other words, worship practices which are not, in and of themselves, offensive to the orthodox doctrine, become an offense when they are instituted because of pressure by heterodox (false-teaching) churches; in such a case, it is sinful to choose to adopt new practices for the purpose of appearing to be in agreement with the false teachers.

However, Article X does not only address cases of persecution. Indeed, §7 in the Solid Declaration tells us: "Likewise, when there are useless, foolish spectacles, that are profitable neither for good order, nor Christian discipline, nor evangelical propriety in the Church, these also are not genuine adiaphora, or matters of indifference." This sentence is of vital importance for our present topic. "Useless, foolish spectacles" are not adiaphoristic; unlike true adiaphora, they are not compatible with balance of Word and Sacrament in the Divine Service. While the majority of Article X deals with the matter of those rites which are, in a time of tranquillity for the Church, truly adiaphora and may be retained by the Lutherans as long as they are not introduced because of persecution, "useless, foolish spectacles" are never adiaphoristic. Because of limitations on time, it is not possible to go into great detail on this point, but I believe the ban on "useless, foolish spectacles" is of great importance in evaluating some of the outside influences which are undermining the historic Lutheran rites.

According to the Apology, man-made ceremonies serve two purposes: "Since ceremonies, however, ought to be observed both to teach men Scripture, and that those, admonished by the Word, may conceive faith and fear, and thus that they also may pray (for these are the designs of ceremonies);..." (XXIV.3). The ceremonies are to teach the Word of God to the people of God. The power is in the Word itself, as the Holy Spirit works through the Word to bring about faith in the hearts of hearers. Where ceremonies struggle against such emphasis on the means of grace, they we need to wonder whether we are dealing with a useless and foolish spectacle.

There is no place for the useless and foolish before God's high altar—by definition they are at odds with the Word and Sacrament; they are not adiaphoristic. Here let our rule be to never permit anything within the Church with which we would not feel comfortable at the foot of the cross.

Conclusion.

In seeking to understand the balance of Word and Sacrament in the Divine Service, our concern is not with counting the number of words in the liturgy or using a stopwatch to track the time. That having been said, reducing access to the means of grace by denying God's people private Absolution and the weekly opportunity to receive the Lord's Supper, risks undermining the balance of Word and Sacrament. The balance is an expression of wholeness and unity, with everything, in Löhe's words, leading us to the mountain peaks of the sermon and the Sacrament of the Altar. In the presence of such precious gold, there is no place for the dross of "useless, foolish spectacles" which will be burned up. Sacramental Preaching, in combination with preaching the propers, goes a long way toward ensuring the preaching of the central articles of the faith and preparing the Christian to receive his Savior as He comes to us with His body and blood in the bread and wine. Pastors must be willing to take—and laymen must be willing to give—the time to teach and preach regarding the blessings of the Sacrament, so that Christians will compel their pastors to offer the means of grace to them. As our Savior comes to us through Word and Sacrament, we receive that which Christ promised: "and lo, I am with you always, even to the end of the age." Amen.

The Limits of Liturgical Innovation in light of Martin Luther's Exhortation to the Christians in Livonia Concerning Public Worship and Unity (1525).

For the true unity of the church it is enough to agree concerning the teaching of the Gospel and the administration of the sacraments. It is not necessary that human traditions or rites and ceremonies, instituted by men, should be alike everywhere. (AL.VII.2-3)

Encourage congregations to provide two kinds of liturgies each Sunday, if they can; there are normally two groups in most congregations with cultural differences with whom to communicate. We dare not take away the rich old liturgy best enjoyed by those of us who were raised on it; we dare not deny Lutheran contemporary worship to those who do not understand or appreciate a liturgy which does not communicate to them. ...

There should be more variety that the traditional "mass" forms of LW that are not reaching or sustaining the real spiritual needs of a growing number of Missouri Synod Lutherans who want to honor and worship the Lord in truth and purity. ...

... I personally am distracted from really praying the Lord's Prayer when I am required to chant it in a 16th Century form. Even the traditional Divine Service may have to see modification or even the burial of the Introit, Gradual, and Prefaces or seek more meaningful worship expressions to replace these liturgical formulations which are increasingly experienced as archaic.[*]

It hardly seems disputable that 'creative' worship has spread within the congregations of the Lutheran Church—Missouri Synod (LC—MS) with a rapidity which surprises both opponents and

---

[*] Waldo J. Werning, *Making the Missouri Synod Functional Again*, (Fort Wayne: Biblical Renewal Publications) p. 299.

proponents of the new liturgies. In less than twenty years, the LC—MS has been transformed from a state of nearly-total liturgical uniformity to one in which such uniformity is often viewed as impossible or even as a hindrance to the Gospel. Those who would cling to the traditional rites are told, "Such liturgy purists in music and style need to recognize that even the selection of the Scriptures in the liturgy is a pattern made by church leaders in a dated past."* The Reformer himself is cited as the basis for such an attitude: "Luther certainly gave the example of Lutherans being free to create liturgies and hymns which pursue a variety of structures that contain a great amount of God's Word."† Therefore, we are to believe, the course is clear for those who wish to be Lutheran: "Lutherans are true to their Biblical heritage in providing such resources and encouraging such rich variety of worship without critics confusing style and substance or fusing style with substance."‡

But is this actually the historic Lutheran position? Certainly the citation from Augsburg Confession VII is often utilized as a justification for wide variations in liturgical practice. But one isolated passage does not make an argument. The following pages will explore Lutheran teaching regarding liturgical innovation and variety, offering an assessment of Martin Luther's "Exhortation to the Christians in Livonia Concerning Public Worship and Unity (1525)," followed by a brief examination of the Augsburg Confession's position on liturgical innovation, as well as statements by American Lutherans and synodical bodies.

I.

Luther's "Exhortation to the Christians in Livonia Concerning Public Worship and Unity (1525)" (referred to hereafter as "Exhortation...") was written in response to the chaos brewing in Dorpat, Livonia as a result of the excesses of Melchior Hoffmann, a radical

---

* ibid., p. 291.
† ibid., p. 296.
‡ ibid., p. 330.

reformer.* Hoffmann, "a furrier from Swabia who believed he had a call to preach the gospel"† had arrived in Dorpat in 1524. The city council demanded that Hoffmann "bring proper recommendations" after his followers engaged in iconoclastic activities ("...attacks on churches and cloisters in which altars, pictures, etc. were ruthlessly destroyed."‡) and Luther's "Exhortation..." was written in response to this request for recommendations.§ Luther's "Exhortation...," although it never mentions Hoffmann by name, falls far short of endorsing this would-be reformer; indeed, Luther assesses actions such as those undertaken by Hoffmann and his followers as evil, as can be seen in the following citations.

> However I have heard through credible witnesses how faction and disunion have arisen among you also, in this way, that some of your preachers do not teach and act concordantly but according to whatever each one thinks is the best according to his own judgment and will. And I do not want to believe evil about this, because we must remember that it will not be any better with us than it was with the Corinthians and other Christians at the time of St. Paul, when divisions and dissension arose among Christ's people. Even as St. Paul, himself, acknowledges and says, I Corinthians 11:19, "There must be divisions and sects, so that those who are approved become known." For Satan is not satisfied with being the prince and god of the world, he also wants to be supreme among the children of God, Job 1:9, and "goes about like a roaring lion seeking whom he may devour." I Peter 5:8.ᶜ

> For when you were papistic Satan certainly left you in peace, and if you still had nothing but false teachers he would not assault you very much with discord and faction. But now that the true seed of God's Word is with you, he cannot leave it alone; he must

* Martin Luther, *Luther's Works*, trans. by Paul Zeller Strodach, rev. by Ulrich S. Leupold, (Philadelphia: Fortress Press) Ulrich S. Leupold and Helmut T. Lehmann, eds., vol. 53, 55 vols., p. 43.
† ibid.
‡ Martin Luther, *Works of Martin Luther*, trans. by P.Z. Strodach, (Philadelphia: Muhlenberg Press, 1932), vol. 6, 6 vols., p. 141.
§ *Luther's Works*, vol. 53, p. 43.
ℭ *Works of Martin Luther*, vol. 6, p. 144–145.

sow his seed there also, even as he does this to us by means of the fanatics. And God tests you thereby to discover whether you want to stand firm.*

Nevertheless, both you and your preachers should use all diligence to the end that everything go harmoniously and unitedly and such work of the devil be opposed and checked. For the reason why God destined the devil to do such things is that we may have cause to exercise ourselves in unity and through that those who are tested may become known.†

Several points can quickly be discerned from these quotations. First, the problem rests with the fact that "some of your preachers do not teach and act concordantly but according to whatever each one thinks is the best according to his own judgment and will." For Luther, the action of these preachers (presumably Hoffmann and his followers) is directly contrary to the unity of the Church. This interference with the Church's unity is no small matter for Luther; indeed, the Reformer identifies such disruptions over and over again as the work of the devil and a cross which God permits to test the faithfulness of his people. Thus Luther clearly infers a difference between his own reforms and those of the radicals: Luther's changes were necessary to safeguard an orthodox divine service, and thus a matter of spiritual life and death; the radicals' variations are a matter of whim.

Now even if the external regulations in the services,—such as masses, singing, reading, baptizing,—do not add anything to salvation, nevertheless, it is unchristian to be disunited over such things and thereby confuse and unsettle the common people, and not the rather to consider the edification of the people to be more important than our own thought and opinion. Therefore I pray all of you, my dear Sirs, let each one surrender his own opinions and get together in a friendly way and come to a common decision as to how you can be united regard these external matters, so that the practice will be the same and uniform among you throughout your district and not so divergent and disordered,—a

* ibid., p. 149.
† ibid., p. 149–150.

different thing being done here and a different thing being done there, thereby displeasing and confusing the people and making them unhappy.[*]

Therefore make and hold mass, sing and read uniformly, according to a common use, the same in one place as in another; because you see that the people so desire it and need it, so that they are not disturbed on account of you but are the rather edified. For you are here for their edification, as St. Paul says in I Corinthians 10:23. Authority has been given to us, not for destruction, but for improvement. If you do not need such unity, thank God for that; but the people need it.[†]

Luther appeals to the establishment of a common liturgical practice as the way in which the unity of the churches of Livonia is to be maintained or restored. Luther's concern here is not for a legalistic rigidity, but rather it is the salvation of the common people. Liturgical diversity will "confuse and unsettle" the laity, it is "displeasing" to the people—Luther's concern is for the faithful, not the Anabaptist mob whose ears itch for something new. Liturgical uniformity and the edification of the laity go hand in hand, and this edification, Luther reminds his readers, is an important reason for the establishment of the ministry: "Authority has been given to us, not for destruction, but for improvement."

For, as has been said, even if the external uses and regulations are free and, taking the faith into consideration, may with good conscience be changed at all places, at all hours, by all persons; still, taking love into consideration, you are not free to use such liberty, but are in duty bound to consider how matters may be made bearable and better for the common people; as St. Paul says, I Corinthians 14:40, "Let all things be done orderly and honorably among you." And I Corinthians 6:12, "I have power over all things but all things do not profit." and I Corinthians 8:1, "Knowledge puffs up, but love edifies."[‡]

* ibid., p. 147.
† ibid., p. 148.
‡ ibid., p. 147.

Now when your people are offended in that you practice so many different customs and rites and are disturbed thereby, it does not help you any when you are wont to assert: "Yea, the external thing is free; here in my own place I am going to do as pleases me."*

This is said to the preachers in order that they regard love and their obligation toward the people, and do not employ faith's liberty but love's servitude or submission toward the people, but keep faith's freedom toward God.[†]

Luther is fully aware that such uniformity involves a sacrifice on the part of pastors. The personal tastes, interests and attitudes—in short, the Christian freedom—of the pastor must be sacrificed for the edification of Christ's Bride, the Church. Thus Luther's famous paradox in "The Freedom of a Christian" holds true in this situation: "A Christian is a perfectly free lord of all, subject to none. A Christian is a perfectly dutiful servant of all, subject to all."[‡] In this earlier work, Luther applies the first sentence to dealing with "the unyielding, stubborn ceremonialists who like deaf adders are not willing to hear the truth of liberty [Ps. 58:4] but, having no faith, boast of, prescribe, and insist upon their ceremonies as means of justification."[§] It is the second sentence which reigns in this situation where one deals with "The other class of men... simple-minded, ignorant men, weak in faith, as the Apostle calls them, who cannot yet grasp the liberty of faith, even if they were willing to do so [Rom. 14:1]."[¶] This need for sensitivity appears only to have increased between the writing of "The Freedom of a Christian" and "Exhortation..."—most likely because Luther has seen the tactics and goals of the radical reformers.

Nevertheless, Luther is careful to maintain that what is not needed is a new Romish legalism about that which is truly *adiaphora*.

---

* ibid.

† ibid., p. 148.

‡ Martin Luther, *Three Treatises*, (Philadelphia: Fortress Press, 1960) p. 277.

§ ibid., p. 311.

¶ ibid., p. 312.

Still in addition to this, the preacher must, nonetheless, be watchful and admonish the people and instruct them diligently so that they do not accept such common uses as required commands, as though it had to be just so, or as though God would not have it any other way; but that one tell them that it is only done in this fashion in order that they might be edified thereby and preserved in orderly practice, so that the unity of the Christian people may be made stable by means of such external things which, indeed in themselves, are not necessary. For since ceremonies or usages are not a necessity, as far as conscience or salvation is concerned and yet are useful and necessary to govern the people outwardly, one should not force them further than this, or permit them to be established further than that they serve to maintain unity and peace among the people. For faith makes peace and unity between God and men.*

Ultimately, there is a profoundly difficult, but quite Lutheran, tension in Luther's thought which require careful analysis when it comes to the question of liturgical uniformity. Several points can be drawn from Luther's discussion of the topic at hand. First of all, such a discussion of liturgical variation is only possible when the Christian doctrine and Christian life are not undermined by the innovations in question. If the faith is endangered, then such variation is automatically out of bounds. What is really under discussion is the matter of a variety of liturgical expressions of the truth of the Gospel. Even here, however, Luther essentially forbids isolated, individualistic innovation because it violates the law of love—even when the changes faithfully express the Gospel. The same Luther who would declare in his Small Catechism, "the preacher should take the utmost care to avoid changes or variations in the text and wording of the Ten Commandments, the Creed, the Lord's Prayer, the sacraments, etc." (SC Preface.7) applied this principle to the worship life of the Church: there should be unanimity of practice in a region to avoid offending or confusing the people. In such a situation the pastor cannot appeal to his Christian freedom, but must yield because of the need of the people under his care.

---

* *Works of Martin Luther*, vol. 6, p. 148.

II.

The Augsburg Confession, one of the primary statements of the Lutheran faith, reflects this pastoral attitude. Certainly the passage from Article VII of the Augsburg Confession is often cited as proof that liturgical uniformity was not required. The discerning eye, however, quickly perceives another dimension to the question. After all, the confessors were quick to point out:

> Among us the ancient rites are for the most part diligently observed, for it is false and malicious to charge that all ceremonies and all old ordinances are abolished in our churches. But it has been a common complaint that certain abuses were connected with ordinary rites. Because these could not be approved with a good conscience, they have to some extent been corrected. (AL. End of First Part.4-5)

> However, it can readily be judged that nothing contributes so much to the maintenance of dignity in public worship and the cultivation of reverence and devotion among the people as the proper observance of ceremonies in the churches. (AL.Corrected Abuses.6)

> Our churches are falsely accused of abolishing the Mass. Actually, the Mass is retained among us and is celebrated with the greatest reverence. Almost all the customary ceremonies are also retained, except that German hymns are interspersed here and there among the parts sung in Latin. (AL.XXIV.1-2)

The confessors did not embrace the idea of doing what suited one's fancy, but rather clung to the ancient ceremonies, only changing that which they found to be in conflict with God's Word; in such cases they were conscience-bound to change the Mass. Dignity, reverence and devotion are all cited as fruit of the right observance of ceremonies. Historically, opponents of the orthodox Lutheran confession have recognized this expectation of liturgical uniformity in the Augsburg Confession and have attacked the confession on account of it. This emphasis on maintaining the ancient usages is among the reasons for Samuel S. Schmucker's rejection of the Unaltered Augsburg Confession:

> 4. That the Confession explicitly asserts that "no perceptible change" had been made in the public ceremonies of the mass, except the introduction of German hymns along with the Latin ones in several places. Hence the inference would necessarily follow, that if they had made no perceptible change in the public ceremonies of the mass, we could make none, if the Confession was strictly binding on us: and as the ceremonies of the Romish mass are the same now as then, the ceremonies which the Confessions prescribes are the same as those now observed in the church, and if we obeyed the Confession, we should have to perform the same without any "perceptible" difference, except the addition of German hymns along with the Latin, which was at that time used in the Lutheran Church.[*]

III.

The importance which early Lutherans placed on such a common orthodox expression of the faith was not lost even in later ages of the Church. Henry Melchior Muhlenberg, for example, stressed the importance of synodical uniformity with regard to liturgical matters:

> We ... consulted together in Providence with regard to a suitable liturgy (*Agende*) which we could introduce for use in our congregations. ... To adopt the Swedish liturgy did not appear either suitable or necessary since most of our congregations came from the districts on the Rhine and the Main and consider the singing of collects to be papistical. Nor yet could we select a liturgy with regard to every individual's accustomed use, since almost every country town and village has its own. We therefore took the liturgy of the Savoy Church in London as the basis, cut out parts and added to it according to what seemed to us to be profitable and edifying in these circumstances. This we adopted tentatively until we had a better understanding of the matter in order that the same ceremonies, forms, and words might be used in all our congregations.[†]

[*] S.S. Schmucker, *American Lutheranism Vindicated*, (Baltimore: T. Newton Kurtz, 1856) p. 95.

[†] "Muhlenberg's Description of Formation of Liturgy, 1748" included in Rich-

Too much was at stake for the fledgling church to allow for liturgical chaos. A clear Lutheran identity was needed. The Swedish order was contemplated because there was already a Swedish Lutheran population in the colonies. It should be noted that the concern here is the same as that of Luther: the edification of the people by use of a uniform Agende which does not reflect only the desires of the clergy (the Swedish rite?), but also weighs the liturgical background of the worshipers and their situation.

Founded in 1820, the Evangelical Lutheran Tennessee Synod confronted a situation quite similar to that which confronts confessional Lutherans today. In the words of one historian, at the close of the eighteenth and the beginning of the nineteenth century, "We had a weak, indecisive pulpit, feeble catechism, vague hymns, and constitutions which reduced the minister to the position of a hireling taker, and made Synods disorganizations for the purpose of preventing anything getting done."[*] A unionistic hymn-book, intended to serve Lutherans and Reformed, was published in Baltimore in 1817, prompting Rev. Shober of the North Carolina Synod to declare:

> This meritorious undertaking paves the way to universal harmony, union, and love among our Lutheran and Reformed Churches, removing all the obstacles which hitherto prevented that happy effect, and establishes a uniformity in that part of divine worship which cannot fail to be highly gratifying to all those who consider brotherly love an indispensable attribute of Christianity.[†]

The unionistic opponents of the Augsburg Confession understood the importance of liturgical uniformity in expressing their fellowship with the Reformed. The significance of this action was not lost on the true Lutherans. Although extremely limited in their resources,

ard C. Wolf, *Documents of Lutheran Unity in America*, (Philadelphia: Fortress Press, 1966) p. 32-33. Italics added.

[*] C. P. Krauth, cited in *History of the Evangelical Lutheran Tennessee Synod*, by Socrates Henkel (New Market, VA: Henkel & Co., 1890), p. 5.

[†] cited in *History of the Evangelical Lutheran Tennessee Synod*, p. 6.

the faithful Lutherans of the Tennessee Synod strove for uniformity in their own ranks. In 1821—only one year after the synod's founding—is was resolved:

> ...that a Liturgy be arranged according to the Scriptures and the Augsburg Confession, that Rev. Paul Henkel be appointed to attend to this matter, for the use of Synod, as soon as practicable, that between two and three hundred copies be printed, and that the expenses be defrayed by the several treasuries.[*]

Charles Porterfield Krauth, best remembered today for his *Conservative Reformation*, was highly critical of the lack of liturgical uniformity he saw in his own congregation. Krauth declared in a sermon in 1860:

> If every congregation settles these matters for itself, there will be as many varieties as there are congregations. ... A member of another Lutheran congregation comes into our vicinity, but he sees at once that the state of things is different from that to which he has been accustomed; the tastes and habits which were cultivated in one Lutheran church, must all be renounced before he can be comfortable in another. Is it wonderful that our people often feel, not as if they belonged to the Lutheran Church, but merely to a particular Lutheran congregation, and if they remove too far from the congregation to worship with it, leave our Church and unite with another? Do we prize so little the distinctive excellencies of our Church, that we are willing to see it going into a state of dissolution for the benefit of other denominations? And the remarks we have just made in regard to a single locality are strengthened when we think of our whole land. Must a Lutheran clergyman learn a new set of usages every time he makes a change; and shall we never have clustering around the service of our Church the potent charm connected with the growth of our habits in it, the feeling that go whither we will, we shall find it the same; shall we never have a unity manifesting itself in uniformity, and see our people everywhere trained in the same way, so that in all their wanderings as soon as they are within the threshold of the Church of their heart they shall feel that they are at home?[†]

---

[*] ibid., p. 45–46.
[†] *Christian Liberty*, (Decatur: Repristination Press, 1997) p. 16–18.

A similar mindset was at work in the decision by the sixth meeting of the Synodical Conference when the Church adopted William Sihler's Thesis 13 of "Theses Concerning Church Fellowship." The text of this was as follows:

> It is furthermore a contradiction of the Confession if a Lutheran body does not insist that in its congregations only orthodox agendas, hymnals, catechisms, and instructional and devotional books be used, or indeed does not exercise its influence to have unorthodox books on hand discarded and orthodox ones introduced.[*]

Again the concentration is the same: liturgy reflects doctrine, which also, with time, affects doctrine in turn. It is not up to the pastor to attempt molding heterodox resources (e.g., The Lutheran Book of Worship) for use in his parish: rather "a Lutheran body"—a synod—insists her congregations (and, therefore, her pastors) use orthodox materials. The matter is too central to the life of the Church to leave it up to the whims and personal preference of individual pastors. As August Vilmar wrote,

> The liturgy is necessary to keep the balance over against the individuality of the preacher, in order that the Word of God may come to the congregation unhindered and unmutilated. In the days of the coarsest rationalism, when nothing but unbelief and human speculation were preached, how many pious souls have lived on and edified themselves with the Gospel in the liturgy, especially in Thuringia and Saxony.[†]

How true the words remain to this day! Christians who continue their membership (for the present) in heterodox church bodies have a particularly great responsibility to maintain the liturgy—the liturgy may be the primary opportunity that they and others in their church have to hear the proclamation of the Word. To abandon the liturgy in the hope of making the church "grow," despite the false doctrine

---

[*] Lewis W. Spitz, *Life in Two Worlds: A Biography of William Sihler*, (St. Louis: Concordia Publishing House, 1968) p. 147.

[†] cited in G.H. Gerberding, *The Lutheran Pastor*, (Philadelphia: Lutheran Publication Society, 1902) 6th ed., p. 290.

proclaimed by a particular pastor or even a whole synod, will not solve the problem; rather, it only risks making matters worse.

The Missouri Synod's Synodical Handbook declares that the Synodical Commission on Worship shall "clear all literature related to corporate Christian worship in liturgics and hymnology made available through the Synod's boards or through Concordia Publishing House" and "recommend worship materials to the church and advise and warn against the use of worship materials which are unworthy of use in the Christian worship of the Lutheran Church;..."[*] Furthermore, "All service books and hymnals which are to be accepted as official service books and hymnals of the Synod shall be given such status only by a convention of the Synod after a process of exposure and testing decided upon by the Synod in convention."[†] This procedure, when adhered to, is in conformity with the principles Luther expounded to the Lutherans in Livonia; indeed, it is the practice of the orthodox Lutheran church throughout the centuries. As Martin Chemnitz wrote to the clergy of Braunschweig when the city council offered him the position of superintendent:

> Likewise, we must all stick together, as we have in the past, and retain the practice that each does not build up himself or act as lord in his congregation and do what he pleases in preaching, administration of the sacraments, liturgical practices, discipline and other aspects of his office, acting only according to his own ideas, but rather all these things shall be and remain the business of the entire ministerium.[‡]

It was understood that everything about the Church should reflect her teaching and unanimity. Unnecessary liturgical divergence brings confusion to the minds of the laity because of the damage done to the concept of the unity of the Church. This is particularly true in an age of confession, whether in the 1520s in Livonia or the 1990s in the United States of America.

* *Handbook of The Lutheran Church—Missouri Synod*, 1992 Edition, (St. Louis: The Lutheran Church—Missouri Synod, 1992) p. 72.
† ibid.
‡ J.A.O. Preus, *The Second Martin*, (St. Louis: Concordia Publishing House, 1994) p. 133.

THE ART OF RHETORIC
AND THE ART OF HYMNODY

*For a bishop must be ... holding fast the faithful word as he has been taught,
that he may be able, by sound doctrine, both to exhort and convict those
who contradict. (Titus 1:7, 9)*

*And when they had laid many stripes on them, they threw them into
prison, commanding the jailer to keep them securely. Having received such
a charge, he put them into the inner prison and fastened their feet in the
stocks. But at midnight Paul and Silas were praying and singing hymns to
God, and the prisoners were listening to them. (Acts 16:24–25)*

Introduction.

It is the calling of a minister of the Gospel to "hold fast the faithful word as he has been taught" (Ti. 1); thus he is called to serve
within a succession of faithful apostolic teaching, keeping the traditions just they have been delivered to him (1 Cor. 11:2). Holding
fast to the Word which he has received, a called servant of the Word
will thus "by sound doctrine, both to exhort and convict those who
contradict" (Ti. 1:9) and he will be one who is ready "in season and
out of season" to "convince, rebuke, exhort, with all longsuffering
and teaching," (2 Tim. 4:2) The Lord of the Church called His holy
apostles to baptize and teach all nations "to observe all things that
I have commanded you" (Mt. 28:20), and thus the teaching of the
holy apostles is none other than the teaching of Christ Himself,
and this apostolic doctrine, together with the teaching of the Old
Testament prophets, constitutes the foundation of Christ's Church:
"Now, therefore, you are no longer strangers and foreigners, but
fellow citizens with the saints and members of the household
of God, having been built on the foundation of the apostles

and prophets, Jesus Christ Himself being the chief cornerstone, in whom the whole building, being fitted together, grows into a holy temple in the Lord" (Eph. 2:19–21).

As David and Solomon prepared for building the first temple, a tithe of of the Levites* was set apart that they might praise the Lord "with musical instruments." It is only fitting, then, that called servants of the Lord so serve Him with music joined to the Word, "speaking to one another in psalms and hymns and spiritual songs, singing and making melody" in their hearts to the Lord (Eph. 5:19). As Christ's Church "grows into a holy temple in the Lord," still the song for the Lord's Day is,

> It is good to give thanks to the LORD,
> And to sing praises to Your name, O Most High;
> To declare Your lovingkindness in the morning,
> And Your faithfulness every night,
> On an instrument of ten strings,
> On the lute,
> And on the harp,
> With harmonious sound. (Ps. 92:1–3)

St. Paul and St. Silas were unjustly imprisoned in Philippi when they cast out the spirit of divination from a slave girl. Held in the stocks in the inner prison, "Paul and Silas were praying and singing hymns to God, and the prisoners were listening to them. Suddenly there was a great earthquake, so that the foundations of the prison were shaken; and immediately all the doors were opened and everyone's chains were loosed." (Acts 16:25) Having presumably heard their prayers and hymns, the jailer asked them, "Sirs, what must I do to be saved?" (v. 30)

---

* "Now the Levites were numbered from the age of thirty years and above; and the number of individual males was thirty-eight thousand. Of these, twenty-four thousand were to look after the work of the LORD, six thousand were officers and judges, four thousand were gatekeepers, and four thousand praised the LORD with musical instruments, 'which I made,' said David, 'for giving praise.'" (1 Chr. 23:3–5)

Songs, hymns and spiritual songs are the conversation of the Church and her consolation in chains. Thus a servant of the Word must be "rightly dividing the word of truth," while shunning profane and idle babblings (2 Tim. 2:15–16)—and these responsibilities are to be as zealously pursued in the sung confession of the faith as in that which is proclaimed from the pulpit. Thus C. F. W. Walther observed in 1885:

> In a proper and pure public service of worship it is not only fitting and necessary that the preacher preach only God's pure Word, but also that the congregation sing only pure hymns. This latter point is so necessary and is without doubt a matter of the greatest importance: that the preacher choose good hymns, and allow them to be sung, which properly prepares for the hearing of the Word of God and best serve to preserve and seal the Word already heard.[*]

St. Paul admonished St. Timothy: "Hold fast the pattern of sound words which you have heard from me, in faith and love which are in Christ Jesus." (2 Tim. 1:13) This "pattern of sound words"— the tradition of apostolic doctrine— is the *norma normans* of all that is taught, confessed, prayed or sung in the Church Catholic.

Rhetoric and the Pattern of Sound Words

As all that is taught, confessed, prayed, and sung within Christ's Church is to be in perfect conformity to the "pattern of sound words," what place is to be accorded to human eloquence? St. Paul wrote in his first epistle to the Church at Corinth:

> And I, brethren, when I came to you, did not come with excellence of speech or of wisdom declaring to you the testimony of God. For I determined not to know anything among you except Jesus Christ and Him crucified. I was with you in weakness, in fear, and in much trembling. And my speech and my preaching were not with persuasive

[*] quoted in *God's Song in a New Land* by Carl F. Schalk (St. Louis: Concordia Publishing House, 1995), 130-1.

words of human wisdom, but in demonstration of the spirit and of power, that your faith should not be in the wisdom of men but in the power of God. (1 Cor. 2:1–5)

St. Paul taught quite clearly that the power which was at work within the Word which he preached to the Church, rested not in his eloquence, but was, in fact, the power of God, which overcame all of Paul's weaknesses in presentation of that Word.

And yet St. Paul, speaking before King Agrippa, declared that he spoke "the words of truth and reason," and Agrippa said to Paul, "You almost persuade me to become a Christian," to which Paul replied, "I would to God that not only you, but also all who hear me today, might become both almost and altogether such as I am, except for these chains." (Acts 26:25, 28, 29) Paul did not deny the persuasive character of that which was proclaimed, and replied to Agrippa with words of profound eloquence. The requirements that a bishop must be "able to teach" (1 Tim. 3:2) and "able, by sound doctrine, both to exhort and convict" also imply that there is a capacity within man, present to a greater or lesser degree, which is necessary in one who is called to teach the Church.

Rhetoric may somewhat simplistically be described as the 'art of persuasion' but a better description would be 'the cultivation of eloquence.' Instruction in rhetoric has figured prominently in Western civilization since the fifth century B.C., beginning with forensic oratory among the Greeks, and expanding its form and function until it was given what has been described as "an excessively large place in the system of Roman education."[*] Indeed, although the Greeks set forth the principles of rhetoric, it was among the Romans that it would establish its most enduring influence: "From its first introduction to the end of Roman civilization it was part of the intellectual background of the educated Roman."[†] Even though Western Christendom would accord rhetoric a more balanced place

---

[*] M. L. Clarke, *Rhetoric at Rome—A Historical Survey* (London: Cohen & West Ltd., 1968) 163.
[†] ibid., 37.

as one of the three subjects of the *trivium* (grammar, logic/dialectic, and rhetoric), the cultivation of eloquence remained a fundamental element of education.

The historic tension within the Church over the role of rhetoric in connection with the proclamation of the Word can be seen in the respective positions of St. Jerome (A. D. 347–420) and St. Augustine (A. D. 354–430). For his part, St. Jerome came to the conclusion there could be no accommodation between reading the Scriptures and study of 'pagan' authors:

> Fasting and penance alternated [for St. Jerome] with the reading of Cicero and Plautus, and when he took up the prophets he was disgusted by their style. Then he fell ill, and in a feverish dream seemed to be brought before the seat of judgment. Asked to give an account of himself he replied: 'I am a Christian.' 'You lie,' answered the judge. 'You are a Ciceronian, not a Christian. For where your heart is, there shall your treasure be.' 'I was silent at once', Jerome goes on, 'and amid my stripes (for he had ordered me to be beaten) I was even more tortured by the burning of my conscience. ... Finally those present threw themselves at the feet of the judge and besought him to make allowances for youth and to allow time for penitence to the sinner, punishing me thereafter if I should ever read books of the Gentiles again. And I who at this moment of crisis would have promised even more, began to swear an oath: "Lord, if ever I possess or read secular books, I shall have denied thee."'*

One of the benefits of this selection from St. Jerome's writings is that it presents the *telos* of the chain of reasoning which rejects the merits of studying rhetoric: in the end, such a person (if he is consistent) rejects all study of 'secular' authors and their writings, narrowing the province of Christian scholarship to the Scriptures and works of undisputed Christian authorship.

Having taught rhetoric in Carthage, Rome, and in the imperial court at Milan while he was still a pagan, St. Augustine

---

* quoted in Clarke, 148.

was intimately aware of the weaknesses and limitations of rhetoric. Nevertheless, when he wrote his fourth book of *De Doctrina Christiana* in 426, Augustine commended the study of rhetoric to his readers:

> For since by means of the art of rhetoric both truth and falsehood are urged, who would dare to say that truth should stand in the person of its defenders unarmed against lying, so that they who wish to urge falsehoods may know how to make their listeners benevolent, or attentive, or docile in their presentation, while the defenders of truth are ignorant of that art? ... While the faculty of eloquence, which is of great value in urging either evil or justice, is in itself indifferent, why should it not be obtained for the uses of the good in the service of truth if the evil usurp it for the winning of perverse and vain causes in defense of iniquity and error?[*]

Indeed, the *Doctor Gratiae* specifically commended the study of rhetoric to the teachers of the Church and corrected those who thought little of its study: "If anyone says, however, that if teachers are made learned by the Holy Spirit they do not need to be taught by men what they should say or how they should say it, he should also say that we should not pray because the Lord says, 'for your Father knoweth what is needful for you, before you ask him,' or that the Apostle Paul should not have taught Timothy and Titus what or how they should teach others."[†] And Augustine commended to his readers the traditional threefold, Ciceronian task of rhetoric, that is, "to teach is a necessity, to please is a sweetness, to persuade is a victory": "He who seeks to teach in speech what is good, spurning none of these three things, that is, to teach, to delight, and to persuade, should pray and strive that he be heard intelligently, willingly, and obediently. When he does this well and properly, he can justly be called eloquent, even though he fails to win the assent of his audience."[‡]

[*] *On Christian Doctrine*, trans. and introduction by D. W. Robertson, Jr. (Indianapolis: Bobbs-Merrill Co., Inc., 1958), 118–9.

[†] ibid., 141.

[‡] ibid., 142–3.

The Lutheran Reformation stands quite firmly within the Augustinian tradition with regards to rhetoric, and eagerly sought to benefit from the wisdom of the writers of classical antiquity. The scholarship of Philipp Melanchthon was particularly significant in this respect; "Indeed, none of the other major framers of Protestant teaching was so thoroughly immersed in Greek and Latin letters as Melanchthon was. Nor was any so naturally disposed to love them as gifts from God, or so masterly in cultivating them, as he was."[*] The fervently anti-intellectual spirit present in so many of the leaders of the Radical Reformation (e.g. Andreas Carlstadt, Thomas Münzer, and the Zwickau prophets) was countered, in part, by Melanchthon's influence.[†]

Melanchthon had been a student of Greek and Latin literature from the earliest days of childhood, being taught by, among others, his uncle Johannes Reuchlin, one of the most prominent German humanists of his generation, as well as the first significant Hebraist of the German Renaissance. During his years at the University in Tübingen (1512–1518), Melanchthon had already turned his attention to the need for a revitalized study of rhetoric. His inaugural speech as a professor at the University of Wittenberg continued to build on this theme[‡] and a work which he had already begun to write on the subject, *De Rhetorica libri tres*, was finished soon after his arrival at Wittenberg and published in 1519.

This work on rhetoric, divided into three parts, contains a section devoted to religious rhetoric entitled "De sacris concionibus." This was Melanchthon's first work on rhetoric and was followed by a textbook on rhetoric in

---

[*] John R. Schneider, "Melanchthon's Rhetoric As a Context for Understanding His Theology," in *Melanchthon in Europe*, ed. by Karin Maag (Grand Rapids: Baker Academic, 1999), 142.

[†] "For in the earliest throes of its nativity, the evangelical movement was prone to ominous anti-intellectual and (its twin) antinomian eruptions. Melanchthon understood better than anyone did (on his own side, at least) that these precipitous pitfalls were always just one misstep off the sheer precipice of Luther's teachings on justification and Scripture." (Schneider, 142.)

[‡] Schneider, 149.

1531. In the *Institutiones rhetoricae* (1521) he developed a genre of rhetoric which is unique to preaching.[*]

Melanchthon grasped that a crucial point in the reform of rhetoric was the linkage between dialectic and rhetoric. As he wrote in *Elementorum rhetorices Libri II* (1531): "the argument is the same for both the rhetorician and the dialectician: the one [dialectic] navigates between the limits of a proposed theme with sails somewhat more tightly drawn; the other [rhetoric] wanders more freely. The language of the one [dialectic] is accommodated to teaching, the other [rhetoric] to moving".[†] Dialectic *teaches*, but rhetoric *moves*.

The 'motive' character of rhetoric, combined with Melanchthon's discussion of a fourth category of Rhetoric, the genus *didaskalikion*, formed the basis of his application of rhetoric to work of the teaching office within the Church.

> Working with the classical categories of rhetoric—demonstrative (otherwise known as epideictic or panegyrical), deliberative, judicial (otherwise called forensic)—Melanchthon believed that demonstrative rhetoric had its own subcategory of didactic (or instructional). By 1521, he had developed this fourth category, the *genus causarum* or *genus didaskalikion* (the teaching form of oratory), as a natural conduit for introducing dialectic into preaching in order to instruct the faithful.[‡]

Melanchthon's *Loci communes* (1521) is, by its very name and structure, organized for this rhetorical purpose: as a 'commonplaces' of rhetorical arguments on various theological topics. By their very nature, the editions of the *Loci communes* were to be a source from which teachers of the Church could gather support to

---

[*] Susan K. Hedahl, "Melanchthon and the Task of Preaching," in *Philip Melanchthon: Then and Now (1497-1997)* ed. by Scott H. Hendrix and Timothy J. Wengert (Columbia, South Carolina: Lutheran Theological Southern Seminary, 1999), 102.

[†] quoted in Hedahl, 103.

[‡] ibid., 102.

teach according to the various topics of Christian doctrine: Lutheran dogmatics began as a source of theological commonplaces for the construction of rhetoric which would move hearers to agreement.

The fundamental dogmatics text for the Church—the catechism—also was constructed to serve the purposes of such theological rhetoric; thus Martin Luther urges the student of the catechism to continued study of its divinely-given 'commonplaces' so that he may answer the devil's rhetoric: "Doubtless He did not so solemnly require and enjoin this [meditation on God's precepts] without a purpose; but because He knew our danger and need, as well as the constant and furious assaults and temptations of devils, He wishes to warn, equip and preserve us against them, as with a good armor against their fiery darts and with good medicine against their poisonous draughts." (LC Preface:14) Again:

> For it is certain that whoever knows the Ten Commandments perfectly must know all the Scriptures, so that, in all circumstances and events, he can advise, help, comfort, judge and decide both spiritual and temporal matters, and is qualified to sit in judgment upon all doctrines, estates, spirits, laws, and whatever else is in the world. ... But now I know of a truth that such indolent epicures and presumptuous spirits do not understand a single psalm, much less the entire Scriptures; and yet they pretend that they know and despise the Catechism, which is a compend and brief summary of all the Holy Scriptures. (LC Preface:17–18)

Melanchthon's rhetorical description of the work of the teaching office— particularly as that work is carried out in preaching— was given confessional status in the Apology of the Augsburg Confession, Article XV:

> Among the adversaries, in many regions during the entire year no sermons are delivered, except in Lent. But the chief service of God is to teach the Gospel. And when the adversaries do preach, they speak of human traditions, of the worship of saints and similar trifles, which the people

128

justly loath; therefore, they are deserted immediately in the beginning, after the text of the Gospel has been recited. ... On the contrary, in our churches all the sermon are occupied with such topics as these: of repentance, of the fear of God, of faith in Christ, of the righteousness of faith, of the consolation of consciences by faith, of the exercises of faith, of prayer, what its nature should be, and that we should be fully confident that it is efficacious, that it is heard, of the cross, of the authority of magistrates and all civil ordinances, of the distinction between the kingdom of Christ, or the spiritual kingdom, and political affairs, of marriage, of the education and instruction of children, of chastity, of all the offices of love. (§42–43)

"The chief service of God is to teach the Gospel"— and the Apology clearly demonstrates what constitutes such teaching in the *topics* of the sermons, which are delineated according to the 'commonplaces' of Christian doctrine. The motive power of such teaching, rhetorically-speaking, is understood to be in the Word itself; thus it is confessed in Apology XIII: "And God, at the same time, by the Word and by rites, moves hearts to believe and conceive faith, just as Paul says (Rom. 10:17): 'Faith cometh by hearing.' But just as the Word enters the ears in order to strike hearts; so the rite itself meets the eyes, in order to move hearts." (§5) In this point, Melanchthon repeats in summary fashion an argument which he had made against the Anabaptists in 1528, who had been denying the motive power of the holy Sacraments.

After I have spoken about the word 'sacrament,' I must also speak in general about the use of the Sacraments. In the first place, therefore, we should know this, that the Sacraments have not been instituted merely for the purpose of being marks to distinguish Christians from Gentiles, as the toga distinguishes Romans from Greeks or as the vesture distinguishes monks. Some do write that the Sacraments have been instituted that we may show the Gentiles through them that we believe

in Christ and that we may profess our faith before men
and by our example invite others to take up the doctrine of
Christ. But we should feel that Sacraments are signs of the
divine will toward us and not merely signs of our profession
toward men. For the fleece was to Gideon, not merely a mark
by which his army would be distinguished from the enemy, as
if by some signal of the camp, but rather it was a sign of the
will of God and a pledge of promised victory. So, also for us,
the Sacraments are signs of God's will, as Christ also teaches
when he says: 'Do this in remembrance of me.' To remember
Christ is not only to teach others, but also to remember the
benefit which we ourselves have received from him through
his death and resurrection, that is, the remission of sins
which we receive through him. As the will of God is shown
in the Word or in the promise, so also it is shown in a sign as
in a picture. *As the Word is perceived in our ears to arouse faith in our
hearts, so a sign occurs to our eyes that it may also arouse faith in
our hearts.* Therefore Augustine wrote that a Sacrament is
the visible Word, because it signifies the same thing as the
promise does, and is, as it were, a picture of the divine will,
just as the Word is the voice of the divine will.*

The very rites of the Holy Sacraments are understood to be visible, divinely-instituted rhetoric, given by God to move the hearts:
"so a sign occurs to our eyes that it may arouse faith in our hearts,"
(1528) or in the words of the Apology, "so the rite meets the eyes, in
order to move hearts." The motive power is in the Word and rite to
accomplish the purpose for which the Lord of the Church has given
them: the minister of Christ teaches the Church the Gospel according to the commonplaces of theology, and through this proclaimed
Word, the Holy Spirit creates faith in those who hear.

---

* from "Answer to the Anabaptists," in Philipp Melanchthon, *Melanchthon—Selected Writings*, trans. by Charles Leander Hill (Minneapolis: Augsburg Publishing House, 1962), 105–6. Italics added.

Faithful Hymnody: "...[T]hat the unlearned be taught."

Not long after Melanchthon wrote his first *loci*, and before Luther wrote his catechisms, Luther had already begun to address the need for the education of the people in the chief articles of the faith through the reform of hymnody as an aid to teaching. In his preface to the 1524 Wittenberg hymnal, Martin Luther commended the singing of the hymns as being of value, in part, for the instruction of the youth:

> And these songs were arranged in four parts to give the young—who should at any rate be trained in music and other fine arts—something to wean them away from love ballads and carnal songs and to teach them something of value in their place, thus combining the good with the pleasing, as is proper for youth. Nor am I of the opinion that the gospel should destroy and blight all the arts, as some of the pseudo-religious claim. But I would like to see all the arts, especially music, used in the service of Him who gave and made them. ... As it is, the world is too lax and indifferent about teaching and training the young for us to abet this trend.*

This first preface sets forth music—together with all the arts—in service of teaching the youth; a combination of "the good" (God's Word) with "the pleasing" (training in good music). In later years, Luther set this point to rhyme in his poem, "A Preface for All Good Hymnals":

> The great good news has set men free
>   From fear that song a sin might be.
> Indeed, its joys please God much more
>   Than others in life's ample store.
> My singing shatters Satan's works
>   And slays the dragon where he lurks.

...

---

* *Luther's Works*, ed. by Ulrich S. Leupold, 55 vols. (Philadelphia: Fortress Press, 1965), vol. 53, 316.

Let music's calming voice be heard
  That hearts attend God's truth and Word.
When harp was played and music woke
  The Spirit through Elisha spoke.*

Johann Walter's 1538 poem "In Praise of the Noble Art of
Music," which was intended to serve as a theology of music,† made
an explicit linkage of the capacity of the Word joined to music to
serve the motive purpose of rhetoric:
  That such unmerited free grace
    (Which God from love for all our race
  Had promised in His Word) might be
    Kept fresh in human memory
  And move the heart to high delight
    In praising God both day and night—
  This is the weightiest reason why
    God music did at once supply.‡

Walter traces this linkage of the Word and music to the proclamation
of the *protevangelion* in the Garden, the first declaration of the
promise that the Seed of the woman would bruise the head of the
serpent. The Word joined to music continues to serve the divinely-
established purpose in the New Testament:
  God for His Gospel oft employs
    The art of music's joyful noise.
  The Apostles teach with clarity
    What music's use and goal should be.
  By singing psalms and hymns and songs
    God's people should do what belongs
  To glad instruction of each other
    Or admonition of a brother.§

* Carl Schalk, *Music in Early Lutheranism*, (St. Louis: Concordia Academic
Press, 2001) 40, 195–6.
† ibid., 29.
‡ ibid., 188.
§ ibid., 192.

132

Walter even made bold to stress the enduring character of music above all other subjects of the *trivium* and *quadrivium*—even the chief fields of higher education, with the exception of theology—declaring that music was destined to endure for life eternal:

> No further need in heaven to harp
> On grammar fine and logic sharp;
> Geometry, astronomy,
> Law, medicine, philosophy,
> All doused, and even rhetoric,
> While music beams from candlestick.*

Of course, since the movement of rhetoric is to move the heart to agreement with what is affirmed, Walter is quite right: music will be joined to the Word in praise of the Holy Trinity long after the time for rhetoric has ended.

The connection of hymns to teaching the Church is made explicit in the Lutheran Confessions. Melanchthon identifies the catechetical purpose of ceremony and hymnody to be the chief reason for their preservation in the Lutheran rite: "All the usual ceremonies are also preserved, save that the parts sung in Latin are interspersed here and there with German hymns, which have been added to teach the people. For ceremonies are needed to this end alone, that the unlearned be taught." (AC XXIV:2–3) This point is reiterated at length in the corresponding article of the Apology:

> Since ceremonies, however, ought to be observed both to teach men Scripture, and that those, admonished by the Word, may conceive faith and fear, and thus that they also may pray (for these are the designs of ceremonies); we retain the Latin language on account of those who are learning and understand Latin, and we mingle with it German hymns, in order that the people also may have something to learn, and by which faith and fear may be called forth. This custom has always existed in the churches.

* ibid., 194.

For although some more frequently, and others more rarely, mingled German hymns, nevertheless the people almost everywhere sang in their own tongue. It has indeed nowhere been written or represented that the act of hearing lessons not understood profits men, or that ceremonies profit, not because they teach or admonish, but *ex opere operato*, because they are thus performed or are looked upon. Away with such pharisaic opinions! (Ap XXIV:3–5)

The hymns—sung in the common language of the people—are present in the divine service so that "the people also may have something to learn, and by which faith and fear may be called forth." In other words, faith is created through the Word contained within the hymns. Luther also understood the hymns to be used to reinforce what was being taught in the catechism and sermons:

Thus there are in all five parts of the entire Christian doctrine which should be constantly practiced and required, and heard recited word for word. For you must not depend upon that which the young people may learn and retain from the sermon alone. When these parts have been well learned, you may assign besides some psalms or hymns, based thereupon, in order to enforce the same, and thus to lead the youth into the Scriptures, and accustom them to make daily progress therein. (LC Short Preface:24–25)

Thus Latin was retained "on account of those who are learning"; the German hymns are presented "in order that the people also may have something to learn". The exclusive language of the *Augustana*— "ceremonies are needed to this end alone, that the unlearned be taught"— teaches that the rite (which explicitly includes the hymnody) shares in the teaching which takes place in the proclamation of the Word and the celebration of the holy Sacraments; in the words of Apology XIII: "But just as the Word enters the ears in order to strike hearts; so the rite itself meets the eyes, in order to move hearts. The effect of the Word and of the rite is the same, as it has been well said by Augustine that a sacrament is 'a visible word,' because the rite is received by the eyes, and is, as it were, a picture of the Word, signifying the same thing as the Word. Wherefore the effect of both is the same." (§5) The preaching of the Word and administration of the Sacraments were established by the Lord "in order to move hearts," that is, to be His instruments to accomplish the rhetorical affects of teaching, pleasing, and persuading and they are set within a received liturgical rite which shares this catechetical function. Understood in its proper rhetorical context, the assertion that the rite was established "to move hearts" is not an 'emotional' aspect, but speaks to the matter of the conversion of the heart; that is, that the one who hears the Word and sees the rite is persuaded by the work of the Holy Spirit through those means. Toward this end, the Apology applies the words of Romans 10:17— "Faith cometh by hearing"— to the Word and Sacraments. However, exercises in rhetoric which do not teach or convey God's Word, though they may persuade, do not offer grace: "For it does not belong to human authority to promise grace. Wherefore signs instituted without God's command, are not sure signs of grace, even though they perhaps instruct the rude, or admonish as to something." (Ap XIII:3)

The Art of Rhetoric and the Art of Hymnody

To speak, then, of hymns as serving to teach the Word and thus to "move the heart" is not simply a matter of affecting emotions (although undeniably music has such as affect); it is, above all, that it serve as the purposes of rhetoric: to teach, to please, to persuade. Toward this end, one must consider both the elements of rhetoric (*partes orationis*), and the its presentation (*officia oratoris*), utilizing Philipp Melanchthon's hymn, *Dicimus grates tibi, summe rerum** as a model for purposes of this discussion.

According to certain classic models of Rhetoric, there are six *partes* to a rhetorical exercise: "The parts of a speech (*partes orationis*) are the *exordium* or opening, the *narratio* or statement of facts,

---

* "Lord God, We All to Thee Give Praise," Hymn 254 in *The Lutheran Hymnal* (St. Louis: Concordia Publishing House, 1941).

the *divisio* or *partitio*, that is, the statement of the point at issue and exposition of what the orator proposes to prove, the *confirmatio* or exposition of arguments, the *confutatio* or refutation of one's opponent's arguments, and finally the *conclusio* or peroration."[*]

The *exordium* serves to introduce the topic of the oration to the hearer, leaving him "attentive, ready to learn and well disposed."[†] In the hymn under consideration, this purpose is served by its first stanza and is, given the brevity of the hymnic form, combined with *narratio*, setting forth the "facts of the case"[‡]:

> Lord God, we all to Thee give praise,
> Thanksgivings meet to Thee we raise,
> That angel hosts Thou didst create
> Around Thy glorious throne to wait.

The topic introduced in this stanza is the praiseworthy character of God's creation of the angelic host. Given this *exordium* and *narratio*, the hymn must set forth the reason why the Church gives thanks for this act of creation to carry out the hymn's rhetorical purpose: the connection between the host around the throne of God and the Church raising its voice in praise of the Lord.

The *divisio*, normally given to the matter under dispute, addresses in this hymn the reconciliation of the role of the angelic host around the Lord's throne and the Church's praise of the Lord for the creation of that host:

> They shine with light and heav'nly grace
> And constantly behold Thy face;
> They heed Thy voice, they know it well,
> In godly wisdom they excel.

> They never rest nor sleep as we;
> Their whole delight is but to be
> With Thee, Lord Jesus, and to keep

* Clarke, 24. It should be observed that different rhetoricians divide the parts in differing ways.
† ibid., 25.
‡ ibid.

Thy little flock, Thy lambs and sheep.

The *divisio* builds from the point of conclusion of the first stanza: the image of the host gathered around the throne of God. There gathered, they behold the face of God, and shine with light and grace—testimony to their nature as a part of God's good creation which remains uncorrupted by sin. Beholding the face of God, "they heed [God's] voice" and excel in wisdom. Thus the hymn confesses that this angelic host hears the Word of God, and has been granted wisdom to understand it. Uncorrupted spirits, recipients of the divine Word, they are not subject to fallen man's need for physical rest, but are given over to the delight of being in the presence of the Lord, and serving His will. At this point, the hymn makes explicit the point that Jesus is the Lord of Hosts, and that the delight of the angelic host is therefore twofold: to abide with Christ, and to do His will in the preservation of the flock, Christ's Church. At this point, the hymn addresses the 'point of issue'—the role of the angelic host in the preservation of Christ's Church. The consolation— "They never rest nor sleep as we"— has immediate application throughout the *divisio* and *confirmatio*, as Melanchthon sets forth the terrific threat which confronts Christ's little flock.

The ancient Dragon is their foe;
His envy and his wrath they know.
It always is his aim and pride
Thy Christian people to divide.

As he of old deceived the world
And into sin and death was hurled,
So now he subtly lies in wait
To ruin school and Church and state.

A roaring lion round he goes,
No halt nor rest he ever knows;
He seeks the Christians to devour
And slay them by his dreadful power.

The 'point at issue' is Satan's war against the Church—the destruction and division which he seeks to unleash on the Christ's Church. The hymns sets forth the angelic host as defenders of Christ's little flock, and the devil as the foe of the Church. The dragon and the angels are at war, and the angelic host know the character of the enemy— "his envy and his wrath ... his aim and pride"— even when the Church is tempted to forget. Satan's opposition to the divinely-established order is manifest in his subtle treachery targeting "school and Church and state," threatening ruin of the three estates established by the holy Trinity for order within this world. The powerful imagery from St. Peter's first epistle of Satan as a lion seeking whom he may devour is utilized, as is the devil's own sleepless pursuit of his destructive aims; as the angelic host "never rest nor sleep as we," for the devil, "no halt nor rest he ever knows". If the hearer was uncertain at the *exordium* regarding the connection between the creation of the angelic host and the Church's song of thanksgiving, these stanzas set forth the alarming *confirmatio*: sleepy Christendom may forget for a time the threatening peril of Satan's treachery, but the angels never sleep, and as they delight to behold the face of Jesus, and watch over His little flock, they ever stand in opposition to the devil's treachery against all order in this fallen world.

Turning to the seventh stanza, one hears the *confutatio*, an answer to all fears aroused by knowledge of the devil's might and treachery:

> But watchful is the angel band
> That follows Christ on every hand
> To guard His people where they go
> And break the counsel of the Foe.

As Christ gave assurance unto His holy apostles— "and lo, I am with you always, even to the end of the age" (Mt. 28:20)—the hymn teaches that where Christ is, His angelic host is present, accomplishing a twofold service to Jesus for the defense of His little flock: (1) to guard His people where they go, and (2) break the counsel of the Foe. Having warned the hearer of the deadly danger posed by the devil, the hymn does not abandon the hearer in despair, but offers the consolation that with the presence of Christ with His Church comes, among other blessings, the care and protection of the angelic host.

The final stanza is devoted to the *conclusio* of the rhetorical structure, offering a repetition of the theme of the *exordium*, but with the weight of the *confirmatio* and *confutatio* reenforcing that theme:

> For this, now and in days to be,
> Our praise shall rise, O Lord, to Thee,
> Whom all the angel hosts adore
> With grateful songs forevermore.

The recipient of the hymn is now given to understand that his praise for the Lord's creation of the angelic host is part of the Church's eternal hymn of praise of the Lord of Hosts precisely because that protection extended by the holy angels is part of Jesus' preservation of His little flock. The Church song shall be joined to that of the angelic host in everlasting praise to the Lord.

As the above analysis demonstrates, despite the poetic structure, and necessary brevity of the hymnic form, Melanchthon's *Dicimus grates tibi* is nevertheless an almost perfect model of rhetorical construction.

Having considered the *partes orationis*, one turns to the *officia oratioris*—the presentation of the hymn.

The functions of the orator (*officia oratoris*), or, as they were sometimes called, the parts of rhetoric, are firstly *inventio*, invention, or, as the textbooks defined it, 'the devising of matter true and probable which will make a case appear more plausible'; secondly, *dispositio*, arrangement; thirdly, *elocutio*, style or presentation; fourthly, *memoria*, memory, and fifthly, *actio* or *pronuntiatio*, delivery. The last two stand apart as being matters more of nature than of art, and some authorities omitted one or both of them from the list.[*]

Applied to the hymn, the first several functions of the orator rest with the hymnist: *inventio* and *dispositio* are in the hands of the author and/or translator of a hymn. The Church must then assess the fruit of such labors, and examining the hymn on the basis of various criteria which contribute to the rhetorical value of the hymn: its faithfulness to the doctrine of holy Scripture, followed by matter such as poetic merit, richness of rhetorical construction, etc.

However, the matter of *elocutio* as it applies to the hymn rests less with the author of the hymn and more with the composer of the accompanying music and the manner in which those who play and sing the hymn apply themselves to their respective endeavors. It is worth noting that there are notable Lutheran composers who have argued that the principles of rhetoric must even be applied to the music which accompanies hymns.[†] Be that as it may, certainly the composition of music, and the manner in which that music is performed and sung, are important elements of the *elocutio* of a hymn. *Memoria* and *actio* are also in the hands of musicians and singers. As with the texts of Scripture and the catechism, committing the text of hymns to memory keeps them at the immediate disposal of the Christian to teach, to please, and to persuade. Despite weaknesses of *elocutio*, *memoria*, and *actio*, the power of the Word to move the hearts of men abides. "So then faith comes by hearing, and hearing by the word of God." (Rom. 10:17) This Word abides and is effective, whether that Word is heard in sermon or liturgy, seen in the rite, or sung and heard in the hymns of the Church.

---

[*] Clarke, 24.

[†] "It is said that Christoph Bernhard, a highly talented pupil of Heinrich Schütz, used to stress that music may well be compared with rhetoric, since it shares many characteristics of rhetorical language and literature. He likely learned this from Schütz, whose compositions are musical rhetoric of a high order. Johann Mattheson, the eminent contemporary of Bach and Handel, went so far as to tell his students that the six elements of rhetoric must be found also in their music." (Walter E. Buszin, "Hymn Tunes in the Service of the Gospel," in *Music for the Church—The Life and Work of Walter E. Buszin* by Kirby L. Koriath (Fort Wayne: Good Shepherd Institute, 2003) 204.

Appendix—"Lord God, We All to Thee Give Praise" (TLH #254)

1. Lord God, we all to Thee give praise,
Thanksgivings meet to Thee we raise,
That angel hosts Thou didst create
Around Thy glorious throne to wait.

2. They shine with light and heav'nly grace
And constantly behold Thy face;
They heed Thy voice, they know it well,
In godly wisdom they excel.

3. They never rest nor sleep as we;
Their whole delight is but to be
With Thee, Lord Jesus, and to keep
Thy little flock, Thy lambs and sheep.

4. The ancient Dragon is their foe;
His envy and his wrath they know.
It always is his aim and pride
Thy Christian people to divide.

5. As he of old deceived the world
And into sin and death was hurled,
So now he subtly lies in wait
To ruin school and Church and state.

6. A roaring lion round he goes,
No halt nor rest he ever knows;
He seeks the Christians to devour
And slay them by his dreadful power.

7. But watchful is the angel band
That follows Christ on every hand
To guard His people where they go
And break the counsel of the Foe.

8. For this, now and in days to be,
Our praise shall rise, O Lord, to Thee,
Whom all the angel hosts adore
With grateful songs forevermore.

The Role of Philosophy in the Theology of Philipp Melanchthon: Is There a Need for Reappraisal?*

Introduction.

Philip Melanchthon (1497-1560) is arguably the most controversial figure in the history of confessional Lutheranism. From his own generation, through mid-nineteenth to early twentieth century America until the present†, Melanchthon has been as fiercely rejected by some Lutheran theologians as he has been defended by others—a reaction which seems oddly out of place when discussing a man noted for his irenic character.

Melanchthon's significant role in the Reformation is beyond dispute; his authorship of a significant portion of the Lutheran Confessions, as well as his writing of the first Protestant dogmatics, the *Loci communes*, and his role as the *praeceptor Germaniæ* would alone be sufficient to grant Melanchthon a place of enduring significance in Reformation history. And yet, the reasons for criticism cited by Melanchthon's critics are also significant and numerous: (1) his apparent equivocation regarding to the real presence of Christ's body in the Lord's Supper and concerning the bondage of the will, (2) his compromising spirit during the Leipzig Interim, and (3) Melanchthon's *variata* edition of the *Confessio Augustana* are among the common criticisms. The complexity of Melanchthon's character and the record of his life's work is such that a brief overview is virtually impossible. This paper, therefore, will be limited primarily to one of Melanchthon's better-received works: his *Loci communes* of

---

* This essay was published previously in the Reformation 1997 issue of *Logia*.

† Matthias Flacius and Nicholas Selnecker, Friedrich Bente and Samuel S. Schmucker and Jaroslav Pelikan and Lowell Green are examples of such competing assessments in these different ages.

1521 (hereafter LC1521). Quirinus Breen has aptly summarized the importance of LC1521 within the 'canon' of Lutheran theology:

Philip Melanchthon was the author of the first book of Protestant theology, which he called *Loci communes rerum theologicarum seu hypotyposes theologicae* (Wittenberg, 1521). As a first it is worth some study, for firsts are likely to be models for later things of their kind. Moreover, while Melanchthon is by some considered to depart from early Protestant thought (cf. Philippism), Luther gave unqualified and almost extravagant praise to his young collaborator's first work. This justifies putting at least the 1521 edition in the fundamental canon of Protestantism. Finally, if such is its importance, Melanchthon's method deserves examination.*

This paper will first provide an outline of Philip Melanchthon's life leading up to the publication of LC1521. This historical section will be followed by an examination of certain highpoints in Melanchthon's theological development leading up to the LC1521. After having examined Melanchthon's historical and doctrinal background leading up to this significant work, we will examine Melanchthon's structure and methodology in the LC1521.

I. Historical Background: Melanchthon's life from 1497 to 1521.
I.1 A Overview of Melanchthon's Life Prior to His Arrival in Wittenberg.

Born in the small town of Bretten, the first-born of an armorer and a mayor's daughter, Philip Schwarzerd's background hardly seemed one which would produce the *praeceptor Germaniae*. However, Melanchthon's great uncle, the Hebraist John Reuchlin, arranged for a private tutor for Philip, his brother George, and an uncle when Philip was only seven years old, thus beginning a life of

---

* "The Terms 'Loci Communes' and 'Loci' in Melanchthon," *Church History*, XVI:4 (December 1947), p. 197.

rigorous academic work.* Philip was engaged in studying Greek by the age of 12, and Reuchlin presenting him with a Greek grammar and Greek-Latin lexicon during Philip's study of the language under private tutelage. Indeed, it was around this time that Reuchlin latinized the name "Schwarzerd" to "Melanchthon."†

Melanchthon entered the University of Heidelberg at age thirteen and received his Bachelor of Arts in June, 1511. Although he soon applied for his Masters, Melanchthon was turned down because "he was still too young and of too childish an appearance."‡ Melanchthon entered the University of Tübingen in 1512 as a result, applying himself to such diverse topics as the classics, Hebrew, philosophy, astronomy, mathematics, and medicine.§ Melanchthon was awarded the Master's degree in 1514 and became a private tutor at the university.⁜

Melanchthon's various activities and accomplishments quickly earned him recognition within the broader circles of Humanism. Erasmus declared of him in 1516: "What promise does not this Philip Melanchthon, a youth, as yet, and almost a boy, give of himself! He is equally at home in both languages [Greek and Latin]. What acuteness of invention, what purity of diction, what memory for recondite matters, what extensive reading, what delicate grace and noble talents he displays!"** Melanchthon was invited to the University of Ingolstadt, but turned down the invita-

* Joseph Stump, *Life of Philip Melanchthon*, (Reading, PA and New York: Pilger Publishing House, 1897), p. 14.

† Stump, p. 17. For more on John Reuchlin and his relationship to the Reformation, see "Reuchlin's Philosophy: Pythagoras and Cabala for Christ," by Lewis W. Spitz, *Archiv für Reformationsgeschichte*, 47:1 (1956), pp. 1-19.

‡ Stump, p. 19.

§ ibid.

⁜ ibid.

** cited in Stump, p. 20. Indeed, Erasmus remarked even as late as May, 1521: "Who, indeed, would not be distressed in spirit if Philip Melanchthon, a youth provided with so many exceptional gifts, was deprived of the public good will of the learned by this storm?" [*Christian Humanism and the Reformation: Desiderius Erasmus, Selected Writings*, ed. and trans. by John C. Olin, (New York, Evanston and London: Harper & Row, 1965), p. 162.]

tion upon the advice of Reuchlin.* Instead, Reuchlin recommended Melanchthon for a position at the University of Wittenberg, declaring to Elector Frederick, "I know of no one among the Germans who excels [Melanchthon], except Erasmus of Rotterdam, and he is an Hollander."† Melanchthon was, of course, extended the invitation and he arrived at Wittenberg—the heart of the coming storm—on August 25, 1518.‡

I.2 Speech at arrival at Wittenberg.

Melanchthon began to make his mark on the University of Wittenberg from his first lecture, "The Improvement of Studies for the Youth"—a somewhat ironic topic for a twenty-one year old man whose appearance betrayed his youth. Martin Luther was apparently "astonished by the learning, the comprehensive grasp, the reasoning power, and the beautiful diction, which Melanchthon's discourse revealed,"§ an assessment echoed by one modern translator, who proclaims it to be "a remarkable literary masterpiece."⁋ Melanchthon's general aim in the work was straightforward: "May it please a few men to remind the youth of this distinguished academy, that whatever high summit of excellent training they reach, they should understand the rationale behind the revival of studies ... And my entire lecture stresses this, so that I may impart to you a zeal for elegant literature (I mean Greek and Latin)."** The content of this lecture will be discussed more fully under II.3.

---

* Stump, p. 21.
† ibid., p. 23.
‡ ibid., p. 25.
§ ibid., p. 27.
⁋ Lowell C. Green and Charles D. Froehlich, *Melanchthon in English*, (St. Louis: Center for Reformation Research, 1982) Sixteenth Century Bibliography #22, p. 12. Ralph Keen offers a somewhat different assessment: "The lecture is written in a very dense Latin style that is difficult to read and would surely have been impossible for part of his audience to understand. ... Melanchthon was still somewhat unskilled as a public speaker and may have been trying to impress; later on his lectures become delightfully clear." (*A Melanchthon Reader*, trans. by Ralph Keen, (New York, Bern, Frankfurt am Main, Paris: Peter Lang, 1988) p. 47.)
** Keen, p. 48.

I.3 Melanchthon's Early Years in Wittenberg.

Melanchthon's work in Wittenberg is well-represented in his first two courses, which he announced in his "The Improvement of the Studies of the Youth": "We have at hand Homer, and we have Paul's letter to Titus." These courses were offered in the winter of 1518.* Stump notes that "As copies of Erasmus's edition of the Greek New Testament were scarce at Wittenberg, he had a special edition of the Epistle to Titus printed for the use of his students. But in addition to the lectures which he had announced, he also undertook, for the present, to give instruction in Hebrew."†

The alliance between Melanchthon and Luther seems to have been virtually unavoidable. Even before Melanchthon's arrival, Schwiebert notes,

> ... Biblical Humanism forced Luther to conclude that Aristotle must go, and with him the whole philosophy and methodology of Scholasticism which would require a drastic revision of the university curriculum. In two years' time the conservative Thomists and Scotists were won over to the new exegetical approach and the Elector was being strongly urged to revise the curriculum purging it of scholastic methodology and introducing Biblical Humanism.‡

* ibid., p. 56, 57.

† Stump, p. 32. Among Melanchthon's other publications during 1518: "...two treatises of Plutarch, a dictionary, a Greek hymn, *Athenagoras*, Plato's *Symposium*, and miscellaneous prefaces and discourses. By January [1519] his three books on rhetoric appeared." (Clyde L. Manschreck, *Melanchthon, The Quiet Reformer*, (New York, Nashville, Tennessee: Abingdon Press, 1958) p. 44)

‡ Ernest G. Schwiebert, "New Groups and Ideas at the University of Wittenberg," *Archiv für Reformationsgeschichte*, 49:1/2 (1958), p. 70. Alister McGrath recounts the following incident in which Luther benefited from the labors of the Humanists: "On 25 September 1516, Luther presided over an academic disputation on the occasion of the promotion of Bartholomaus Feldkirchen to the degree of Bachelor of Divinity. ... In the course of this disputation, Feldkirchen argued that the treatise *de vera et falsa poenitentia* should not be ascribed to Augustine, and supported this assertion by arguing that Augustine taught that man could not fulfil the commandments of God through his own reason and strength. These assertions outraged Karlstadt,

The common reforming thrust of Melanchthon and
Luther was observed by students. As one Swiss student wrote in
1520: "Luther is lecturing on the Psalms, while Philip is treating
St. Paul. Melanchthon is, so to say, Luther's traveling companion
in Christ. The same enthusiasm unites the two, the same reliabil-
ity as scholars, the same working together in all undertakings and
teachings."*

Although Melanchthon began lecturing on Titus in the
winter of 1518, nearly a year passed before he held a theological
degree. Melanchthon, "almost against his will," was awarded the
Bachelor of Theology in September, 1519 in recognition of his at-
tainments.† However, Melanchthon never accepted the Doctor of
Theology degree "because he did not want to assume the responsibility which he believed doing so would involve."‡

who insisted that both Augustine and the scholastic theologians had been seriously misrepresented during the course of the debate. Luther then proceeded
to challenge Karlstadt to confirm his assertions, a challenge which Karlstadt
had little option but to accept. Unfortunately, Karlstadt did not have access to
an edition of Augustine, and was obliged to travel to the Leipzig book fair on
13 January 1517—some four months after the disputation—to purchase one.
Significantly, Karlstadt, like most theologians of the early sixteenth century,
was obliged to read his Augustine at second hand, in the form of collections of
'sentences' extracted from his works, or references made to him in the writings
of other theologians (such as those of Thomas Aquinas or Duns Scotus, with
whose writings contemporary records indicate he was well acquainted). ... By
April 1517, it is clear that Karlstadt had decided that Luther was right in his interpretation of Augustine, and published 151 theses defending an Augustinian
theology over and against that of his former scholastic mentors, particularly
Capreolus. In these theses, Karlstadt defended the supreme authority of scripture, and a derivative authority of the fathers, particularly Augustine. In many
ways, this may be seen as a humanist programme. Indeed, there are excellent
reasons for suggesting that, at this stage, Karlstadt saw himself as developing
a theological programme similar to that already associated with Erasmus." *The
Intellectual Origins of the European Reformation*, (Cambridge, Massachusetts and
Oxford, England: Blackwell Publishers, 1987) p. 61-2.

* Schwiebert, "New Groups and Ideas at the University of Wittenberg," p. 71.
† Stump, p. 36.
‡ ibid.. Melanchthon's view regarding the doctorate is interesting, given the
prominent position into which he was virtually swept after Luther's death.

Luther, however, did not doubt Melanchthon's God-given capacity for theological understanding, especially when in came to the study of St. Paul's epistles. In fact, Luther stole a copy of Melanchthon's lectures on Corinthians and published them in the spring of 1521!* As Luther wrote in the volume's preface:

Why did you suffer me to ask, command, and urge you so often to publish? This is my defense against you: I am willing to be, and to be called, a thief, fearing neither your complaints nor accusation. ...

The Scripture, you say, must be read without commentaries. You say this correctly about Jerome, Origen, Thomas, and the like. They wrote commentaries in which they give their own teaching. ... Nobody should call your annotations a commentary, but a guide to reading the Scripture and learning Christ—something which no commentary has hitherto presented.[†]

Melanchthon indisputably proved himself a faithful fellow laborer with Luther during the early years of the Reformation. Whether writing in defense of Luther at Leipzig or against the Paris theologians, Melanchthon was quickly drawn to a place of leadership in the Reformation. In conclusion, it is worth noting that Melanchthon introduced additional reforms to the curriculum of the University of Wittenberg when he became rector in 1523, "throwing out the last vestiges of Scholasticism, establishing an improved *Pedagogium*, and instituting *Rhetoren* in the two principal dormitories."[‡] Both Luther and Melanchthon remained cognizant of the need for academic reforms to, by God's grace, mirror and support the reforms being carried out in the Church.

* Manschreck, *Melanchthon, the Quiet Reformer*, p. 92.
† ibid.
‡ Schwiebert, "New Groups and Ideas at the University of Wittenberg," p. 72-73.

II. Doctrinal Background: Melanchthon up through 1521.

II.1 Melanchthon and John Reuchlin.

Melanchthon profited greatly from the influence and support of his great uncle, John Reuchlin. (Certainly the relationship between these men merits more discussion than can be allowed here.) It should be recognized that the benefits of this relationship were by no means 'one way': Reuchlin also gained from Melanchthon. Melanchthon delved into Scripture and the Church Fathers as part of his studies during his years in Tübingen (Fall 1512-Summer 1518). Melanchthon's interest in religion was by no means limited to academic pursuits, however: the young scholar supported his great uncle in contending with the Dominicans who "insisted on the burning of all Jewish books and documents."[*] This support, aside from Melanchthon's personal views concerning the Jews and regardless of his view of Hebraic studies, was probably reinforced by his familial relationship to John Reuchlin. Unfortunately, "Reuchlin considered the Cabala, not Hebrew for its own sake, his major concern."[†] However, for Melanchthon (and Luther) the motivation was different: "Both Luther and Melanchthon appreciated Reuchlin's contribution to language study which was so crucial also in the reformer's drive *ad fontes*. ... Luther and Melanchthon disparaged cabalistic nonsense, though Melanchthon found some good in it."[‡]

As was observed above, Reuchlin helped secure the position at the University of Wittenberg for Melanchthon. The closeness of the familial bond was severed, however, when Reuchlin accepted a position at the University of Ingolstadt in 1519. Reuchlin urged Melanchthon to follow him to Ingolstadt, promising Melanchthon

---

[*] Stump, p. 20.

[†] Lewis W. Spitz, "Reuchlin's Philosophy: Pythagoras and Cabala for Christ," p. 7. Indeed, "The *De arte cabalistica*, 1517, reveals Reuchlin as a matured Hebraist and the leading Christian expert on the Cabala. ... The Cabala was Reuchlin's major source. He viewed it as a symbolic reception of divine revelation, which leads to the salvation-bringing contemplation of God." (Spitz, p. 8)

[‡] ibid., p. 16.

that Eck was willing to forgive him.* Melanchthon declined Reuchlin's request, responding, "I love my native land certainly, but I must consider what Christ has called me to do more than my own inclinations. Trusting in the Holy Spirit, I shall do my work here until the same Spirit calls me away. I ask not to live happily but righteously and Christlike."† In response, Reuchlin "requested Philip never to write him again lest he be suspected of sympathy for a heretic!"‡ Furthermore, Reuchlin withdrew his promise of his library, willing it instead to the monks of Pforzheim.§ It would be decades before Melanchthon's anger would entirely pass: "Melanchthon, in turn, ignored [Reuchlin's] death and did not relent until thirty years later..."❡ Given the violence of Melanchthon's separation from the greatest Humanist influence in his life, Manschreck writes with justification: "Nothing could more forcefully have indicated the commitment of Melanchthon to the evangelical reform movement, nor have demonstrated so effectively that humanism was not his final standard."**

II.2 Eramus and *sola fide*.

Erasmus, like Reuchlin, had a significant influence on the young Melanchthon. Melanchthon readily admitted this influence, writing in 1519: "I myself know how much all students owe to Erasmus, and most of all myself."†† Melanchthon's bond with Erasmus was more of a scholarly, rather than personal, nature—a sharp contrast with Melanchthon's relationship with his great uncle. Melanchthon and Erasmus corresponded until Erasmus' death.‡‡

---

* Manschreck, *Melanchthon, the Quiet Reformer*, p. 53.
† quoted in Manschreck, *Melanchthon, the Quiet Reformer*, p. 53.
‡ ibid.
§ ibid.
❡ Spitz, "Reuchlin's Philosophy: Pythagoras and Cabala for Christ," p. 16, n. 59.
** Manschreck, *Melanchthon, the Quiet Reformer*, p. 53.
†† Lowell Green, "The Influence of Erasmus upon Melanchthon, Luther and the Formula of Concord in the Doctrine of Justification," *Church History*, 43:2 (June, 1974), p. 189.
‡‡ ibid.

152

Aside from the influence Erasmus had on Melanchthon the Humanist, he also seems to have played a role in the development of Melanchthon the Theologian. Of course, Erasmus' 1516 Greek text of the New Testament was of great significance to Melanchthon and Luther. However, Erasmus may have had a more specific influence on Melanchthon's theological development: the distinction between *imputare* and *reputare* in holy Scripture, and the significance of this distinction for a right understanding of Christian righteousness.

Lowell Green observes that "The terms *imputare* and *reputare* had often been confused before Erasmus."[*] Erasmus, however, "distinguished between *reputare* and *imputare* at least as early as 1503. He wrote in his Enchiridion: 'Christ will fight for you and will impute his gift to you as merit (*liberalitatem suam tibi pro merito imputabit*)'..."[†] Again,

> In [Erasmus'] exegesis of Rom. 4:3-8 in the first edition of his *Novum Instrumentum* he pointed out that in translating the Greek verb, *elogísthe*, verse 3, several translations were possible: *reputatur*, *imputatur* or *acceptum fert* (to be reputed, to be imputed, or to be held acceptable). In contrast to the Vulgate and Valla, Erasmus insisted that the verb in this passage must be translated as *imputatur* or *imputatum est*.[‡]

Based on this and other examples,[§] Green concludes that "it seems that Erasmus never realized the implications of forensic justification. Nevertheless it cannot be denied that he provided the grammatical foundation upon which they [Melanchthon and Luther] built their teaching of justification."[⁋]

It has been rightly observed that "To some degree, Melanchthon advanced beyond Luther in areas such as the doc-

* ibid., p. 185.
† ibid., p. 187.
‡ ibid.
§ see Green, "The Influence of Erasmus upon Melanchthon, Luther and the Formula of Concord in the Doctrine of Justification," p. 187, n. 14.
⁋ Green, "The Influence of Erasmus upon Melanchthon, Luther and the Formula of Concord in the Doctrine of Justification," p. 187.

trine of Law and Gospel, which is already evident in the 1521 *LC*. ... Melanchthon's emphasis on Law and Gospel, while having roots in the teaching of the early Luther, in some ways refined and certainly helped and guided Luther. Note the fine material on this point in Melanchthon's *LC* of 1521."* It should be recognized that Erasmus, albeit in a limited fashion, helped make this development possible by doing the grammatical work necessary to lay the biblical foundation for forensic justification.

II.3 Melanchthon's Rejection of Scholasticism: The Subordination of Philosophy to Theology.

First as a humanist, and then as a reformer and humanist, Philip Melanchthon was an unflinching enemy of the Scholastic theologians. This facet of Melanchthon's thought—particularly in its more humanist orientation—can readily be seen in his inaugural lecture at the University of Wittenberg, "On Correcting the Studies of Youth":

> German youth elsewhere, a few years ago, undertook an auspicious debut in the learned arena, and not a few have returned in mid-course with a virtually barbaric dismissiveness, saying that the revival of literary studies is more difficult than useful: Greek is seized upon by some with idle minds to be used for ostentatious display. Hebrew letters are of dubious value. Meanwhile literature perishes from lack of genuine cultivation, and philosophy is abandoned by those who turn to contentions about other things. When such a horde of illiterate people prepares to foregather, who fails to perceive that the champion they counter needs more than one ally?

> ...

> I believe that it was about eight hundred years ago that the world was set into commotion by the Goths and Italy devastated by the Lombards, just as Roman literature was destroyed along with Rome herself, and at once the furor of war

---

* J.A.O. Preus, *The Second Martin*, (St. Louis: Concordia Publishing House, 1994) p. 65.

destroyed the libraries and killed the Muses with inactivity. ... [A]t about that time Gregory whom they call the great and I call the leader of the parade and the torchbearer of the dying theology--otherwise a man of outstanding piety--was administrator over the Roman church, and held up the decline in that most unhappy century, as much as he could by teaching and writing.

...

...some men, led either by lust for subtleties or love of dispute, fell to Aristotle, albeit mutilated and mangled and obscure even to some Greeks, to whom he seemed like Apollo himself, rendered into Latin that would try even the conjectures of the raving Sibyl. Yet here incautious men entered. Gradually the better disciplines were neglected, we left Greek learning behind, and everywhere bad things began to be taught as if they were good. From this proceeded Thomases, Scotuses, seraphic doctors, cherubic doctors, and the rest of their followers, more numerous than the offspring of Cadmus.*

Melanchthon, in describing the problem, began to propose a solution:

It was not possible, when the Greeks were held in contempt, for a single philosopher to be of any use to humane studies; and concern for sacred things as well slowly died. This latter situation has crippled the true Christian rites and customs of the church; the former has crippled the study of literature. Perhaps a fairer destruction could have taken place in other circumstances. For they would have been able easily to establish the literature that had fallen into disuse, the rites of the pure church, and with good literature--if any remained preserved--to correct the ruinous customs of the church, to stir up the fallen spirits of men, and to strengthen them and set them in order.†

* Keen, p. 47-49.
† ibid., p. 50.

Central to Melanchthon's guide to reform was a restoration of the ancient letters:

> Greek literature is to be joined to Latin, that you may read philosophers, theologians, historians, orators, poets, to pursue, wherever you turn, the real thing and not the shadow of things, as Ixion when he was to meet with Juno fell upon the cloud .... And when this journey, as it were, is prepared by compendia, you proceed, as Plato says, to philosophy. For I am clearly persuaded of the view, as one who likes things that are distinguished, that the mind must previously be exercised prudently and sufficiently by the human disciplines (for such I call philosophy) in order to excel, whether it be in the sacred things or the marketplace. ... But select the best things from the best sources, both those things that pertain to knowledge of nature and also to the forming of manners. Greek learning is especially necessary for this, for it embraces the universal knowledge of nature, so that you may speak fittingly and fluently about morals.[*]

Melanchthon's concerns in 1518 are much more in keeping with those of the humanists. The decay of letters and piety are the primary focus for Melanchthon. While certainly the study of holy Scripture was a vital component in the restoration of the sacred (e.g. the lectures on Titus), Melanchthon's focus is still more humanist than it would be in the months and years to come.

Melanchthon-as-reformer is much more in evidence in his baccalaureate theses of September, 1519. By this point the Leipzig disputation (June-July 1519) has passed and Melanchthon has drawn the unpleasant attention of John Eck.[†] Not too surprisingly,

[*] ibid., p. 54.

[†] see Stump, p. 34-35. Melanchthon commented regarding the debate: "Indeed, that province of debate was first undertaken for no other reason than that it might be made known openly what a great difference there is between the old theology, that of Christ, and the new, Aristotelian doctrine." ("Letter on the Leipzig Debate, 1519" in *Melanchthon: Selected Writings*, trans. by Charles Leander Hill,

therefore, the theses stress points which would become significant Reformation themes. For example, the theses stress salvation *sola gratia*:

> 6. The Law, therefore, causes us even to hate God.
>
> 7. Just as hate is not the beginning of love, so servile fear is not the beginning of filial fear.
>
> 8. It follows that servile fear is not the beginning of repentance.
>
> 9. Therefore the gracious act of Christ is righteousness.
>
> 10. All of our righteousness is a gracious imputation of God.
>
> 11. Therefore it is true that even good works are sins.[*]

The presentation of salvation by the "gracious imputation of God" is particularly significant. Lowell Green observes: "[in] the *Baccalaureate Theses* of 1519, Melanchthon presented the earliest Reformational assertion of justification by the free imputation of Christ's merit."[†]

The baccalaureate theses also uphold the *sola Scriptura* principle for determining the articles of faith.

> 16. It is not necessary for a Catholic to believe any other articles of faith than those to which Scripture is a witness.
>
> 17. The authority of councils is below the authority of Scripture.
>
> 18. Therefore not to believe in the "*character indelibilis*," transubstantiation, and the like is not open to the charge of heresy.[‡]

By January 25, 1520, the Day of the Conversion of Paul, Melanchthon's understanding of the radical distinction between biblical theology and scholastic theology had grown even further, as he demonstrated in "Paul and the Scholastics," his oration for that

---

(Minneapolis: Augsburg Publishing House, 1962) p. 22.)

[*] "Baccalaureate Theses, 1519," in *Melanchthon: Selected Writings*, p. 17.

[†] Lowell Green, *How Melanchthon Helped Luther Discover the Gospel*, (Fallbrook, California: Verdict Publications, 1980) p. 125.

[‡] Hill, *Melanchthon: Selected Writings*, p. 18.

day. Melanchthon's study of the Pauline epistles—a work begun at Tübingen—was having an effect on him: "I am of the opinion that Christ, and therefore the sum of our salvation, cannot be known so accurately from the writings of anyone else, or from the commentaries of any other, as they can from those of Paul." This point is eminently personal for Melanchthon: "As a boy I did some damage to my mind in preoccupation with the literature of the philosophers, which, I hope, the doctrine of Paul some day will repair."† The error of the Scholastics stands in contrast to such a spirit of reverence toward the Pauline epistles: "With what great damage the schools of theology have neglected Paul up to now, I shudder to say. For after having condemned the doctrine of Paul, they embraced Aristotle, and scarcely is the name of Christ left. Certainly his grace is unknown, and it is from this alone that his divinity can properly be learned."‡

Nevertheless, Melanchthon had not abandoned his high estimation of the importance of the secular arts: "Philosophy should be sought—and by this term all antiquity especially has been included—in order that from that source one may seek a form of the better life."§ However, "By the consensus of all the wise, the very best kind of discipline has always been considered to be that most adapted to the improvement of character and the pursuits of life. In this connection I shall show just what we who have been washed in the blood of Christ actually owe to Paul. It is not right for Christians to seek a form or plan of life from philosophers but from the divine books."ℂ Ultimately, the *sola Scriptura* principle must be upheld: "... I propose principles for dispute in order to urge that no man should seek a judgment about sacred matters from any other source except holy Scripture. ... I take the position that it does not matter if anyone does not believe anything except what Scripture teaches."**

* "Paul and the Scholastics," in *Melanchthon: Selected Writings*, p. 33.
† ibid., p. 38.
‡ ibid., p. 41.
§ ibid., p. 33-34.
ℂ ibid., p. 34.
** ibid., p. 52.

The key elements of Melanchthon's theological methodology, *sola Scriptura*, with a heavy Pauline emphasis, and a firm understanding of salvation as being *sola gratia*, naturally coupled with a unflinching belief regarding man's utter depravity, were now in place. The background was set for the LC1521.

III. An examination of the Methodology of the *Loci communes* of 1521.
III.1 Historical background of this work.

As was the case with some of Melanchthon's earlier published works of theology, LC1521 began with the surreptitious publication of lecture notes. Melanchthon had begun lecturing on Romans in the summer of 1519 "at the insistence of Luther" and, as had been the case with his course on Titus, Melanchthon prepared a Greek text of Romans for his students.* When certain students, who Melanchthon deemed to be "blessed with more zeal than judgment," printed his lecture notes on Romans it became necessary, Melanchthon believed, to publish this work in a more acceptable form.† As Melanchthon explained in his dedicatory epistle:

> Last year, while expounding the Epistle of Paul to the Romans, I arranged in a methodical manner so to speak, the most common topics of theological science. In addition, I set in order the medley of the epistle itself. This laborious study, though prepared for the sole purpose of indicating to those whom I privately taught the nature of the argument of the Pauline disputation and its manner of refutation (και ελεγχον) in as fruitful a way as it possibly could be done, was nevertheless circulated by some unknown persons. In a word, whoever published it, I approve their zeal more than their judgment. Especially is this the case, since I had written it in such a way that, without the Epistle of Paul it could not have been properly understood, what theme I had followed throughout the entire work.

---

* Manschreck, *Melanchthon, the Quiet Reformer*, p. 83.
† ibid., p. 82.

Now because it is not within my power to suppress a book made almost for common use, it seems best to revise and re-arrange it. For indeed, many things contained therein wanted a more accurate argument, and likewise many things, revision. Moreover, because it concerns the whole argument, the principal topics of Christian discipline are indicated in order that the youths may understand both what things are to be sought out in the Scriptures, as well as learn under what base hallucinations they labor everywhere in theological science, who have handed down to us the subtle pratings of Aristotle, instead of the doctrine of Christ.[*]

Thus what began as lecture notes on Romans became the first work of Lutheran systematics. First published in April, 1521, two Wittenberg editions were published before the end of the year and an additional edition was produced in Basel. "By the end of 1525 eighteen Latin editions had been published in addition to various printings of Spalatin's German translation of it. Throughout Germany and in foreign lands the book won acclaim, for it was something radically new in theological science—a system of doctrine drawn from the Scriptures!"[†]

III.2 Melanchthon's use of the terms 'Loci communes' and 'Loci' and the relationship between philosophy and theology.

Quirinus Breen draws attention to the importance of Melanchthon's understanding of the terms 'loci communes' and 'loci', and relates this usage to a difference between Aristotle and Cicero with regards to the meaning of this terminology:

> To Aristotle [*topoi* or *loci*] are merely points of view from which a probable proposition may be looked at. His aim is to make dialectics as responsible to truth as it

---

[*] *The Loci Communes of Philip Melanchthon*, trans. by Charles Leander Hill, (Boston: Meador Publishing Company, 1944) p. 63-64.

[†] Manschreck, *Melanchthon, the Quiet Reformer*, p. 82.

is possible. He knew there had always been a relation of dialectics to rhetoric—that rhetoric dresses up dialectical propositions for purposes of persuasion. Thus he wanted to make rhetoric more responsible to the truth; but he was aware that through rhetoric exactitude or precision cannot be attained in knowledge. The basic difference in Cicero is that he does not believe in any but probable statements. Therefore with him dialectics is everything as a means of discovering knowledge. The chief tool of dialectic as a finder of knowledge is the topic or *locus*. The *loci* are now no longer mere points of view. They are *sedes argumentorum*, i.e., the veins within a subject matter in which we dig for knowledge of it. They are the pits from which we pull up learning. Bearing in mind that Cicero's *loci* discover for us the only kind of knowledge that exists, it is understandable that he magnified the *loci* far beyond the bounds set by Aristotle.[*]

Breen believed that the difference between the methodologies of the orthodox and the heterodox could be framed in terms of the difference between Aristotle's and Cicero's *loci*:

That which kept churchmen from falling into the New Academy was the belief that there are things that are certain, namely, the body of the received faith. After Anselm, largely speaking, those were considered heretics who dealt with the articles of faith by means of dialectics, that is, as probable propositions; while those were considered orthodox who held that the articles of faith are in part expressible in propositions necessarily true.[†]

Breen attempts to place Melanchthon's LC1521 within the Ciceronian camp by drawing attention to his use of *hypotyposes* as a synonym for *loci*; a term which (Breen observes) Quintilian

---

[*] Breen, "The Terms 'Loci Communes' and 'Loci' in Melanchthon," p. 201.
[†] ibid.

says means a "picturesque discription [which] cannot be regarded as a statement of facts."* Breen therefore concludes: "I take it that Melanchthon intended the *loci communes* to be understood rhetorically."† Melanchthon's *Erotemata Dialectices* (1549) is cited as further proof, as he there defines "a dialectical *locus*" as "a *sedes argumenti*, or rather, an index pointing out where is the source whence the material is to be drawn by which a proposition in question is to be confirmed; so that, if you should seek confirmation of this proposition: Glory is to be sought, some source is to be pointed out whence the confirmation is to be drawn."‡ "This," Breen declares, "is thoroughly Ciceronian."§ All of this seems directed toward placing Melanchthon into the same category with the 'Ciceronian' medieval heretics who questioned the articles of the faith. Nevertheless, Breen concedes a certain 'Aristotelianism' to Melanchthon: "Melanchthon in fact distinguishes between propositions which are probably true and those which are certainly true. This is certainly Aristotelian. ... As long as there is a belief in Scripture as revelation, there will be a decent respect for Aristotle somewhere."❡

The nature of Breen's objection to Melanchthon is more clearly presented in his essay, "The Two-Fold Truth Theory in Melanchthon."** For Melanchthon, philosophy, like any other field of human endeavor, ultimately functions in the service of the biblical theology. Thus, "Never are we ushered into the realm of reason as a promised land in which the mind may find full play for its natural gifts. Melanchthon fears the apparent frivolity and irreverence which are sometimes the by-product of unfettered mental activity."†† Breen objects: "Yet this is a danger that must be risked."‡‡ Breen continues:

---

* ibid., p. 203.
† ibid.
‡ ibid., p. 205.
§ ibid.
❡ ibid., p. 206.
** *The Review of Religion* IX (Jan. 1945).
†† ibid., p. 131.
‡‡ ibid.

The point is important, for Melanchthon's caveats spring from a suspicion that reason in full play might damage the faith. And this is of the essence of the two-fold truth theory. The classroom in philosophy at Wittenberg was not free. This is regrettable, for that lowered philosophy to a technique of propaganda. Be the cause never so good, philosophy will not serve as mere apologist. ... To Melanchthon philosophy was a kind of automaton in the service of theology.[*]

This understanding of Melanchthon's approach to philosophy leads Breen to conclude:

> Melanchthon's works on theology are fundamentally rhetorical, or homiletical. They are handbooks for preachers. Their rhetorical character fits their author. ... His theological *loci* are intended to show the preacher the veins of Scripture which can be fruitfully worked for the rebuke of sinners and the consolation of believers. The *loci* are also shot through with warning, comfort, and practical admonition; while later editions get more dialectical, he seldom misses an opportunity to give an [sic] homiletical turn to an argument.[†]

Breen rejects Melanchthon's rhetorical approach and the reason is simple: Breen rejects Melanchthon's *sola Scriptura* principle.

> ...the question arises whether the theological *loci* or topics constitute a true body of theological knowledge or whether they are a body of Melanchthonian opinions. That is, who or what determines the *loci*? Who or what determines that Scripture alone, and not the living church also, provide the subject matter of theology? Or, who or what determines that the basic topics (*supremi loci*) pointed out by Luther—namely, law and gospel, sin and grace—are

---

[*] ibid., p. 132.

[†] Breen, "The Terms 'Loci Communes' and 'Loci' in Melanchthon," p. 207.

indeed more fundamental than St. Thomas' *locus* of God as Being, or than Calvin's *of the glory of God?* And who or what determines that natural reason does not play an indispensable role in theology? Surely, Melanchthon's theology is in the state of opinions largely.*

For all of Breen's blustering, his insights into Melanchthon's rhetorical methodology disproves the common Protestant assumption that Melanchthon's humanism or his 'Aristotelian argumentation' undermined biblical truth.† Breen's objection to Melanchthon is that Melanchthon's *Loci communes* (and other writings) operate from the assumption that their presentation of biblical truth is accurate and his argumentation therefore draws upon all areas of knowledge, including exegesis, history, philosophy, patristic study, natural science, to give the reader support in defending true doctrine. As Melanchthon declared,

> In theological matters we especially seek two different things: one, how we shall be consoled in regard to death and the judgment of God; the other, how we shall live chastely. One is the subject of true, evangelical, Christian preaching, to the world and to human reason unknown; that is what Luther teaches, and that is what engenders righteousness of the heart, in which good works then originate. The other is what Erasmus teaches us—good morals, the chaste life. It is also what the heathen philosophers knew about.

---

* ibid., p. 208.

† For example, "Melanchthon even came to use rational proofs for the existence of God in his commentary on Romans and later editions of the *Loci Communes*. These proofs were structured just as those used by Aquinas and the Scholastics, whom he had once condemned. Melanchthon employed such concepts as the orderliness of nature, the rational nature of man, the necessity of a single first cause, and the teleological goal of a final cause, asserting that each of these necessitates the existence of God, therefore God exists. ... Because he elevated the role of natural reason, Melanchthon, like the scholastics before him, necessarily held revelation not in a position superior to reason but coordinate with reason." (Jonathan Selden, "Aquinas, Luther, Melanchthon, and Biblical Apologetics," *Grace Theological Journal* 5:2 (1984), p 195.

What, however, has philosophy in common with Christ, blind reason with the revelation of God? Whoever follows this knows only sophistication; he does not know faith. If love does not proceed out of faith, then it is not genuine, only an external, Pharisaic hypocrisy...*

Breen, however, desires philosophy to be freed from the 'shackles' of theology, at least from a theology normed by the principle of *sola Scriptura*.

In light of the above discussion, it is not surprising that Melanchthon's approach in LC1521 is self-consciously centered on the Scriptures. As Melanchthon declares in the dedication of LC1521:

> Moreover, because it concerns the whole argument, the principal topics of Christian discipline are indicated in order that youths may understand both what things are to be sought out in the Scriptures, as well as learn under what base hallucinations they labor everywhere in theological science, who have handed down to us the subtle pratings of Aristotle, instead of the doctrine of Christ.
>
> I am indeed treating everything sparingly and briefly, due to the fact that I am discharging the duty of an Index rather than a commentary. Hence, I am only stating the nomenclature of the topics, to which that person roaming through the Divine Scriptures may be directed. I do not wish to lead them away from scriptures to some obscure and intricate argument of my own; but if possible that I might incite them to the Scriptures.
>
> For on the whole, I am not quite equal to the commentaries, not even to those of the Ancients. So far from that am I, that I would not by any longer writings of mine, restrain anyone from the study of the Canonical Scripture.

* *Corpus Reformatorum* vol. 20, p. 700 in Clyde Manschreck, "The Bible in Melanchthon's Philosophy of Education," *The Journal of Bible and Religion*, 23:3 (July 1955), p. 204.

On the contrary, I would desire nothing quite so much if it were possible, as that all Christians be thoroughly conversant with the divine letters alone, and be wholly transformed into their nature. ... He is mistaken who seeks the form of Christianity in any other source than Canonical Scripture. For indeed how much do the Commentaries lack the purity of Canonical Scripture? In Canonical Scripture, one will find nothing but what is worthy of honor, while in the Commentaries how many things depend upon the valuation of human reason!*

Thus Melanchthon clearly subordinates philosophy and the testimony of the fathers to the authority of Scripture. Again, Melanchthon says of the fathers:

If you take away from Origen his absurd allegories and his forest of philosophical sentences, how little will be left! And yet, the Greeks with great unanimity follow him, as do certain of the Latin writers like Ambrosius and Jerome, men who seem to be pillars. And after these, almost every author, the more recent he is, the more adulterated.

... Finally, it cannot be but that human writings often entangle even the cautious reader.†

It is not that these other sources are worthless, but rather that they are flawed and derivative, and thus pale when compared with Scripture, which is flawless and the source of Christian doctrine.

Melanchthon clearly demonstrates his methodology in his first *locus*, "On the Powers of Man, Especially Free Will." First, Melanchthon sets aside argumentation from the Church fathers:

Augustine and Bernard wrote on Free Will but the former, indeed, retracted his writings in many ways in the later works which he wrote against the Pelagians. Bernard is not like him. There are some works on this subject even

---

* *The Loci Communes of Philip Melanchthon*, p. 64-65.
† ibid., p. 65.

among the Greek authors, but they are rare. Since I shall not follow human opinions, I shall set forth the subject with simplicity and clarity, a thing which authors both ancient and modern have almost obscured. And they have done so because they interpreted the Scripture in such a way as to wish to satisfy simultaneously the judgment of human reason.[*]

Philosophy is rejected as a source of truth regarding the Free Will:

Within this topic, although Christian doctrine differs from philosophy and human reason, philosophy has gradually crept into Christianity, and the impious dogma of Free Will has been received and the beneficence of Christ has been obscured by that profane and animal wisdom of human reason. ... That which is designated "reason" has been taken over from Platonism, and is especially pernicious. For just as in these latter times the church has embraced Aristotle in preference to Christ, so immediately after the inception of the church, Christian doctrine was weakened through the fusion [infusion?] of Platonic philosophy. And so it happens that besides the Canonical Scriptures, there are no genuine letters in the church. In general, whatever has been handed down by way of commentaries, smells of philosophy.[†]

In conclusion, therefore, regardless of what may be argued concerning the nature of later orthodox Lutheran dogmatics, it should be conceded that Melanchthon's LC1521 reflects its author's understanding of the subordination of all fields of study to the revelation of Scripture. In this respect, the LC1521 is a good example of the virtues of humanist studies in the service of biblical theology.

---

[*] ibid., p. 69-70.
[†] ibid., p. 70-71.

III.3 The Structure of LC1521 and Melanchthon's Methodology.

The structure of LC1521 is quite different from the structure of later versions of the *Loci communes*—indeed, its structure does not even follow the outline of the "principal heads of theological science" which Melanchthon provides in LC1521.* Melanchthon observes that "In the individual sciences certain topics or places are wont to be sought, whereby the whole of each science is comprehended. These topics are to be considered a goal to which all our studies may be directed. Now in theology, we see that the ancient authors aimed at this indeed cautiously and prudently."† Several points need to be observed here: Melanchthon is recognizing a need for a structured study of theology and not only, for example, a treatment of these topics as they appear in the course of the exegetical study of particular books of sacred Scripture. Furthermore, Melanchthon is aligning himself with the delineation of topics provided by the "ancient authors." Melanchthon is careful, however, to distinguish his work from that of the later theologian of the Eastern and Western Churches: "Of more recent authors, John of Damascus and Peter Lombard both foolishly did so [that is, sought the topics of theology]. For John of Damascus plays the philosopher too much, while Peter Lombard chose to heap up the opinions of man rather than to present the judgment of Scriptures."‡

Melanchthon provides the list of topics "in order to indicate at least, on what topics the whole scheme hangs, and to the end that they ['the studious'] may understand whither they must direct their studies."§ Not all of the topics were equally open to being understood or explained—some could only be confessed. As Melanchthon wrote:

> As certain of these are straightway incomprehensible, so on
> the contrary, there are some that Christ has willed the en-

---

* See Appendix A for a comparative list of the actual contents of LC1521 versus the "principal heads of theological science." Appendix B provides a comparison of the contents of LC1521, and the 1543 and 1555 versions of *Loci communes*.
† *The Loci Communes of Philip Melanchthon*, p. 66.
‡ ibid.
§ ibid.

tire company of Christians to know fully. The mysteries of divinity we have the more rightly adored than investigated. On the other hand, they cannot be put to test without danger, because not rarely holy men indeed have attempted to do so.[*]

Therefore LC1521 could be expected to avoid speculative theology, self-consciously not going beyond the limits of the biblical revelation. Again, Melanchthon declares: "...there is no reason why we should put much labor on the greatest topics such as, God, on the Unity and Trinity of God, on the great mystery of Creation, and on the mode of Incarnation. I ask you, what did the Scholastic theologians gain so many years ago, when they busied themselves with these topics alone?"[†] These Scholastic labors are all the more troublesome for Melanchthon because they led, he believed, to a neglect of the Gospel: "And moreover, their folly might have gone unnoticed had not their foolish disputations for a time obscured to us the Gospel and the Benefits of Christ. ... Whoever is ignorant of the remaining topics such as the power of sin, the law and grace, I do not see how I may call him a Christian."[‡] Thus we again see that pastoral concern, not an academic's need to theorize about the mysteries of the faith, motivated Melanchthon's authorship of LC1521, for the structure of the this work reflects Melanchthon's pastoral concerns, setting forth and defending the scriptural teaching regarding "the power of sin, the law and grace." LC1521 was not intended to serve as a reference work on the various *loci* of theology.[§]

The structure of LC1521 reflects the points emphasized

---

[*] ibid., p. 67.

[†] ibid., p. 67-68.

[‡] ibid., p. 68.

[§] Appendix B readily demonstrates that later editions of the *Loci communes* reflected more of a balance between pastoral and academic emphases—a balance carried over in works such as Martin Chemnitz' *Loci Theologici*, which was Chemnitz' lectures/elaborations on the 1548 edition of the 1543 revision of the Melanchthon's *Loci communes*. Melanchthon's motivations for a later shift in emphasis and the effect this shift had on Chemnitz and later Lutheran Orthodoxy (1580-ca. 1713) is a topic worthy of further research.

above. LC1521 does not have *loci* for any of the following topics: God, Unity, Trinity, or Creation. Instead of beginning his work with a *locus* on God (his practice in the 1543 and 1555 *Loci communes*), Melanchthon begins instead with a discussion of the bondage of the will and predestination. Indeed, Melanchthon was aware of the radical nature of this approach: "But I may seem foolish to discuss in the very outset of this work, a topic so difficult as that of predestination, and yet, what consequence in saving will there be, whether I treat in the first or last topic, a matter which falls into every department of my disputation?"[*] Starting from this base, Melanchthon's progress through the themes of sin, Law, Gospel, grace, faith, love and "On the Old and the New Man" reflects an approach in LC1521 which begins with the fallen state of man and then progresses through the *ordo salutis*.[†] It is also worth noting that there is similar structure at work in LC1521 and articles II through VI of the Augsburg Confession, which treat "Of Original Sin," "Of the Son of God," "Of Justification," "Of the Ministry of the Church," and "Of the New Obedience." The pastoral focus of LC1521—man's fallen state and the atonement which restores man to a right relationship with God and makes good works possible as a result—is at work in the *Confessio augustana*. The inclusion of an article on God stressing His Unity and Trinity as confession's first article, however, could signal the tension between the topical and pastoral approaches Melanchthon delineates in LC1521.

Conclusion.

Melanchthon's various editions of the *Loci communes* are worthy of further attention from confessional Lutheran theologians. Melanchthon's authorship of three of Lutheranism's symbolical writings indicates the importance of studying his private writ-

* *The Loci Communes of Philip Melanchthon*, p. 74.

† There is a certain parallel here to Nicholaus Hunnius' classic delineation of the *ordo salutis* as consisting of Christ being brought "near to the sinner: a. by the calling, b. by repentance, c. by justification, d. by conversion, e. by renewing, f. by the new birth, g. by the union with Christ." (*Epitome credendorum*, trans. by Paul Edward Gottheil, (Nuremberg: U.E. Sebald, 1847) p. 124-125.)

ings (especially the 1521 and 1535 editions of the *Loci communes*) in the effort to come to a better understanding of our dogmatic heritage. The late-J.A.O. Preus has well-summarized the importance of Melanchthon's *Loci communes* as one of the key works handed down by a central Lutheran father:

> In addition to Melanchthon's important contributions to Luther's translation of the Bible, his theology is best known from three works, two of them of a confessional nature and one which he set for teaching purposes. The first two, his best known and most widely used, were the Augsburg Confession and its Apology, and the third was his *Loci Communes*. Each of these works is a classic and each has been received and honored in Lutheran circles and more widely for over four centuries.
>
> Melanchthon's greatest work beyond the Augsburg Confession and its Apology, the *Loci Communes* (LC), was first published when he was 24 years old. In 1521 two editions appeared, and during the first period of the *Loci*, 1521-25, no less than 18 Latin and several German editions appeared.*

Melanchthon would continue to rework the *Loci communes* for more than three decades. The *Loci communes* underwent three major rewrites before the end of Melanchthon's life: one in 1535, another in 1543, and a final revision in 1555. Nevertheless, LC1521's origins in a study of St. Paul's doctrine in his Epistle to the Romans should not be forgotten. With perhaps a little hyperbole, it could be claimed that Lutheran dogmatics sprang from a study of St. Paul.

No one was more aware of the significance of Melanchthon's *Loci communes* than Luther himself. Luther observed in his *Bondage of the Will* (1525) that Erasmus' views on the freedom of the will "have been refuted already so often by me, and beaten down and completely pulverized in Philip Melanchthon's *Commonplaces*—an unanswerable little book which in my judgment deserves not only to be immortalized but

---

* J.A.O. Preus, *The Second Martin*, p. 64.

even canonized."* Even after a major re-write (and with another about to be released) Luther could declare in the winter of 1542-43:

> If anybody wished to become a theologian, he has a great advantage, first of all, in having the Bible. This is now so clear that he can read it without any trouble. Afterward he should read Philip's *Loci Communes*. This he should read diligently and well, until he has its contents fixed in his head. If he has these two he is a theologian, and neither the devil nor a heretic can shake him. The whole of theology is open to him, and afterward he can read whatever he wishes for edification. ...
>
> There's no book under the sun in which the whole of theology is so compactly presented as in the *Loci Communes*. If you read all the fathers and sententiaries you have nothing. No better book has been written after the Holy Scriptures than Philip's. He expresses himself more concisely than I do when he argues and instructs. I'm garrulous and more rhetorical.†

The above pages have traced Melanchthon's intellectual and theological development up to his writing of LC1521. We have seen the development of a theologian who was able to bring the work of humanist studies into the service of the Reformation and we have briefly examined the influence this development had on the first work of Lutheran dogmatics. The convergence of the *sola Scriptura* principle and Melanchthon's pastoral concern resulted in a work aimed at more than being a theological resource book—it was directed toward the salvation of its reader. The author contends against Scholasticism's 'philosophizing' because it directs the student away from the Gospel and because the Scholastics speculated about mysteries of the faith which should be adored, not probed. Melanchthon's LC1521 was 'rhetorical' in the best sense of the

---

* Martin Luther, *The Bondage of the Will*, trans. by Philip S. Watson, (Philadelphia: Fortress Press, 1972) vol. 33, 55 vols., p. 16.

† Martin Luther, *Table Talk*, ed. and trans. by Theodore G. Tappert, (Philadelphia: Fortress Press, 1967) vol. 54, 55 vols., p. 439-440.

term—its aim was not the discovery of the truth, but the presentation and defense of the truth against error.

The Decree of Uppsala (1593) and the Confessional Lutheran Church in Sweden

A common denigration of the Evangelical Lutheran Church is that it is a "German church"—a church to be listed among the ranks of the "Protestants," albeit with a predilection for ethnic foods and a religious form of "October Fest" known by the name of "Reformation Day." Usually those who charge Lutherans with being a Germanic sect combine that charge with demands that Lutherans divest themselves of their confessional heritage as an element of their ethnic baggage which hampers the ecumenical imperative. Samuel S. Schmucker, one of the nineteenth century fathers of "American Lutheranism," was fond of disparaging recent Confessional Lutheran immigrants for being 'too German,' and certainly our own age has not lacked for those who would mock defenders of our confessional heritage as "Hyper-European".*

Perhaps this paper will do little to divest the Evangelical Lutheran Church of the accusation of its "European" character, but it is intended to give its hearers an opportunity to broaden their knowledge of the Lutheran Reformation period outside of Germany by looking at the early history of another major branch of the Evangelical Lutheran Church.

Today, the five largest Lutheran churches in the world are: (1) the Church of Sweden (6.8 million), (2) the Evangelical Luther-

---

* The presenter has even had the occasion to hear a sermon by a synodical official who mocked a chapel filled with seminarians, commenting to the effect that all their 'white faces' made him 'sick.' It is uncertain how this word of Law was to lead to amendment of life on the part of the hearers, since, the rhetorical question posed in Jeremiah 13: "Can the Ethiopian change his skin or the leopard its spots?," (v. 23 NKJV) is presumably answered in the negative by members of all ethnic groups.

an Church in America (4.8 million), (3) the Evangelical Lutheran Church of Finland (4.55 million), (4) the Evangelical Lutheran Church in Denmark (4.5 million) and, (5) the Church of Norway (3.9 million). In comparison to the 20 million Lutherans in the Nordic countries, there are approximately 12.6 million Lutherans in the various German churches of the Lutheran World Federation (even counting officially 'Union' churches).[*] It is not our intention here to examine the relative claims of these church bodies as authentic adherents of the dogmatic standard of the Evangelical Lutheran Church, the Book of Concord (1580).[†] But clearly it is to our detriment when we ignore the history of such a significant portion of the Evangelical Lutheran Church and one of the most significant documents in the history of the Lutheran Church in Sweden and Finland: the Decree of Uppsala (1593).

A Brief Overview of the History of the Reformation in Sweden to the Council of Uppsala

Just as the Reformation in Germany occurred in close connection with the political movements of the time, the origins of the Swedish Reformation were connected to Sweden's independence from Denmark and the rise of the Vasa line of kings.

The missionary effort in Sweden began in earnest during the life of St. Ansgar (801-865; Festival Day February 3). King Björn of Hauge requested missionaries be sent to Sweden, and Ansgar and two assistants were sent north by King Louis the Pious (778-840) in 829 for that purpose. A small congregation was established in 831, where Ansgar served for six months, before he was called to serve as Bishop of Hamburg. In 847, the bishoprics of Bremen and Hamburg were consolidated under Ansgar's authority as

---

[*] These statistics have been gathered from the website of the Lutheran World Federation (lutheranworld.org).

[†] In fact, the presenter is prepared to defend the thesis that none of these bodies consistently uphold the faith which Luther and his noble coadjutors boldly confessed.

metropolitan bishop, and he renewed the mission work in Sweden, spending two years there, from 848–850.

The process of the Christianization of Sweden was, perhaps, a slow one; whereas Norway 'converted' during the reign of King Olaf Tryggvason (A. D. 995-1000), and suffered a brief relapse into paganism until the reign of Olaf Heraldsson (1015–1028),[*] Adam of Bremen described the pagan temple which was still standing in Uppsala in 1070. The archdiocese of Uppsala was established in 1164—over three centuries after Ansgar began his missionary efforts in that area of Sweden.

Following the conversion of the Scandinavian peoples, a period of political consolidation led to the political unification of Norway, Iceland, Sweden-Finland, and Denmark in the Kalmar Union (1397–1524).[†] In the words of one historian of the Reformation, "At the time of the dawn of the Reformation the affairs of Scandinavia were in singular and, as it appears, hopeless confusion."[‡] However, the "union" actually amounted to Danish rule over all the Nordic peoples, and it was the brutality of Christian II, who reigned as King of Denmark from 1513 to 1523, which brought the union to an end.

Danish power had been declining in Norway and Sweden, and the Sture branch of Sweden's aristocracy essentially ruled Sweden at the beginning of the reign of Christian II. King Christian sought to exploit the tension between the Stures and the Trolles, another noble family which supported the Kalmar Union. When Sten Sture the Younger (1493–1520) imprisoned Gustav Trolle, the archbishop of Uppsala, after a power struggle in November 1517, Pope Leo X excommunicated Sture, and Christian II invaded Sweden. What Christian couldn't have imagined was that this move

---

[*] Olaf II is also revered as Saint Olaf (Festival Day July 29).

[†] Iceland came under Norwegian rule in 1262, Norway came under Danish control after the death of Olaf IV in 1387, as did Sweden-Finland after 1389. The Kalmar Union was formalized in 1397 by means of the Treaty of Kalmar (named for a Swedish castle near the Danish border).

[‡] Ludwig Häusser, *The Period of the Reformation (1517-1648)*, ed. by Wilhelm Oncken (New York: Robert Carter and Bros., 1874) p. 143.

would lead to the rise of the royal family which would unify Sweden as a kingdom and as a significant power within Europe.

The brutal centralizing policies of Denmark's King Christian II (1513-23), which culminated in the summary execution of 82 leading Swedish noblemen in the 'Stockholm Bloodbath' of November 1520, broke the leadership of the Sture clan and nearly neutralized the resistance of the nobility as a whole. Leadership of the opposition after the Bloodbath devolved by default to a young nobleman from Dalarna: Gustav Eriksson Vasa.[*]

With the death of Sten Sture the Younger in 1519, and in the aftermath of the Stockholm Bloodbath the following year, Gustav Vasa (1496–1560) led a successful revolt against Christian II. Gustav I was elected regent in 1521 and became king by action of the Swedish parliament in June 1523.

Ironically, it was Pope Clement VII who pushed Gustav toward the Lutheran Reformation. Archbishop Trolle had supported Christian II's claim as king of Sweden following the death of Sten Sture the Younger; an action which contributed to Trolle being exiled after the Stockholm Bloodbath. When Clement VII insisted that Gustav reinstate Gustav Trolle as archbishop, Gustav assumed control of the affairs of the Church.[†]

Thus the Reformation in Sweden was begun by Gustav Vasa, who, after the fashion of the German princes, did not hesitate to use his power to seize the property of the Church.

Already harboring Lutheran sympathies, in 1527 the king convinced the Diet at Västerås to agree to royal seizure of church properties and revenues. The king generously remanded much of the property gained at Västerås to the care of his nobility, but the monarchy profited dramatically: the proportion of farms in Swe-

---

[*] Paul Douglas Lockhart, *Sweden in the Seventeenth Century* (Hampshire, England: Palgrave Macmillan, 2004)

[†] Robert Murray, *A Brief History of the Church of Sweden—Origins and Modern Structure* (Stockholm: Diakonistyrelsens Bokförlag, 1961), p. 23-4.

den and Finland owned by the crown grew from 3.5 percent to 21.3 percent.*

Fortunately, the pattern of princely usurpation seen throughout Protestant Europe did not come to the same end in Sweden that it did in other nations. The difference was the formative influence of two brothers, Olavus Petri (1493-1552) and Laurentius Petri (1499–1573), both of whom studied at the University of Wittenberg, and later became steadfast Lutherans.

Gustav appointed Olavus Petri to the Cathedral in Stockholm in 1524. Olavus published a Swedish translation of the New Testament in 1526 (an effort which led to the publication of a Swedish translation of the whole Bible in 1541), a *Manual* of Lutheran liturgical rites in 1529, and a Swedish Mass in 1531.[†] However, Olavus paid a price for his steadfast Lutheran confession: he was eventually sentenced to death in 1539 for his opposition to Gustav's attempts to subvert the authority of the Church and place it entirely under the power of the king, and he remained in prison under sentence of death for several years before he was eventually pardoned.

Following the Council of Uppsala (1531), Laurentius Petri was consecrated as Archbishop of Uppsala by Petrus Magni, the Bishop of Västerås—through whom the apostolic succession was continued in the Church of Sweden. Laurentius served for 42 years as the Archbishop of Uppsala and his influence on the future of the Swedish Church was even more marked than that of his brother. For purposes of this presentation, we draw particular attention to his Church Order of 1571, which the Decree of Uppsala would uphold as the standard for Lutheran practice in Sweden. Concerning this Church Order it has been observed:

> This document, according to its author's testimony the mature fruit of thirty years' labour, gathers up in itself the positive results of the whole Swedish Reformation. By its loyalty to

---

* Lockhart, p. 7.
† Murray, p. 25.

conservative Lutheranism in general and above all to the best traditions of the Reformation in Sweden, by its author's spirituality, tact and soundness of judgement, it stands as one of the greatest of all the existing monuments of a truly evangelical *via media*.[*]

Or, in the words of another historian of the Swedish Church:

> Laurentius Petri was well aware of the risk that the Reformation might evolve in a subjective and individualistic direction. To avoid this he worked for many years toward giving the Church of Sweden a ratified code of canon law and a fully established liturgy. ... The Church emerges clearly autonomous, though in a co-operative relationship with the State. ... Each parish is self-governed, and the parishioners play an important role in its administration. The canonical hours and a whole series of ceremonies and holidays that had been abolished in Germany were retained in Sweden. In many respects the Church of Sweden acquired in Laurentius Petri's Church Ordinance the character it still [1959] possesses.[†]

When speaking of the Reformation in Germany, there are several critical moments which appear most central to the "conversion" of the states which made up the Schmalkaldic League. The Diet of Augsburg gave the league its creedal statement—the Augsburg Confession—and those territories which were later aligned with the league all subscribed the confession as a condition of membership; the extended period of relative peace from the organization of the league in 1531 until the outbreak of the Schmalkald War in 1547 provided an opportunity for territorial churches to be reformed in keeping with the confession, and often modeled the reforms of their Church Orders on those which had already been carried out in Electoral Saxony.

---

[*] Yngvi Brilioth quoted in Eric Yelverton, *An Archbishop of the Reformation* (Minneapolis: Augsburg Publishing House, 1959) p. 17.
[†] Murray, p. 33.

It might best be said that the Reformation came to Sweden in stages, and began by reforming the liturgy, and later formally adopting the doctrinal standard which had already long been confessed in the practice of the Church. The reform of the Mass (including communion in both kinds), the marriage of priests, the publication of the Scriptures in the vernacular, the reform of catechesis—all of these were accomplished within years of the reforms at Wittenberg. Thus, for example, in 1536, a synod meeting at Upsala made Olavus's Mass and *Manual* obligatory for the whole of Sweden.*

The Lutheran Confessions explicitly uphold the traditional grades of ministry, particularly the division (by human authority) between bishops and pastors.† However, the greed of the princes often pitted them against the called leaders of the church, as the secular powers sought to seize the wealth of the Church. In this regard, Gustav Vasa was not dramatically different from his contemporaries elsewhere in Europe, such as Henry VIII of England, who seized the assets of the monasteries between 1536 and 1539, and Christian III of Denmark, whose 1536 decree seized all spiritual and temporal power from the bishops.‡ It was after the crown had seized the assets of the Church that Christian III constructed his new church, with superintendents in the place of the former

---

* Murray, p. 29.

† "But this is their opinion, that the power of the Keys, or the power of bishops, according to the Gospel, is a power or commandment of God, to preach the Gospel, to remit and retain sins, and to administer sacraments." (AC XXVIII:5) "To this we answer, that it is lawful for bishops or pastors to make ordinances that things be done orderly in the Church..." (AC XXVIII:53) "Concerning this subject, we have frequently testified in this assembly that it is our greatest wish to maintain Church polity and the grades in the Church, even though they have been made by human authority." (AP XIV:24) "First, therefore, we will show from the Gospel that the Roman bishop is not by divine right above other bishops and pastors." (TR 7)

‡ L. A. Anjou, *The history of the reformation in Sweden*, trans. by Henry M. Mason (New York: Sheldon & Co. 1859), p. 338.

bishops (though in time the superintendents had the historic title restored to them) who called priests to the parishes of their super-intendencies.[*]

A similar threat loomed over the Swedish Church, and would reappear periodically until the Council of Uppsala. As one historian of the Swedish Church has observed, "Gustav Vasa became increasingly antiepiscopal in his latter years. Finally, Laurentius Petri was the only one whom he addressed by the title of bishop, in itself quite indicative of the primate's status and importance. ... After Gustav Vasa's death the episcopate rapidly regained its leadership status in the life of the Church."[†]

Following the death of Gustav I, the king's eldest son, Erik, became king. The eight years of the rule of Erik XIV were marked by efforts by the Calvinists to interfere with the Church of Sweden, only to be rebuffed by Archbishop Laurentius and the other bishops. A case in point is witnessed in the Diet of Arboga (April 1561):

> The king laid before the clergy orally, and afterward in writing, interrogatories respecting the elevation of the sacrament (that is, of the bread and wine in the Lord's Supper), the use of images, the altar, the mass cloths, and the lighting of candles at the time of divine service. Were these to be retained or rejected? The answer was, that the elevation of the sacrament was an indifferent ceremony, and might be omitted where it could be so done without scandal, but that the worship of it, by which was to be understood the kneeling at its reception, should be retained, because there is the body and blood of the Lord, "which is worthy of all honor and reverence;" that images were not sinful of themselves, but all worship of them should be forbidden; that *one altar was necessary* in every church, but no more; that mass clothes and wax lights were things indifferent, which any congregation might at pleasure retain or reject.[‡]

---

[*] ibid., p. 341.

[†] Murray, p. 32.

[‡] Anjou, p. 355-6.

On each of these points, the Calvinist and Romanist positions are clearly avoided and the biblically Lutheran practice is upheld. Again, in 1562, Laurentius Petri wrote in defense of retaining the exorcism in Baptism, as well as defending "the consecration of the sacrament, and the kneeling at its reception, the allowableness of the use of images, and the liberty of the church in things indifferent."* The king was clearly convinced to firmly uphold the Lutheran doctrine and "was determined not to leave Calvinism any influence within his kingdom..."†

Erik's reign was a relatively brief one because of the ongoing conflict in which he engaged with his own brothers and the nobility, and he was deposed and imprisoned in 1568. At that point his brother, John, assumed the throne, and reigned as John III from 1568 until his death in 1592.

As difficult of Erik's reign had been, John's posed far greater difficulties. In the words of one historian, "King John's self-confidence in his own theological acumen, and his lofty ideas of the width and weight of his kingly episcopal rights, was for the leader of the church no less dangerous than the terrible power of his father had proved."‡ Like his father Gustav, John believed himself to have authority, and used imprisonment and the threat of imprisonment in the attempt to shape the Church to his will. Coupled with his notions regarding the Church and her teaching, one had a rather lethal combination.

John imagined it was possible to accomplished a reunion of the Roman and Evangelical Churches on the basis of a chimerical *consensus quinque saecularis*—the consensus of the first five centuries—the same notion which gave rise to the heretical views of Georg Calixtus in the Syncretistic Controversy of the seventeenth century. He was influenced in this line of thought through the writings of the Romanist apologist George Cassander, who, among other things, made his own revision of the Augsburg Confession which

* Anjou, p. 357.
† Anjou, p. 362.
‡ Anjou, p. 456

was acceptable to neither party. The results of John's romanticism was the exile of faithful Lutheran priests, the influence of Jesuits upon John's council, his son's conversion to Romanism, and division among the people.

In 1577, John introduced his infamous "Red Book," a liturgy intended to undo some of Larentius Petri's reforms of the Mass. What followed was the Swedish equivalent of the Augsburg Interim, and the Church was divided for seventeen years. Those clergy committed to upholding the received Lutheran rite often fled to the territories controlled by Duke Karl (Charles)—another of the sons of Gustav Vasa. Some of the most steadfast Lutherans—including priests such as Abraham Andreae—had to flee abroad.

As John's life drew to an end, he appears to have recognized the error of his ways, and began to release some of those who had been imprisoned, and, most importantly, expressed his agreement with a Church Council to accomplish a reconciliation within the Church. John's son and heir apparent, Sigismund, had become king of Poland in 1587, and was a committed papist, having been educated by the Jesuits. When John died on November 17, 1592, both sides realized that they would have to move quickly in determining the future of Sweden.

The Council of Uppsala

Before the end of November, Duke Karl had begun work on creating a unified front against the future king, and "One of the initial tasks of the interim government was to find a legal manner in which to forge a national resistance front against any innovations Sigismund might be pleased to initiate within the temporal and spiritual field upon his arrival."* Two major issues pressed for resolution by a Council: election of a new archbishop (Andreas Larentii Björnram had died on New Year's Day 1591), and repeal of John's "Red Book." Duke Karl and the interim government pledged "to protect every man in the true religion, in the clear and pure word

---

* Oskar Garsten, *Rome and the Counter-Reformation in Scandinavia* (Oslo: Universitetsforlaget, 1980), p. 96.

of God, *according to the Augsburgh [sic] Confession,*" and the Church
Council was scheduled to convene on February 25, 1593, the First
Sunday in Lent.

The Council of Uppsala was well attended: four bishops
were present, as were the four professors of the college of Uppsala,
twenty-two masters, and 306 priests, as well as Duke Karl, and nine
members of the council of the kingdom.†

The decision regarding whom to elect to serve as archbishop was deferred to the end of the council. Thus the Council was
chaired by a prolocutor rather than a president, because "The term
president (praeses), was avoided as a term of worldly power, or a
Calvinistic form of expression, implying a free election for the time
being."‡ Professor Nicolaus Olai Botniensis, one of the theologians
who had been persecuted for opposing John's liturgy, was elected
prolocutor on March 2. Botniensis "was not acting out of character
when on 3 March he reminded the Assembly of the importance
of the Councils of Nicea, Constantinople, and others, both as an
element to heal theological divisions and as a doctrinal bastion constructed to resist opposition from without."§

On March 3, the Council began a review of the Augsburg
Confession, covering the first nine articles,€ and then continued on
March 5 with the rest of the *Augustana*.

After the reading of the Augsburgh confession,
and the examination of it, were completed, bishop Petrus
Jonae rose up and asked the council of the kingdom and
the rest of the assembly, if they received the confession
which had been now critically examined and approved, and
would hold fast to it, even if it should be God's will that
they should on that account somewhat suffer. All arose and
declared unanimously that they would not deviate there-
from, but be ready for it to stake their life and blood. Then

* Anjou, p. 597. Italics in original
† Anjou, p. 599.
‡ Anjou, p. 601.
§ Garstein, p. 100.
€ Anjou, p. 605.

the prolocutor exclaimed with a loud voice, "*Now is Sweden become one man, and we all have one Lord and God!*"[*]

And thus, Garstein observed, "the *Confessio Augustana Invariata* had officially become recognized as the cornerstone of Swedish Church doctrine."[†]

The next day, the "Red Book" was discussed, and *no one* could be found to defend it. Those who had defended the liturgy during the reign of King John publicly repented. The penitents included three bishops. "Mutual reconciliations took place among the clergy, and promises to bury the past in oblivion. The question being then put by the prolocutor, whether they would abandon the liturgy, and the answer being unanimously in the affirmative, the session was closed by reading the confession of the diocese of Strängness on the liturgy."[‡]

Having subscribed the *Augustana*, repealed the "Red Book," and reinstated the 1571 Church Order of Laurentius Petri, the council elected Abraham Andrae as the new archbishop—the man John most bitterly rejected would lead the Swedish Church after John's demise.[§]

Karl had hoped that the Council of Uppsala would restraint his papist nephew. What Karl found, however, was that once begun, the Council could not be controlled by him. His own inclinations were more influenced by Reformed thinking that probably even he realized, and he demanded three liturgical changes before he would subscribe the decrees of the council: (1) the removal of the exorcism from the baptismal rite; (2) the elimination of salt and candles from the baptismal rite; (3) the elimination of the elevation from the Mass.[¶] The Church, however, was unmoved and retained these adiaphoron to uphold Christian freedom. The Duke caved.

---

[*] Anjou, p. 607

[†] Garstein, p. 101.

[‡] Anjou, p. 609.

[§] Garstein, p. 106. Abraham Andrae received 243 votes out of 306 clergy; only clergy voted in the elction of a bishop or archbishop.

[¶] Anjou, p. 620.

Thus, "The decree of the council of Upsala was a solemn protest against the principles of 1539, that there was a right in the king to determine what the religion of the land should be, and the council itself, indeed, was still more a protest."[*]

When Sigismund arrived in Sweden on September 30, 1593, he faced the secular authorities and Church in unified opposition to his efforts to allow for Roman Catholic services in Sweden. The bishops held their ground, and "nothing was conceded beyond what had already been conceded—the right of the king to have the papal service performed in his own court."[†]

It is hard to overemphasize the Decree of the Council of Uppsala in the unity of the confessional Lutheran Church of Sweden:

> In the final event the Uppsala Declaration was endorsed by no fewer than seven bishops, 1,556 members of the clergy, 233 representatives of the Nobility (including Duke Charles and fourteen members of the Council of the Kingdom), 137 officials, the mayors and councils of 36 cities and towns, and finally the civil officers representing 197 provinces and counties. With this broad backing from practically every level of Swedish society the Declaration of the Uppsala Assembly emerged to become the Magna Charta of religious independence in Protestant Sweden.[‡]

The Seven Points of the Decree of Uppsala

It has become customary[§] to treat of the decree under seven major points. We shall examine these in turn.

[1]   First, that we all unanimously abide by the pure and saving Word of God, found in the writings of the holy prophets, evangelists and apostles; that in all our churches it shall be taught,

---

[*] Anjou, p. 598.

[†] Anjou, p. 627

[‡] Garstein, 108-9.

[§] e.g., Anjou, 623-4, Garstein 107-108. See attached text of the *Decretum Upsaliense.*

believed and confessed that the Holy Scriptures were given through the Holy Spirit, and that they contain completely everything belonging to the Christian doctrine concerning God Almighty and our salvation, concerning virtue and good words, and that they are a foundation and support to a pure Christian faith, a canon whereby to judge, discern and prevent all disagreement in religion; that no explanations by the holy fathers or others are necessary, whoever they may be, who have added that which is not in harmony with the Holy Scriptures; that no man is allowed to explain God's Word according to his own mind, in which respect no regard or approval shall be given the highness, reputation or authority of any person; that nothing but the Holy Scriptures, as it has been said before, [shall have this authority].

John III had sought the *consensus quinque saecularis* as the basis of the interpretation of Scripture, and guide to the public teaching of the Church; in this he had been influenced by Georg Cassander, and the writings of Vincent of Lerin, which had been published in Swedish for the first time in 1576, the year before the release of his "Red Book."* John's effort to established his liturgy on Vincent's notion of early Church Tradition as the two standards of doctrine was as doomed to failure as Cassander's "consensus," Calixtus' Syncretism and Frederick's Prussian Union. The Decree clearly repudiates any private interpretation, including that of a 'Vincentian Canon': "no man is allowed to explain God's Word according to his own mind, in which respect no regard or approval shall be given the highness, reputation or authority of any person". The perspicuity and sufficiency of the Sacred Scriptures are thus clearly confessed in the first point of the Council of Uppsala.

---

* Anjou, p. 472.

[2]   Moreover, we consent and acknowledge that we will abide by the Apostles', Nicene and Athanasian symbols, and also by the oldest and true Unaltered Augsburg Confession, which was delivered by Electors and States to Charles V. at the great Diet of Augsburg, A. D. 1530.

Although the Church of Sweden had been reformed in keeping with Lutheran teaching beginning in the 1520s, nevertheless it is by this Decree that Sweden officially subscribed the *Augustana*, understanding this confession to stand together with the ecumenical creeds as an exposition of the Holy Scriptures. As noted previously, the first task undertaken by the council following selection of a prolocutor was an examination of, and subscription to, the Unaltered Augsburg Confession. The brevity of the article makes it clear that in the intention of its formulators, this point needed no further explanation.

[3]   Likewise, we acknowledge and will keep that religion both in doctrine and ceremonies printed in the ritual of 1572, and which prevailed in the kingdom during the latter part of the reign of our blessed king Gustaf, of blessed memory and in high favor with God, and during the lifetime of our blessed archbishop, Lars Petri Nericiani the elder.

    But as there are retained in it some ceremonies which are used at the administration of Baptism and the Lord's Supper, such as the use of salt, candles and the elevation of the Host, also moving the missal from one corner to the other of the altar, and ringing of bells at the elevation of the Host—all of which have been laid aside in most of the Evangelical churches because they have been much misused, and more evil has come from the abuse than good from a right use of the ceremonies,—

Therefore, it is publicly and unanimously decided that all pastors and also bishops in their visitations, shall diligently teach the people and admonish them faithfully not to abuse the ceremonies. Should they find that the abuse cannot be abolished unless the ceremonies be dispensed with, then may the bishops, with a few from each chapter in every diocese, convene with others of the most learned of the clergy, and consider, consult and decide upon how these ceremonies, before mentioned, may in time (without offense and tumult) and with quietness, be laid aside.

Concerning exorcism, we confess that we do not consider it so necessary at baptism that without it baptism would not be perfect; but as this ceremony well agrees with the baptismal act, reminding not the child, but those present, about the condition of man before baptism and about the efficacy of baptism, therefore we may in true Christian liberty very properly use it in our churches. But in order that no one may take offence at the words that seem too severe, thinking that they mean a bodily possession, we have agreed to change them thus: viz. for *"Farhä ut,"* etc., substitute *"Vik här¨efran."* Yet we do not hereby condemn the churches in foreign countries and such persons in our kingdom as retain them and are nevertheless one with us in faith.

The order of the points reflects the ordering events at the Church Council. The "Red Book" having been abolished, the 1572 Church Order was restored. The Council teaches a very valuable lesson regarding adiaphora: rather than abandoning such things, the bishops and pastors were to "diligently teach the people and admonish them faithfully not to abuse the ceremonies." This is very much in keeping with the spirit of the *Augustana*, "among us, in large part, the ancient rites are diligently observed. For it is a false and malicious charge that all the ceremonies, all the things instituted of old, are abolished in our churches." (Jacobs, p. 46)

Even where changes were carried out—such as the change in the words of exorcism—it is for the purpose of teaching the people. The change in emphasis in the exorcism from "begone thou foul spirit" to "may he depart hence" is so that "no one may take offense at the words that seem too severe, thinking that they mean a bodily possession".

[4]   In regard to the liturgy which has been used by some of the clergy in the kingdom, and which has been found to be a root and cause of much evil and disturbance in matters of religion within the kingdom, and since it has been shown by the Word of God that it is in every respect superstitious, and in reality conformable to the Popish mass, which is offensive, opposed and derogatory to the merits of Christ our Saviour, serving as a gate and entrance for other horrible Popish heresies,—we have completely and sincerely, with heart and mouth, disapproved said liturgy and all its evil consequences in doctrine, ceremonies, discipline, or whatever it may be called, and unanimously and earnestly pledged ourselves never to receive, approve or use it.

Where there had been deviation from the historic rite, there was repentance over the offense which had been given by the surrender in matters where no compromise could be tolerated: where it is "offensive, opposed and derogatory to the merits of Christ our Savior". As the experiences of the Swedes under King John bore a resemblance to the plight of the German Lutherans under the Augsburg Interim, so the Decree comes to conclusions which are analogous to the pronouncement of Formula of Concord X: "So also by such yielding and conformity in external things, where there has not been previously Christian union in doctrine, idolaters are confirmed in their idolatry..." (SD §16)

[5]   Neither shall we receive or approve any other Popish doctrines or heresies, whatever they may be called, but reject them all together as human devices, contrived for worldly honor, dominion, power, and riches, through which men are often misled.

Likewise, we reject entirely the heresies of the Sacramentarians, Zwinglians, Calvinists and Anabaptists, and all other heresies, whatever be their name, which we at no time will approve or agree to.

A clear confession is marked not only by what is *confessed*, but also by what is *rejected*. Certainly, the Council of Uppsala bore witness to this fact in its action regarding the Church Order. But also, just as it clearly *subscribed* the *Augustana*, it was necessary to condemn those heresies condemned by confessional Lutherans in all times and places.

[6]   Finally, we have found that the principles of church discipline and a just church penance are in substance printed in the aforesaid ritual. But as it has for some time been very much neglected, we have each and every one, in his estate and dignity, promised to see to it that it be hereafter kept more diligently and faithfully, and be sincerely put into practice, and, where circumstances demand it, that which is furthermore necessary may be added by the common consent of the bishops and chapters. And although it should not

be tolerated or allowed that such should settle in the kingdom who hold false doctrines and are not one in faith with us, in order that they may be lead others astray, yet that trade and commerce may not be hindered, we agree that those who have any heretical doctrines shall not be allowed or permitted to hold any public meetings in houses or otherwise; and in case any should be found guilty of that or of speaking evil of our religion, they shall be duly punished.

Thus church discipline was preserved from interference by the secular authorities. As the Lutheran Confessions teach, "The Gospel has assigned to those who preside over churches the command to teach the Gospel, to remit sins, to administer the sacraments, and besides jurisdiction, viz. the command to excommunicate those whose crimes are known, and again of absolving the repenting. And by the confessional of all, even of the adversaries, it is clear that this power by divine right is common to all who preside over churches, whether they be called pastors, or presbyters, or bishops." (Treatise §60-61)

The restrictions on residence by false teachers was upheld; as was observed above, even the king was only permitted to hear his Romish priests within his own chambers.

[7] And in order that it may be known and manifest to all what we at this meeting have considered and decided upon, it shall, as early as possible, be printed and published.

This point anticipated the action in which King Sigismund engaged upon returning to Sweden. However, by that date the decree was too widely dispersed to recall. How sad that in our own age there has been such neglect of a confession of Lutheran doctrine and practice which was won at such a great cost. Thus this presenter commends the Decree of Uppsala to you for further reflection, that we might learn from our forefathers of blessed memory, and conform our lives and conversation to their godly example.

CAPITAL PUNISHMENT:
A SCRIPTURAL PERSPECTIVE[*]

Introduction

Although plans for this presentation were made several months ago, one must thank the Supreme Court for their perfect sense of timing, since their announcement of their decision regarding the legality of lethal injection as a form of capital punishment emphasizes the timeliness of our topic today.

In a sense, one might wonder what point there is to discussing Capital Punishment. Surely every thinking person has long ago reached a settled view on the morality or immorality of the state punishing a crime by ending the life of the perpetrator of that crime? In fact, the matter has been debated for generations, and, when it comes to legislation, the victory seems to have gone to those who oppose what has come to be called, "the death penalty." One article summarizes the global status of capital punishment as follows:

> Among countries around the world, almost all European and many Pacific Area states (including Australia, New Zealand and Timor Leste), and Canada have abolished capital punishment. In Latin America, most states have completely abolished the use of capital punishment, while some countries, however, like Brazil, allow for capital punishment only in exceptional situations, such as treason committed during wartime. The United States (the federal government and 36 of its states), Guatemala, most of the Caribbean and the majority of democracies in Asia (e.g. Japan and India) and Africa (e.g. Botswana and Zambia) retain it.[†]

---

[*] This paper was originally presented to the Houston-area businessmen's luncheon on April 18, 2008.

[†] http://en.wikipedia.org/wiki/Capital_punishment (referenced April 1, 2008)

The same article notes that "91% of all known executions [in 2006] took place in six countries": China (at least 1,010), Iran (177), Pakistan (82), Iraq (at least 65), Sudan (at least 65), and the United States (53).* If the number of executions in 2007 and 2008 continue this general global trend, one might almost begin to wonder at the continuing debate.

Consider for a moment that opponents of capital punishment often chide American Conservatives for their 'inconsistency' or 'hypocrisy' in vehemently opposing abortion at the same time that they support capital punishment. Leaving aside for the moment the profound moral confusion—indeed, mental muddle—which is readily evident in such a comparison, one might refute such mock outrage by an appeal to cold statistics. According to the most recent statistics available from National Right to Life,† 1,206,000 abortions took place in the United States in 2005, which means an average of 3,304 abortions a day, or roughly 138 abortions every hour of every day in *Anno Domini* 2005. This means that there were almost certainly over 2.5 times as many abortions *an hour* in America as there were death row criminals who endured having their sentenced carried out in the entire *year* of 2006. I suspect that if only 53 legal abortions took place per year in the United States, abortion would probably never have become a major political issue, and the number of people vocally committed to the "Pro-Life" movement—if such a movement existed at all—would be vanishingly small. Perhaps this bespeaks a greater moral zeal on the part of the opponents of capital punishment, or perhaps it bespeaks a certain weakness with figures combined with utter ethical confusion. Certainly, virtually all would concede that those who are *justly* convicted of a crime which carries the death penalty are rightly described as "wicked" individuals, whereas unborn children are, according to the legal (if not accurate, theologically-speaking) description, "innocent." If one

* ibid.

† http://www.nrlc.org/press_releases_new/Release012208.html (referenced April 7, 2008)

is morally outraged by the perception that both abortion and capital punishment constitute the unjust taking of a human life—and one cannot charge Conservatives with hypocrisy for separating the two issues, if one is unwilling to wed them in one's own moral calculus—then given the finite time available to contending against two perceived moral evils, how much time should such a person devote to combating capital punishment, when abortions are 22,754 times as frequent in our country, and an abortion ends a life which is, by any legal definition, innocent of any crime against positive law?

However, the reality is that this is not a debate rooted in such reasoned argument, but in a visceral perception of an inherent injustice to the penalty. For many opponents of capital punishment, the state's imposition of the death penalty is considered a travesty, whereas the termination of a pregnancy is upheld by the same individuals as a sacrosanct right of free women.

Matters of morality and justice must ultimately be resolved not in the realms of "personal choice" or "feelings" but in divine Law and positive law. As I am not a *juris doctor* but rather a steward of the mysteries of God, I will leave matters of positive law to those who are better qualified to speak on such a topic, and confine my observations today to the Word of God. Nevertheless, there is certainly cultural relevance to such an examination. The Christian faith is foundational to our civilization; there was a time not long removed when the West was called Christendom, and there are still many who maintain that these United States were once a Christian nation. The Scriptures of the Old and New Testament are foundational to all who would be called Christians, and must rightly be received as they claim regarding themselves: "All Scripture is given by inspiration of God, and is profitable for doctrine, for reproof, for correction, for instruction in righteousness, that the man of God may be complete, thoroughly equipped for every good work." (2 Tim. 3:1–17 NKJV) It is, then, to the Holy Scriptures that we turn our attention.

The Old Testament

Man was originally created sinless—in his unfallen state, Adam and his wife were made in the image of God. The divine Law consisted of the commandment and promised punishment: "Of every tree of the garden you may freely eat; but of the tree of the knowledge of good and evil you shall not eat, for in the day that you eat of it you shall surely die." (Gen. 2:16–17 NKJV) The fall of man occasioned the beginning of death in this world. The divinely-decreed punishment for sin was death. St. Paul expresses the universality of this divine punishment in his Epistle to the Romans: "Therefore, just as through one man sin entered the world, and death through sin, and thus death spread to all men, because all sinned—". (Rom. 5:12) There is a crucial point to be understood in this: all human beings, on account of being born of the line of Adam, are born subject to death on account of their sin. Everyone born of Adam who has thus far died, endured the death penalty for sin. "For the wages of sin is death, but the gift of God is eternal life in Christ Jesus our Lord." (Rom. 6:23)

The story of Cain and Abel is, one may presume, so well known as to not need to be repeated on this occasion. Instead, I would have us consider the crime of Cain, and the punishment which the Lord imposed upon him. Cain murdered his brother, and sought to conceal his crime. The Lord said to Cain: "What have you done? The voice of your brother's blood cries out to Me from the ground. So now you are cursed from the earth, which has opened its mouth to receive your brother's blood from your hand. When you till the ground, it shall no longer yield its strength to you. A fugitive and a vagabond you shall be on the earth." And Cain said to the LORD, 'My punishment is greater than I can bear! Surely You have driven me out this day from the face of the ground; I shall be hidden from Your face; I shall be a fugitive and a vagabond on the earth, and it will happen that anyone who finds me will kill me.' And the LORD said to him, 'Therefore, whoever kills Cain, vengeance shall be taken on him sevenfold.' And the LORD set a mark on Cain, lest anyone finding him should kill him." (Gen. 4:10–15) From this first example of murder in the antediluvian world, we witness the Lord take the step of specifically preserving Cain from being slain by those who would otherwise avenge themselves on him.

Wickedness attended the line of Cain, so that in the sixth generation, Lamech, Cain's descendant, said to his wives:"Adah and Zillah, hear my voice; wives of Lamech, listen to my speech! For I have killed a man for wounding me, even a young man for hurting me. If Cain shall be avenged sevenfold, then Lamech seventy-sevenfold." (v. 23–24) Thus this descendant of Cain boasted in his wickedness.

In time, the wickedness of men grew so that"Then the LORD saw that the wickedness of man was great in the earth, and that every intent of the thoughts of his heart was only evil continually. And the LORD was sorry that He had made man on the earth, and He was grieved in His heart." (Gen. 6:5–6) Thus the Lord resolved to drown that ancient world in the flood, leaving alive eight souls of men, Noah and his three sons, and their wives.

Whereas in the world before the flood, there is no sign of a divinely-established authority among men with authority for capital punishment, this situation changes in the world after the deluge. We read in Genesis 9 that the Lord said to Noah, "Surely for your lifeblood I will demand a reckoning: from the hand of every beast I will require it, and from the hand of man. From the hand of every man's brother I will require the life of man. Whoever sheds man's blood, by man his blood shall be shed; for in the image of God He made man. And as for you, be fruitful and multiply; bring forth abundantly in the earth and multiply in it." (v. 5–7) Traditionally, this commandment to Noah has been understood as establishing the authority of law, even over life. Thus, for example, Luther observes in his Genesis commentary:

> But here Jehovah establishes a new law, requiring the murderer be put to death by man—a law unprecedented, because heretofore God had reserved all judgment to himself. When he saw that the world was growing worse and worse, he finally enforced punishment against a wicked world

by the flood. Here, however, God bestows a share of his authority upon man, giving him the power of life and death, that thus he may be the avenger of bloodshed. Whosoever takes man's life without due warrant, him God subjects not only to his own judgment, but also to the sword of man. Though God may use man as his instrument in punishing, he is himself still the avenger. Were it not for the divine command, then, it would be no more lawful now to slay a murderer than it was before the flood.

    This is the source from which spring all civil laws and the laws of nations. If God grants man the power of life and death, he certainly also grants power in matters of lesser importance—powers over property, family, wife, children, servants and fields. God wills that these things shall be under the control of certain men, who are to punish the guilty.[*]

The universal character of the commandment should be noted, as the commandment was given before the division of the nations at the Tower of Babel; it is also not an aspect of the Old Testament ceremonial law given to Israel. It would have been universal in application from the time of the flood until the death and resurrection of Christ Jesus.

    As pertains to the Law specifically given to Israel, it is well beyond the scope of this presentation to offer a comprehensive survey of the Law given to Moses. However, we will highlight several points. First, let us consider the *lex talionis* (the "law of retaliation") which is given three times, once each in Exodus, Leviticus and Deuteronomy. In Exodus 21, the Lord sets forth a series of crimes and their prescribed punishments. Several crimes are specifically punished with death, such as premeditated murder, striking or cursing one's father or mother, or kidnapping a man with the intention of selling him into slavery. Following discussion of a case of a child born prematurely on account of injury to the mother, we read: "But

---

* *Commentary on Genesis*, trans. by John Nicholas Lenker, vol. II (Minneapolis: The Luther Press, 1910) p. 276–277.

if any harm follows, then you shall give life for life, eye for eye, tooth for tooth, hand for hand, foot for foot, burn for burn, wound for wound, stripe for stripe." (v. 23–25)

In Leviticus 24, the penalty for blasphemy is specified as death by stoning: "And whoever blasphemes the name of the LORD shall surely be put to death. All the congregation shall certainly stone him, the stranger as well as him who is born in the land. When he blasphemes the name of the LORD, he shall be put to death. Whoever kills any man shall surely be put to death. Whoever kills an animal shall make it good, animal for animal. If a man causes disfigurement of his neighbor, as he has done, so shall it be done to him—fracture for fracture, eye for eye, tooth for tooth; as he has caused disfigurement of a man, so shall it be done to him. And whoever kills an animal shall restore it; but whoever kills a man shall be put to death. You shall have the same law for the stranger and for one from your own country; for I am the LORD your God." (v. 16–22) Thus we see that Israel was to recognize a uniform code of justice in their midst, with foreigners enjoying the same protections as the people.

In Deuteronomy 19, there is consideration given to a circumstance where a person would try to manipulate the authorities through false testimony; in such a case, the one who was guilty of such false witness would be liable to the punishment which they sought to have inflicted upon another. "And the judges shall make careful inquiry, and indeed, if the witness is a false witness, who has testified falsely against his brother, then you shall do to him as he thought to have done to his brother; so you shall put away the evil from among you. And those who remain shall hear and fear, and hereafter they shall not again commit such evil among you. Your eye shall not pity: life shall be for life, eye for eye, tooth for tooth, hand for hand, foot for foot." (Deu. 19:18–21)

Thus we behold a system of justice which was uniform, fair, based upon sufficient evidence, with gradated punishments according to the nature of the crime, which included the divinely-mandated punishment of death for certain select crimes. It was, no doubt, a Law in which the death penalty held a prominent place, but which was reserved for select crimes. The Lord God who gave commandment, "You shall not murder" (Exo. 20:13) is the One who also commanded that murderers shall be put to death according to the manner prescribed by the Lord.

The New Testament

Beyond doubt, there are many who attempt to drive a wedge between the Old and New Testaments. Certainly there are elements of the Old Testament Law which, having been fulfilled by the Christ, are no longer part of the life of the Church. After all, St. Paul wrote to the Colossians: "So let no one judge you in food or in drink, or regarding a festival or a new moon or sabbaths, which are a shadow of things to come, but the substance is of Christ." (Col. 2:16–17) Where there were those who attempted to demand that Gentile converts undergo circumcision (as was required under the Law given to Abraham and Moses), St. Paul strongly rebuked them and declared, in part, "For in Christ Jesus neither circumcision nor uncircumcision avails anything, but faith through love." (Gal. 5:6)

But the moral Law is not abolished. As Jesus declared in His Sermon on the Mount: "Do not think that I came to destroy the Law or the Prophets. I did not come to destroy but to fulfill." (Mat. 5:17) Again, "Whoever therefore breaks one of the least of these commandments, and teaches men so, shall be called least in the kingdom of heaven; but whoever does and teaches them, he shall be called great in the kingdom of heaven." (Mat. 5:19)

What we find, then, is that Christ fulfills the Law: the sacrificial system pointed to Him, but now He has made the one perfect sacrifice for sin. Thus, for example, we read in Hebrews 9: "But Christ came as High Priest of the good things to come, with the greater and more perfect tabernacle not made with hands, that is, not of this creation. Not with the blood of goats and calves, but with His own blood He entered the Most Holy Place once for all, having obtained eternal redemption. For if the blood of bulls and goats and the ashes of a heifer, sprinkling the unclean, sanctifies for the purifying of the flesh, how much more shall the blood of Christ, who through the eternal Spirit offered Himself without spot to God, cleanse your conscience from dead works to serve the living God? And for this reason He is the Mediator of the new covenant, by means of death, for the redemption of the transgressions under the first covenant, that those who are called may receive the promise of the eternal inheritance." (Heb. 9:11–15) Thus Christ Jesus is the Redeemer, having by means of His death redeemed those who were under the first testament, and now those who have come to faith under the new.

The Law—the commandments of God—has not been abolished; Jesus made atonement for sin, so that all who repent of their sin and believe in Him are delivered from condemnation and receive eternal life in Him. But God's Word warns very strongly against any Antinomian sentiment; thus St. Paul wrote to the Romans: "Therefore the law is holy, and the commandment holy and just and good." (Rom. 7:12)

There is a Gnostic notion common in our society which wants to do away with the notion of 'sin' and 'punishment' (civil or eternal) altogether. Gnosticism maintains that it is through 'knowledge' (*gnosis*) that man is redeemed from life in this world; man's soul is trapped in matter ('like a gem in the mud') and that through *gnosis* the soul can be freed from the flesh. I believe that a gnosticizing tendency is at work when people view the penal system as a 'correctional' system, aimed not at punishment for crimes, but at 'education.'* The 'death penalty' has become the target of such fury because it is not intended to educate but to punish; conservatives miss the mark, I believe, when they argue for the death penalty primarily in terms of educational (i.e. 'deterrent') purposes. Such 'educational' arguments concede more than they gain, in my opinion; and they also veer away from the foundation in the divinely-established authority of the state to punish evildoers.

Jesus firmly upheld the authority of the state when He said to the Pharisees and Herodians, "Render therefore to Caesar

---

* Please note: this does not mean that a principled argument against the death penalty cannot be made. Rather, our contention here is primarily with those who are opposed to punishment per se.

the things that are Caesar's, and to God the things that are God's."
(Rom. 22:21) It is only when Caesar intrudes upon that which
is God's—such as worship, as the Caesars demanded for themselves—that the faithful may not comply with Caesar's authority.

Tax collectors and soldiers came to St. John the Baptist,
and thus we read in Luke 3: "Then tax collectors also came to be
baptized, and said to him, 'Teacher, what shall we do?' And he said
to them, 'Collect no more than what is appointed for you.' Likewise
the soldiers asked him, saying, 'And what shall we do?' So he said to
them, 'Do not intimidate anyone or accuse falsely, and be content
with your wages.'" (v. 12–14) Notice that these two governmental
activities—collecting taxes and waging war—are linked on this occasion, and St. John attacks neither governmental activity; instead,
he commands individuals not to abuse their authority through graft
or 'shaking people down.' The authority to wage war—in which
soldiers most certainly aim to kill the enemy, not educate him—is
morally closely aligned to the authority of the state to put criminals
to death.

St. Paul makes the same linkage of authority—taxation and
the 'power of the sword'—when he wrote to the Church in Rome:

> Let every soul be subject to the governing authorities. For
> there is no authority except from God, and the authorities
> that exist are appointed by God. Therefore whoever re-
> sists the authority resists the ordinance of God, and those
> who resist will bring judgment to themselves. For rulers
> are not a terror to good works, but to evil. Do you want
> to be unafraid of the authority? Do what is good, and you
> will have praise from the same. For he is God's minister to
> you for God. But if you do evil, be afraid; for he does not
> bear the sword in vain; for he is God's minister, an avenger
> to execute wrath on him who practices evil. Therefore you
> must be subject, not only because of wrath but also for con-
> science' sake. For because of this you also pay taxes, for they
> are God's ministers attending continually to this very thing.
> Render therefore to all their due: taxes to whom taxes are

due, customs to whom customs, fear to whom fear, honor to whom honor. (13:1-7)

Now, the very Roman officials about whom he wrote unjustly put St. Paul and many other martyrs to death. Certainly such officials brought judgment upon themselves for such misuse of the authority which had been given to them; nevertheless, such abuse does not destroy the proper use, and St. Paul specifically designates the authority of the state as 'bearing the sword' as God's minister against those who practice evil. Similarly, St. Peter declared in his first Epistle: "Therefore submit yourselves to every ordinance of man for the Lord's sake, whether to the king as supreme, or to governors, as to those who are sent by him for the punishment of evildoers and for the praise of those who do good. For this is the will of God, that by doing good you may put to silence the ignorance of foolish men—as free, yet not using liberty as a cloak for vice, but as bondservants of God. Honor all people. Love the brotherhood. Fear God. Honor the king." (1 Pet. 2:13-17)

Themes of submission, honor and taxation may not sound like music to the ears of most Americans, but this is precisely because we have become a people obsessed with license, not liberty, for whom the highest virtue is often seen to be ethical irresponsibility.

Some may object, "But Jesus said, 'Love your enemies.'" True. Jesus declared, "But I say to you, love your enemies, bless those who curse you, do good to those who hate you, and pray for those who spitefully use you and persecute you, that you may be sons of your Father in heaven; for He makes His sun rise on the evil and on the good, and sends rain on the just and on the unjust." (Mat. 5:44-45) Thus the Lord, in His providential care, cares for all, and yet that does not overturn His divine judgment against sin. Christians are to love their enemies, and they are to render obedience to the authorities and be subject to them. Your forgiveness toward your enemy does not mean he has been absolved of what he owes to the state.

Consider the two men who were crucified with Jesus. St. Luke tells us that one of the crucified criminals began to blaspheme

Christ, "But the other, answering, rebuked him, saying, 'Do you not even fear God, seeing you are under the same condemnation? And we indeed justly, for we receive the due reward of our deeds; but this Man has done nothing wrong.' Then he said to Jesus, 'Lord, remember me when You come into Your kingdom.' And Jesus said to him, 'Assuredly, I say to you, today you will be with Me in Paradise.'" (23:40–43) Jesus does not contradict the man's assertion that he has been "justly" sentenced to death for his sin, and he does not confuse being absolved before the divine judgment—trusting in Christ Jesus as His Savior from eternal condemnation—with being absolved from responsibility under Caesar's Law.

Jesus said to Pontius Pilate: "My kingdom is not of this world. If My kingdom were of this world, My servants would fight, so that I should not be delivered to the Jews; but now My kingdom is not from here." (John 18:36) Those who dream of theocracy confuse the two kingdoms; so do those who confuse absolution from sin with nullification of punishment under law.

From the time of Noah until now, the Lord has given responsibility to human authority to punish wrongdoing, even unto death. The 'death penalty' is not under assault because it is racially or economically biased—all incarceration and civil penalties (such as fines) are similarly flawed and we do not throw out all law simply because someone may have unjustly received a speeding ticket. No human system of justice is without flaws and a requirement of absolute perfection is neither required nor possible for the legitimacy of the established authorities. Rather, keeping with the words of St. John, we expect them to not knowingly defraud people, or to deliberately subject the innocent to unjust punishment.

The 'death penalty' is under attack because the notion of *punishment* is under attack. In an degenerate culture where 'niceness' is more important than justice and truth, the battle has easily favored those who advocate an abandonment of punishment and the rise of the correctional state. A man who has been punished has, in the old phrase, 'paid his debt to society'. But the correctional state is concerned not with punishment, but reeducation. The correctional state does not seek to punish, but to convert.* Conversion is a concern of religion—even the ersatz religion of modern democratism.

The Gnostics are not concerned about a handful of criminals suffering execution for their crimes; they are outraged by the notion that there is guilt and punishment, and that Lord has established order and authority in this world in service of Him, to punish evildoers and protect those who do good. Our civilization is built on a very specific understanding of the origin of law, and the divine Lawgiver who has set order in the world. Those who desire to preserve our civilization must understand the true character of this conflict, and permit and uphold the justice of Caesar's sword.

---

* This does not deny that there is something quite educational about being punished; but the educational aspect is secondary.

THE CHURCH-STATE RELATIONSHIP AND AUGUSTANA XVI IN THE WRITINGS OF C. F. W. WALTHER AND S. S. SCHMUCKER

It is paradigmatic that two men of such opposite points of view as Carl Ferdinand Wilhelm Walther (1811–1887) and Samuel Simon Schmucker (1799–1873) became dominant figures in American Lutheranism* during the crucial decades surrounding the Civil War. These two men stood as near-polar opposites on almost every theological issue of their day, of which original sin, baptismal regeneration, confession and absolution, the Lord's Supper, and confessional subscription are only a few examples. The conflict between "Old Lutherans" and "American Lutherans" fixed the course of American Lutheranism throughout the following decades along a more confessional path than had obtained previously, with the result that some consider Walther "the dominating figure throughout the whole period"[†] of confessional revival, while Schmucker found the controversy had "alienated many of his former friends and clouded the evening of his days."[‡] In the words of another author:

> If we want to generalize about nineteenth-century American Lutheranism, we have to say that it is not so much the story of the Gettysburg tradition as it is the story of the triumph of confessional orthodoxy. This Lutheran

---

* We have in mind here the phenomena of the Lutheran faith in America, not the more narrow category of liberal "American Lutheranism" as represented by the *Definite Platform* and the *American Recension of the Augsburg Confession*. This will be the application throughout this article, with exceptions designated by quotation marks.

† O. W. Heick, and J. L. Neve, *A History of Christian Thought*, 2 vols. (Philadelphia: Muhlenberg Press, 1946), 2:305.

‡ Abdel Ross Wentz, *The Lutheran Church in American History* (Philadelphia: United Lutheran Publication House, 1923), 170.

"success story" is in turn preeminently the story of Walther and the Concordia tradition.*

Nevertheless, the influence of these two men can be found, partially, in the scope of their vision:

> Both Schmucker and Walther were dedicated according to their own lights to the task of building a vital Lutheranism on American soil in accord with the demands of the particular situation here. Both men intended to take seriously what it meant to be Lutheran. Furthermore, neither man wanted to be parochial, and thus both were interested in the ecumenical task — even if they saw the task in two radically different perspectives.[†]

The "radically different perspectives" of these two men on the issues mentioned above have often been pointed out, and these issues were, no doubt, the central points in the struggle between "Old Lutherans" and "American Lutherans." The debate, after all, centered on the worship life of the Church, particularly upon the marks of the church, the Word and the Sacraments. It is also true, however, that many other issues divided the two sides, even when their confessional statements were virtually identical. This study will examine the views of Schmucker and Walther concerning the Church-State relationship, or more specifically, the life of the Christian under secular authority. This task will be accomplished by first comparing the general statements of the two theologians, followed by an examination of their views on a number of practical issues of their day.

Church and State in the Theology of Walther and Schmucker

At first glance one might not expect to see much difference between the views of Schmucker and Walther, since both men

---

* Leigh D. Jordahl, "Schmucker and Walther: A Study of Christian Response to American Culture," in *The Future of the American Church*, ed. Philip J. Hefner (Philadelphia: Fortress Press, 1968), 82.
† Jordahl, 81.

claimed to base their teaching on the Lutheran Confessions, without any great modification. As will be shown below, both theologians upheld the view that Augustana XVI teaches obedience to the state in all matters, unless commanded to sin, and both believed that the Scriptures and the Lutheran Confessions taught a separation of Church and State.

Walther professed to ground his views in the Lutheran symbols when defending a careful division of secular authority from that given to the Church. For example, in his address to the eighth Western District Convention on May 15, 1862, Walther's central task was explaining how to abide by the teachings of the *Treatise on the Power and Primacy of the Pope* within the American setting. Of particular concern for Walther was this passage:

> Especially does it behoove the chief members of the church, the kings and the princes, to have regard for the interests of the church and to see to it that errors are removed and consciences are healed. God expressly exhorts kings, "Now therefore, O kings, be wise; be warned, O rulers of the earth" (Ps. 2:10). For the first care of kings should be to advance the glory of God. Wherefore it would be most shameful for them to use their authority and power for the support of idolatry and countless other crimes and for the murder of the saints (Tr, 54).

Walther admitted that "it was mainly through the service of those God-blessed princes, whom the Lord used as instruments, that the church of the pure confession became firmly rooted and was allowed to grow" during the years of the Reformation and immediately following, but he explained that:

> Princes should indeed be guardians of the church, and their queens its wet-nurses — but by no means by taking the governance of the church into their hands, transplanting secular force into the church and bringing it to bear in their shame. In the church they are not strictly speaking princes and princesses but, the *Treatise on the Power and Primacy of the Pope* rightly says, distinguished members of the church.

210

One must not misunderstand the passage quoted from the *Treatise on the Power and Primacy of the Pope* in a caesaro-papist manner, as though Christian government still had some inherited natural right to interfere forcibly in the administration of the church. *

Walther cited Luther to defend his contention that it is not the duty of government to repress heresy:

One cannot oppose heresy with force. Another strategy is needed. This is a battle and a matter different from those dealt with by the sword. . . .

No matter how much one esteems the piety of a prince who proves himself to be the guardian and patron of the church by sincere love and care, the danger is always near that he will exceed the proper limit established by God and introduce secular power into the church — to the unspeakable harm of souls.†

Indeed, Walther declared American religious freedom to be among the blessings of God:

He has let us enjoy not only the pure milk of the gospel according to our Lutheran Confessions but besides this, in a measure such as was not the case even at the time of the Reformation, the freedom to establish this doctrine in life and to found truly evangelical and apostolic congregations which rule themselves after the norm of God's Word.‡

The value of American religious freedom for maintaining a right relationship between church and state is a common theme in Walther's sermons. Walther observed during his Fourth of July address in 1853:

* C. F. W. Walther, "Church and State," trans. Robert Ernst Smith, in *Essays for the Church*, 2 vols. (St. Louis: Concordia Publishing House, 1992), 1:65–66.
† Ibid.,67.
‡ Ibid., 68.

State and church, the civic and religious life are here separated from one another in such a way that the state does not inquire how its citizens come to God or what they trust for their salvation. . . . I maintain that this religious freedom is one of the brightest stars in the banner of our new fatherland . . . .

As the church cannot be a state, so also the state cannot be a church. A state is certainly not an institution of God by which its citizens are to be led to *eternal life*.*

Again:

What then is the most glorious, the greatest, yes, the only thing that the state can grant the true religion? Not privileges, but *liberty*; not government regulations which enforce beliefs of religion, but *freedom* of religion to proclaim these doctrines to the whole world; not the protection and spreading of religion with temporal power, but freedom of religion to defend itself and to reach out with the weapon of the persuasive Word; not control of the state, but *freedom* to live in the state, to have a hospitable reception, a place of refuge, a lodging-place.†

Walther also echoed the Confessions concerning the loyalty due to the civil authorities. According to Augsburg Confession XVI, "Christians are necessarily bound to obey their own magistrates and laws, save only when commanded to sin; for then they ought to obey God rather than men. Acts 5, 29." This theme was repeated by Walther in a sermon on 1 Peter 2:1–10:

What if [the state] uses its powers in *behalf* of criminals and *against* the pious, does not punish the evildoers and praise the upright? Should a Christian obey it even then?

I reply: If it commands you to sin, to do something against your faith and a good conscience, then you dare not

* C. F. W. Walther, *The Word of His Grace: Occasional and Festival Sermons*, trans. and ed. Evangelical Lutheran Synod Translation Committee (Lake Mills, Iowa: Graphic Publishing Company, 1978), 153–154.
† Ibid., 157.

obey it; then it no longer commands in the name of him whose place it takes; then what Peter said to his government applies when it ordered him to be silent about the name of Jesus: "We ought to obey God rather than men." Acts 5,29. But if it does not order you to sin, then obedience is due it, even if it acts unjustly; for it is God's will that its laws be held sacred even when it is administered by impious people.*

Schmucker also believed in a clear division between the two kingdoms, with Christians owing allegiance to the ecclesiastical and civil authorities. This focus was reflected in early ecumenical works such as his *Fraternal Appeal to the American Churches*. Schmucker's proposed "United Protestant Confession" appended to this *Fraternal Appeal* addressed the Christian's relationship to civil government in its tenth article:

> God the supreme Lord and king of all the world, hath ordained civil magistrates to be under him, over the people, for his own glory and the public good; and to this end hath armed them with power, for the defense and encouragement of them that do good, and for the punishment of evil-doers. The power of the civil magistrate extendeth to all men, as well clergy as laity in things temporal; but hath no authority in things purely spiritual. Christians ought to yield obedience to civil officers and laws of the land: unless they should command something sinful; in which case it is a duty to obey God rather than man.†

Although the precise terminology is not the same, it can be seen that this article contains much in common with Article XVI of the Augsburg Confession. The chapter entitled "Of Political Affairs" in Schmucker's *Lutheran Manual* begins by running Article

* C. F. W. Walther, *Standard Epistles* (Fort Wayne: Concordia Theological Seminary Printshop, n.d.), 243.
† S. S. Schmucker, *Fraternal Appeal to the American Churches, with a Plan for Catholic Union on Apostolic Principles* (New York: Taylor & Dodd, 1839), 134.

XVI in parallel columns of Latin and English, with the next seventeen pages structured as a commentary on this article, clause by clause.[*] In his dogmatics textbook, *Elements of Popular Theology*, Schmucker cites the entire unaltered text of Article XVI at the head of his chapter on civil government.[†] The clear implication is that the chapter will be a commentary on this article. Indeed, Schmucker's alterations to Article XVI in his *American Rescension* were not as drastic as those found in other articles. Schmucker insisted that aside from the removal of the condemnatory clauses (as he had done throughout the *Augustana*) the American Recension deviates from Article XVI only in his removal of the term *imperial*.[‡]

Schmucker's presentation of this article of faith did not vary much in the years following the "American Lutheranism" controversy, as can be seen in his 1860 *Evangelical Lutheran Catechism*. Chapter XXIV "Of Civil Government" stresses the central doctrinal points found in the Augustana, as becomes evident from a comparison of its six questions with the text of Article XVI:

Q304. Whilst Christians faithfully discharge their obligations to the church, do they not also owe some duties to the civil government under which they live?

Q305. What duties does God enjoin on civil rulers?

Q306. May Christians accept civil office?

---

[*] S. S. Schmucker, *Lutheran Manual on Scriptural Principles: or, The Augsburg Confession Illustrated and Sustained* ... (Philadelphia: Lindsay & Blakiston, 1855), 178–195. The text concerning this article is virtually the same as that found in *Elements of Popular Theology*. The format is different, however, and a discursus on Christians and "just war" is included.

[†] S. S. Schmucker, *Elements of Popular Theology: With Occasional Reference to The Doctrines of the Reformation, As Avowed before the Diet at Augsburg in MDXXX. Designed chiefly for Private Christians and Theological Students* (Philadelphia: Smith, English & Co., 1860), 326.

[‡] S. S. Schmucker, *American Lutheranism Vindicated* (Baltimore: T. Newton Kurtz, 1856), 62. The original text reads: "*Of Civil Affairs* they teach that lawful civil ordinances are good works of God, and that it is right for Christians to bear civil office, to sit as judges, to judge matters by the Imperial and other existing laws ..." *Concordia, or Book of Concord. The Symbols of the Ev. Lutheran Church* (St. Louis: Concordia Publishing House, 1922), 14 (English only edition).

Q307. Ought there to be any connection between church and state, as in Europe?

Q308. What other duties do Christians owe to their civil magistrates?

Q309. Are Romish priests exempted from the jurisdiction of the civil courts, as their standard authors claim?

As found in the other examples, Schmucker emphasized the independence of the two powers and the obligation owed to the civil authorities. In answer to question 304, the catechumen is told, "Yes; they are to regard civil government as a divinely appointed institution, whose powers are to be employed in accordance with God's word, for the benefit of the people, and whose lawful requisitions they are religiously bound to obey." Again, in response to question 307 we read: "No. The Savior says: 'My kingdom is not of this world'; nor has he authorized civil rulers, as such to exercise control over the church."[*]

Given the above preliminary analysis, therefore, one could expect general agreement between Walther and Schmucker on the relationship between Church and State to be reflected in their practical application. This, however, does not prove to be the case.

The Form of Government: Divinely Ordained?

Although the confessional approach expressed in Schmucker's *Elements of Popular Theology* and *Lutheran Manual* might appear similar to that of Walther, the author's views express a clear distinction between himself and the Saxon emigrant theologian. This difference is clearly delineated in Schmucker's willingness to esteem one *form* of government as more pleasing to God than another. Although Schmucker stated, "The Confessors do not pronounce any particular kind of government of divine origin," he went on to declare that the "Democratic or Republican form of government ...

[*] S. S. Schmucker, *Evangelical Lutheran Catechism, Designed for Catechumens, and the Higher Classes in Sabbath-Schools* (Baltimore: T. Newton Kurtz, 1860), 116–118.

is doubtless the most perfect form of government, as it secures in the highest degree the rights and happiness of all its citizens. Of this fact the history of our own favored country affords demonstrative proof."* Schmucker even proposed that "had the divine Savior prescribed any form, it doubtless would have been the republican; for such is essentially the form of government which he gave to his church. ..."† When Schmucker cited "our illustrious fathers" he quoted the Declaration of Independence, not Luther or the Lutheran fathers of the Age of Orthodoxy!‡

For Schmucker, the democratic republic was to be considered among the principles defended by the confessors at Augsburg:

> It is certainly commendable, that living under a government so defective, the confessors should have uttered not a word inconsistent with the purest principles of republicanism; nay, that they even asserted to the face of the Emperor, their right to resist such laws as they deemed sinful.§

Again:

> [T]he seeds of liberty, civil as well as religious, were sown by the Reformers; and the same principles which led them to protest against the corruptions, and resist the encroachments of the Papal hierarchy, led our fathers to erect the standard of liberty on these Western shores, exploded the absurd doctrine of passive obedience to kings, taught the crowned heads of Europe that their subjects have rights, which can no longer be trampled on with the impunity of the dark ages.¶

One can see a tension in Schmucker's thought. Although admitting God did not establish a particular form of government, nevertheless he dismissed the "passive obedience" given to kings as

---

* Schmucker, *Elements of Popular Theology*, 328.
† Ibid., 330.
‡ Ibid., 332.
§ Ibid., 327.
¶ Ibid., 328.

216

an "absurd doctrine" and told the reader, in essence, that the American form of government really is the way Jesus would want it done.

However, Walther's views on this matter were quite different. For Walther, it was not the pastor's place to establish God's attitude toward any particular form of government. As Walther observed in his "Fourth of July Address":

> If now you should desire that I blend my voice in the accustomed fashion of those who appear before the citizens of this land on this day; that is to say, should you expect of me that I present a eulogy on the ingenuity of man which has erected the astounding, great, glorious, and richly blessed edifice of this republic, then you would, of course, soon be disappointed in me.
>
> I am a Christian! ... as a Christian I could never be a priest who would lay the offerings of praise and thanksgiving on altars erected to mortal men ...
>
> You would still less expect of me that I should point out the advantage of our republican constitution over the monarchies of our former fatherland ... You know that I am a theologian, a preacher of religion, a servant of the church. In considering this union of States today, I am naturally going to do so in relation to religion, to Christianity, to the church.[*]

In his sermon on 1 Peter 2:11–20, Walther denounced the "spirit of rebellion and insurrection" in which men

> revile heads of government; yes, they pour upon them the vilest mockery and ridicule in words and writing. To be a king and to be a tyrant, to rule the people and to oppress them are considered synonymous. To exterminate all kings and privileged groups and grant democratic freedom to all people has been called the goal toward which the world is moving. When it has been attained the golden age will have come.

---

* Walther, *The Word of His Grace*, 152–53.

And what is the definition of a republic? A state where one can do what he wishes. Therefore the laws of the government are no longer considered sacred; if one conforms to the law it is only because one still feels himself too weak to oppose the power of the government. ...

Yes, it is true that God has not decided whether the families of a country should unite to form a monarchy in which one person rules, or an aristocracy, where a group rules, or a republic in which the people themselves rule through elected officials. But *wherever governmental authority is established, it cannot be overthrown by force; it should be held sacred; God should be honored in his substitute and given that absolute obedience which children give their fathers.*[*]

Although Walther might personally have preferred a democratic republic over other forms of government, he did not presume a divine concurrence with his opinion. In fact, Walther demonstrated an awareness of the danger of Antinomianism inherent in democracy, to which Schmucker seems to have been oblivious.

The Relationship between the Faith, the Reformation, and Civil Rights

As was noted above, Schmucker professed in *Elements of Popular Theology* that "the seeds of liberty, civil as well as religious, were sown by the Reformers."[†] These civil liberties, he believed, had been best exhibited in the American republic. Schmucker asserted further on in the same work:

Let the American patriot recollect the language of his fathers, "that all men are created equal," and have unalienable rights, among which is "liberty." Let him remember, that with these words on their lips, they invoked the blessing of Heaven on their struggle, and that He who rules in the

---

[*] Walther, *Standard Epistles*, 239–240, 242. Italics added.
[†] Schmucker, *Elements of Popular Theology*, 328.

218

heaven of heavens heard their cry."*

A government's ability to protect and expand the rights of its citizens was Schmucker's primary test of its legitimacy, and a government that fails to deliver in this respect may not be able to claim the loyalty of its citizens: "Under any one of these [various] forms of government the principles of the Reformers would have led them to remain obedient, *if it were administered in such a manner as to secure the rights and promote the happiness of its members*."[†]

This call to patriotic vigilance was specifically applied to the pastoral office in *The Christian Pulpit, the Rightful Guardian of Morals, in Political No Less than in Private Life*, when Schmucker called upon pastors "to hold up to the view of our rulers and fellow citizens [their duty] in their political action to recognize the universal brotherhood and equality of man in civil rights."[‡]

The alleged link between the Reformation and civil liberties is maintained throughout Schmucker's writings. In his *Discourse in Commemoration of the Glorious Reformation of the Sixteenth Century*,[§] Schmucker pronounced American civil liberties to be among the fruits of Protestantism: "Such was the glorious Reformation of the sixteenth century . . . . The fruits, both civil and religious, of this Revolution, we, in these United States, most richly enjoy."[¶] Roman Catholicism's "very essence is an admixture of *civil* and religious despotism."[**]

The last feature of the Reformation to which we shall advert is, that it has delivered the civil government of the

* Ibid., 336.

† Ibid., 328. Italics added.

‡ S. S. Schmucker, *The Christian Pulpit, the Rightful Guardian of Morals, in Political No Less than in Private Life* (Gettysburg: H. C. Neinstedt, 1846), 17. Cited in Abdel Ross Wentz, *Pioneer in Christian Unity* (Philadelphia: Fortress Press, 1967), 263.

§ S. S. Schmucker, *Discourse in Commemoration of the Glorious Reformation of the Sixteenth Century* (New York: Gould & Newman, 1838). Schmucker actually begins this discourse with the words "When in the course of human events"!

¶ Ibid., 8.

** Ibid., 70. Italics in the original.

countries which embraced it, from papal tyranny, and has given a new impulse to civil liberty, which has been felt throughout the Christian world.

Since the relative tendencies of Protestantism and Popery have been fully developed and attentively studied, no fact in the philosophy of history is more fully established than that the former is intimately allied to civil liberty; and the latter to civil despotism.[††]

How much, how incalculably much the Protestant nations have gained by the Reformation, is demonstrated by their manifest and striking superiority to their Catholic neighbours in every thing relating to civil rights and liberty, to internal improvements, to domestic purity and happiness...[‡‡]

[E]ven the venerable patriot Lafayette was constrained to exclaim to different American citizens, "If the liberties of your country are destroyed, it can only be by the *popish clergy*;" it becomes us to lend respectful attention to this subject, and in a suitable Christian manner, endeavour to resist the encroachments of the enemy.[§§]

As was the case concerning the form of government, Walther's views on civil rights were rather different from those held by Schmucker. Unquestionably, Walther upheld the Christian's use of his civil rights. In fact, he supported Protestant-run newspapers to counter "the other political papers in the west [that] are openly organs of anti-Christianity" in order "to provide in the upstanding families a Christian outlook on current events and to effect a conscientious use of civil rights and privileges among the people."[¶¶]

[††] Ibid., 96.
[‡‡] Ibid., 98.
[§§] Ibid., 124–125. Italics in the original.
[¶¶] C. F. W. Walther, *Selected Letters*, trans. Roy A. Suelflow (St. Louis: Concordia Publishing House, 1981), 146. Note: Walther was quite concerned about the effect secular papers were having on his parishioners: "our own Lutherans are in the political domain completely led by atheistic newspapers which determine

While opposing any attempt by the Church to turn to the State in search of "hand-outs" or other support (for fulfilling her obligation to care for the poor, for example), such was not the case for individual Christians *as citizens*:

> That which is not a duty or a right of Christians, but only duties and rights of citizens, is something else again. Therefore we read that the apostle Paul as citizen appealed to Caesar (Acts 25:11) and appealed to his full citizen's rights (Acts 16:35–40).[*]

At the same time, however, Walther denounced the post-Civil War Missouri constitution for containing "a notorious declaration of inherent, inalienable human rights."[†] This opposition to "inalienable human rights" and particularly the idea of equality was Walther's first point of attack in his four sermons on Communism and Socialism:

> The first thing we have to consider is:
>
> 1. It is a fact that men are not equal.
>
> Throughout the creation every thing differs from everything else. God is accordingly not an equalizer, but one who creates dissimilar things. Man cannot, to save his life, make two things equal. The principle that all things shall be made alike is not founded in nature. The same is evident in man. … It would therefore be altogether unnatural to place human society in such a condition that all would be equal.[‡]

Walther opposed a similar "spirit" which he believed was at work in the American Civil War, a spirit "possessing and poisoning

---

their attitudes and from which they naturally absorb much more than politics, as you can well imagine" (150).

[*] Ibid., 82.

[†] C. F. W. Walther to Fr. Brunn, 8 Nov. 1865, *Briefe*, 1: 235, 236. Trans. Robert W. Paul in Carl S. Meyer, ed., *Moving Frontiers* (St. Louis: Concordia Publishing House, 1964), 238.

[‡] C. F. W. Walther, *Communism and Socialism* (Hill City, MN: Hope Publicity Bureau, 1964), 25–26.

increasingly more hearts, which wrings from us anew the cry of the blessed martyr Polycarp:'God, what times hast Thou allowed me to experience!'"* Walther continued: "And should we say, what is this spirit for? — It is the spirit of the first French Revolution, whose motto was:'Liberty, Equality, Fraternity' ... these heralds explicitly declare:'What are a million men against an idea!'"† Walther discerned echoes of Münzer and the "Twelve Articles of the Schwabian Peasants" in this quest for "Liberty, Equality, Fraternity," and

> this spirit, which confuses Christian liberty with civil equality, is blowing over the entire country as a hot wind by which even many of the few plants which Christ had planted in these last days through his Word and Spirit wither and dry up. It is the revived spirit of Carlstadt.‡

In short, Christians should avail themselves of the rights given them as citizens, but they should not consider such rights intrinsically "inalienable," standing higher than the state itself. The state stands higher than those rights it may choose to grant or remove. Any effort "to exterminate all kings and privileged groups and grant democratic freedom to all people" was rejected by Walther, as was the idea that "To be subject to an *unjust* government because it is of God and endure oppression at its hands without rebelling is now deemed weakness, cowardice unworthy of a free man, yes insanity."§ Schmucker's priorities were precisely the reverse of Walther's in this regard, and this brings us to the next point.

Christians and Revolution

The views of both Walther and Schmucker were closely tied to their assessment of the primacy of civil rights. Walther rejected his generation's revolutionary spirit in the strongest terms:

God's Word tells us that one of the things which will an-

* "Vorwort der Redaction ..." *Der Lutheraner* 19 (3 Sept. 1862), in *Moving Frontiers*, 236.
† "Vorwort der Redaction ..." *Der Lutheraner* 19 (3 Sept. 1862), 1. [Passage not included in *Moving Frontiers* translation.]
‡ "Vorwort der Redaction ..." *Der Lutheraner* 19 (3 Sept. 1862), in *Moving Frontiers*, 236.
§ Walther, *Standard Epistles*, 240.

222

nounce the end of the world is that after a great fall from
the faith there will be rebellion even against civil government, the sanctity of governmental authority will be denied
and everywhere there will be bloody persecution. ... If we
compare the state of affairs in our day with this picture, we
can see that also this prediction is being literally fulfilled
before our very eyes.*

Walther viewed the drive for "equality" and "human rights" as indi-
visible from revolution against divinely-established authority. Because people consider man to be the source instituting government,

Many say: By nature every person is free, subject to no one,
his own lord. It is only by common consent, they claim, that
a few rule, the rest let themselves be ruled, that a few govern, the rest are subject to them. Subjects, therefore, always
have the right to overthrow the government. The right of
revolution is a holy inalienable right of all nations. ...

This, however, is a great ruinous error. God is
not a God of confusion but order. God did not create two
things to be on the same level. Throughout the entire world
we find an endless gradation, in which one thing is subor-
dinate to another. The whole creation is not a disconnected
mass of things and beings, but an orderly *kingdom* divided
into countless provinces. ... Everywhere [God] has his sub-
stitutes clothed with his majesty who rule and govern.†

The focus was the same as in Walther's argument against
Socialism: revolution against authority is built upon the false premise that creatures are meant to be equal. They are not equal, and
attempts to create a false equality lead to bloodshed and chaos and
the violation of God's Law because one is fighting against the very
order of creation. Even if a government is impious and oppressive, a
Christian must be obedient. Only a command to sin may (and then

* Ibid., 239.
† Ibid., 241.

must) be disobeyed. Any other act of rebellion, no matter how noble the cause seems to the "old Adam," is a sin so serious that Walther links it to the "apostasy" of his age. As Walther explained,

> [I]f it does not order you to sin, then obedience is due it, even if it acts unjustly; for it is God's will that its laws be held sacred even when it is administered by impious people.
>
> With absolute clarity this says that Christians are to obey not only a good and gentle, but also a false and malicious, not only a pious but also a godless, not only an upright and fair but also an unjust and unfair government; for conscience's sake toward God they are to endure all injustice without resisting by force.*

Walther clung tenaciously to these fundamental principles even when threatened during the Civil War. As Walther declared to J. C. W. Lindemann,

> We are in grave danger because we do not go along with the Republican mob, this revolutionary party which has now hoisted the banner of loyalty with unspeakable hypocrisy. We simply rely on the Word—"Be subject to the government which has *power* over you" — not *right*, for where would we be then?†

He expressed this sentiment even more bluntly in a letter to Gustavus Seyffarth dated June 17, 1862: "Whatever our administration does in this war, we subject ourselves to that, according to Romans 13,1."‡

Walther did not draw his definition of rebellion narrowly, either. In a sermon on the text "Render therefore unto Caesar the things which are Caesar's," (Mt 22:21) he included any avoidance of civil laws to be an act of rebellion:

---

* Ibid., 243.

† *Letters of C. F. W. Walther: A Selection,* ed. and trans. Carl S. Meyer (St. Louis: Concordia Publishing House, 1969), 104.

‡ *Correspondence of C. F. W. Walther,* ed. and trans. Roy A. Suelflow (St. Louis: Concordia Seminary, 1980), 61.

Our government was instituted by the will of the majority of all the people and is answerable to it. Yet it is God's ordinance and servant. God has given the sword of protection and vengeance, the scales of justice, into its hands. We should consider its laws holy and inviolable, its commands God's commands, its laws God's laws. ... Yes, we should be ready to sacrifice our very life if our government demands it to preserve the common good, to go in battle against the country's enemy. It is no small sin to transgress a command of our government which we placed over ourselves, to make out a false tax return, or to transgress in a business deal its laws confirmed by God.[*]

Schmucker took a dim view of honoring authority when he believed civil rights to be at stake. He attempted to tie his view to that of the Reformers, declaring that "Under any of these [various] forms of government the principles of the Reformers would have led them to remain obedient, *if it were administered in such a manner as to secure the rights and promote the happiness of its members.*"[†] Considering Luther's well-documented reaction to the Peasants Revolt in 1525, it is hard to include Luther among whatever "Reformers" Schmucker had in mind. After all, while it is certainly true that Luther chastised the rulers, and even declared that they *deserved* to face revolt because of their sins, nevertheless he steadily maintained that to engage in such a revolt was sinful.[‡]

Schmucker, however, made no effort to specify precisely whom he had in mind. Instead, he continued by asserting that "it is

[*] C. F. W. Walther, *Standard Gospels* (Fort Wayne: Concordia Theological Seminary Printshop, n.d.), 346.

[†] Schmucker, *Elements of Popular Theology*, 328. Italics added.

[‡] For example: "Third, you say that the rulers are wicked and intolerable, for they will not allow us to have the gospel; they oppress us too hard with the burdens they lay on our property, and they are ruining us in body and soul. I answer: The fact that the rulers are wicked and unjust does not excuse disorder and rebellion, for the punishing of wickedness is not the responsibility of everyone, but of the worldly rulers who bear the sword." Martin Luther, "Admonition to Peace: A Reply to the Twelve Articles of the Peasants in Swabia," AE 46:25.

a principle maintained by the ablest writers on political philosophy, that resistance to any existing government becomes proper *and a duty,* only when the grievances actually endured or with certainty foreseen, outweigh the hazards of anarchy and violence always attendant on revolutions." Schmucker went on to declare:

> The Confessors inculcate the justice of revolution in those governments which fail to accomplish the just end of their establishment.
>
> But if rulers transgress their duty, and require aught that is improper, we are commanded to obey God rather than man. ... Combination among the oppressed is necessary to a successful resistance of existing governments, and therefore proper. And combination of the oppressed to resist their oppressors is rebellion; its successful termination, revolution.
>
> Thus to withdraw and renounce his allegiance to any government, by which he is wantonly and seriously oppressed, is doubtless the indefeasible right of man; but it is based in the laws of nature, not in the provisions of the Constitution ....*

Here one finds a far different approach from Walther's, even though some of the terminology is similar: Rebellion is justified in the face of oppression when the authorities require that which is "improper" and when the benefits "outweigh the hazards."

While Walther appealed to Scripture, Schmucker defended this "indefeasible right" on the basis of natural law and political philosophy. The ultimate decision whether a government stands or falls Schmucker declared to rest in the hands of the people, while Walther proclaimed this power belongs to God alone. In conclusion, then, it is clear that the views of these two men on the relationship between the governing authorities and civil rights were intimately linked to their beliefs concerning the right of the people to revolt. There is little hope for reconciling these two views, for

---

* Schmucker, *Elements of Popular Theology,* 330–331, 341.

they approach the question of authority from two fundamentally different perspectives.

Slavery and Abolition

The interrelated issues of slavery and abolitionism are perhaps the two where the contrast between the two theologians is the most striking. For Schmucker, slavery was an "abstract injustice and criminality in the sight of God ... an evil moral, social and political, that no republican government can consistently cherish — that no Christian nation can rest quiet under its influence."[*] Schmucker was an abolitionist who became a slaveholder by marriage,[†] although he did speak "of his slaves as servants, treated them kindly, provided them with spiritual ministry, and arranged for their elementary education."[‡]

Walther, on the other hand, once commented concerning Christian liberty: "For whoever is free of God becomes a slave of his own impulses, but whoever is a servant of God is a free man even if he were the slave child of a negro."[§] In essence, to be a Christian makes a man free in a way beyond any earthly freedom, and it is a freedom that no one can take away. Walther maintained:

> abolitionism, which holds and declares slavery as an essentially sinful relationship and every master of a slave thereby as a malefactor and therefore wants to abolish the former under all circumstances, is a child of unbelief and its unfolding, rationalism, deistic philanthropism, pantheism, materialism, atheism, and a brother of modern socialism, Jacobinism, and communism.[¶]

---

[*] "Dr. Schmucker's Letter" from *The Colonization Herald*, 1838, contained in the Corpus of American Lutheranism, Reel 34, Unit X.

[†] Virginia did not allow their manumission—Schmucker freed several slaves the next year when he moved to Pennsylvania. For an extensive treatment of this incident, see Paul P. Kuenning, "American Lutheran Pietism, Activist and Abolitionist" (Ph.D. diss., Marquette University, 1985), 236–243.

[‡] Wentz, *Pioneer in Christian Unity*, 317.

[§] Walther, *Selected Letters*, 59.

[¶] "Vorwort," *Lehre und Wehre* 9 (Feb. 1863): 34, trans. in *Moving Frontiers*, 234.

Walther's rejection of abolitionism was not rooted in a pro- slavery mentality, as some have charged,* but in his hatred of rebellion of all kinds. Because, he believed, there was nothing in the New Testament condemning slavery, and since no one was forced against conscience to own slaves, there could be no justification for the tactics of the abolitionists. As Walther explained in 1869:

> What God permits the Christians in the New Testament to do and does not command them to put aside, but rather to control, cannot be sinful in itself. That is what God does with regard to slavery, which is nothing else than (to put it in Melanchthon's words) the legal deprivation of the capacity to possess property and to determine for oneself the type of occupation which one wishes to follow and the right to live in a place chosen by oneself.
>
> Insofar as this was ordered by law in America, American slavery was not sinful. But whatever was added to it contrary to God's order was just as sinful, godless and damnable as Roman slavery at the time of the apostles. Whatever the apostles did not condemn in Roman slavery, we may not condemn if we wish to be Christians. But anything of a sinful nature connected with American slavery we may not excuse, gloss over, or justify.[†]

It has been observed by Walther's defenders that the Missourian aligned himself with the South during the Civil War. This loyalty was not based on any love of slavery, but was rooted in two biblical principles: (1) being subject to those in authority (Rom 13), and (2) the conviction that the Scriptures did not condemn slavery, and thus Christians dared not go beyond God's Word. As one author has explained:

> Walther in his personal convictions indeed sympathized with the southern States. He had two reasons. In the first

---

* See Paul P. Keunning, *The Rise and Fall of American Lutheran Pietism* (Macon, GA: Mercer University Press, 1988), 134.

† Aug. R. Suelflow, "Walther the American," in *C. F. W. Walther: The American Luther* (Mankato, MN: Walther Press, 1987), 25.

place, he and many of the fathers of our church were in favor of states' rights. ... In the second place, while not favor-
ing slavery, Walther took the position that slavery in itself
was not against the Word of God ... and he was horrified
to read in so many church papers misinterpretations of
the Bible, especially of St. Paul's and St. Peter's letters. But
he never brought his political convictions to bear on the
church and church conditions.[*]

Walther felt a great loyalty to the State of Missouri, declaring to
Theodore Buenger in 1861, "I am a Missourian and therefore will
never be moved to separate my fortune from that of my state unless
I am forced. This state has so far protected me in life and property,
so in the time of need I will not become unfaithful to it."[†] This loyalty placed Walther in considerable danger, as can be seen in another
letter from the same year to Pastor J. M. Buehler:

Since it seems that the battlefield would be fixed here under
the very windows of the college (even Commander Boern-
stein, lying in the Marine hospital, putting his hands on a cannon, swore to shoot up this secessionist nest, as he loves to call
our college), and since the governor presented a prospect of
a military bill in our legislature, we have felt conscience-
bound to close down the institution till further notice ...[‡]

---

[*] Ludwig Ernest Feurbringer, *80 Eventful Years* (St. Louis: Concordia Publishing
House, 1944), 225–226. As noted above, other writers such as Paul Kuenning have
charged that "Walther was convinced that the Scriptures upheld the American system of servitude, and he published several articles in his magazine, *Der Lutheraner*,
by Dr. Wilhelm Sihler of Fort Wayne containing a definitive defense of slavery as an
institution." Kuenning goes on to declare, however, "The official position of the Missouri Synod, typical of orthodoxy, was to remain silent on the subject, maintaining
that the consideration of 'secular' matters by ecclesiastical bodies was improper"
(134). Kuenning seems unaware that *Der Lutheraner* was an "official" publication
of the Missouri Synod, so his charge that the Missouri Synod was "silent" is inconsistent with his own account. As to the charges of Walther's support for the
"American system of servitude," we shall allow Walther's 1869 remarks to stand.
[†] *Correspondence of C. F. W. Walther*, 57.
[‡] Walther, *Selected Letters*, 149.

If Walther's views on secession were still unclear, he went on to note:
We have declared that if a state secedes from the Union,
naturally the individual citizen will not revolt but will either emigrate or will subject himself to the seceding state
government, according to the Bible passage: "Be obedient to
the power that has authority over you." It does not say "Has
the right over you."[*]

Schmucker, however, saw slavery as the great "exception" to
American civil rights, a phenomenon that he believed demanded a
solution. Slavery was "a reproach to our political system, and a violation of the rights of 'equal' man!"[†] This conclusion led Schmucker
to become a moderate advocate of two proposed solutions: slave
resettlement in Africa and abolitionism. Schmucker's support for
resettlement, however, was quite mild. Although an "active member"
of the American Colonization Society who "always regarded colonization as entitled a place, not indeed as in itself a remedy for American slavery, but as a source of much good for Africa,"[‡] Schmucker
had his doubts concerning the practicality of the concept. Schmucker
believed that "African colonization" neither "can or will be extended so
far as to remove entirely the negro from our land."
Whilst voluntary colonization, in Africa and elsewhere,
ought to be encouraged; it seems almost certain that a portion of our coloured population will always remain amongst
us. Colonization, moreover, if conducted with any view to
the entire removal of our slave population, will require a
previous system of legislation for the manumission of the
whole mass of slaves. This ought to be a simultaneous step.
But when laws for the abolition of slavery shall have been
enacted, the inadequacy of foreign colonization will appear
as clear as demonstration. Many will moreover be unwill-

---

[*] Ibid., 150.
[†] Schmucker, *Elements of Popular Theology*, 332.
[‡] "Dr. Schmucker's Letter" from *The Colonization Herald*, 1838, contained in the
Corpus of American Lutheranism, Reel 34, Unit X.

230

ing to remove across the Atlantic, to an unknown land; and coercion would be unjust.*

The primary aim for Schmucker was the abolition of slavery, leaving the option of colonization up to those who had been freed. Schmucker was by no means as extreme as other abolitionists, however, observing that "our Southern fellow-citizens are also often unjustly censured; for not only had the present generation no agency in introducing slavery into the land; the majority of them profess themselves favourable to emancipation in general." In rebuttal to his fellow abolitionists, Schmucker observed that "this great work has difficulties more formidable than some Christians in non-slaveholding states suppose." Indeed, the involvement of the North in the import of slaves meant that "the North comes in for a large portion of the guilt." In summary: "But in this noble enterprise there should be as little crimination as possible."† Even as the Civil War loomed, Schmucker took a moderate approach to the treatment of slave-holding states, urging teamwork in this task rather than division.

It is worth noting, in conclusion, that Schmucker's life was placed in some danger during the Civil War when Confederate troops overran the Schmucker home during the battle of Gettysburg. Cannon fire had been turned on his home, seminary records were damaged, and a portion of Schmucker's personal library and furniture was destroyed. Schmucker had already fled the area, however, having been warned that Confederate soldiers planned to "arrest" him.‡

Conclusion

It can be seen that the views of both men with regard to slavery and abolitionism were consistent with their views on other church-state issues. Fundamentally, the difference between these two theologians centered on their view of civil rights and the relationship of such rights to the established order. These views, in

* Schmucker, *Elements of Popular Theology*, 334–335.
† Ibid., 332, 333, 336.
‡ Wentz, *Pioneer in Christian Unity*, 326–329.

turn, were shaped by the status attributed to the republican form of government. For Walther, although he undeniably praised its benefits, the republic was seen as one option among many and its rise and fall were in the hands of the Creator. Schmucker's views in this regard displayed a greater tension, in which one might speak of the republic knowing a particular "divine favor," but not "divine mandate."

Throughout a survey of Schmucker's work one is struck by his adoption of the *Weltanschauung* of nineteenth-century American liberalism. A great proportion of the treatment of political affairs in *Elements of Popular Theology* is applicable only within the immediate setting of his generation's debate over the intent of the United States Constitution and the Declaration of Independence. The result of this approach is that such materials rapidly lose their value outside of their immediate cultural and historical context. By narrowing his vision of the Reformers to the narrow context of the American republic, Schmucker lost his ability to address himself to the church catholic. This may be considered a symptom of Schmucker's greater failure to equal Walther's success in "building a vital Lutheranism on American soil in accord with the demands of the particular situation here"—his focus was simply too narrow to meet the "ecumenical task."[*]

Walther, however, by consciously repristinating aspects of the teachings of Luther and the Lutheran Confessions concerning the Church-State relationship, particularly the emphasis on the authority of the State,[†] aligned himself with a strain of teaching deeply rooted in the Lutheran dogmatic tradition. Walther's exegesis of certain key passages (such as Romans 13 and 1 Peter 2) and his ability to explain the teachings of the Lutheran symbols within the American context allow Lutherans easier access to their Church's traditions, whereas Schmucker's views on a wide variety of issues simply stray too far from the historic Lutheran norm.

---

[*] Jordahl, 81.

[†] For example, Walther, "Church and State," 65–67.

232

JAMES D. HEISER, is the Bishop of the Evangelical Lutheran Diocese of North America (ELDoNA) and Pastor of Salem Lutheran Church (Malone, Texas). He also serves as Dean of Missions for The Augustana Ministerium and as a member both of the Board of Directors and Steering Committee of The Mars Society.

Heiser earned his B.A.–Political Science at George Washington University (Washington, D.C.) and his M.Div. and S.T.M. from Concordia Theological Seminary (Fort Wayne, Indiana).

Heiser is the author of seven books: one examining the views of Russian Eurasianist Alexander Dugin (*"The American Empire Should Be Destroyed"—Alexander Dugin and the Perils of Immanentized Eschatology*), one recounting the course of the Hermetic Reformation (*Prisci Theologi and the Hermetic Reformation in the Fifteenth Century*), a collection of essays concerning the Office of the Holy Ministry (*Stewards of the Mysteries of God*), two books of essays pertaining to space exploration and theology (*A Shining City on a Higher Hill* and *Civilization and the New Frontier*) and two books on the crises of the Modern age (*A Time for Every Purpose Under Heaven* and *The One True God, the Two Estates and the Three Kingdoms*). He is also the author of hundreds of published articles.